PENN IN INK

PENN IN INK

Pathfinders, Swashbucklers, Scribblers & Sages:
Portraits from *The Pennsylvania Gazette*

S M Hughes

SAMUEL HUGHES

The essays in this book were originally published in *The Pennsylvania Gazette*. Reprinted here by permission.

University of Pennsylvania, Pennsylvania Gazette, Benjamin Franklin, Thomas Evans, Zane Grey, Doc Holliday, Ezra Pound, William Carlos Williams, Noam Chomsky, Zellig Harris, Scott Nearing, Stephen Glass, Leon Higginbotham, Paul Korshin, Robert Strausz-Hupé, Kathleen Hall Jamieson, Alan Kors, Martin Seligman, Josephine Roberts, Lady Mary Wroth.

This book was printed in the United States of America.

To order additional copies of this book, contact:
Xlibris Corporation
1-888-795-4274
www.Xlibris.com
Orders@Xlibris.com
28547

CONTENTS

DEDICATION

For Pat,
whose keen eye and uncommon sense
helped guide these essays through their wayward youth.

FOREWORD

I t isn't easy to say just what sort of book this is. It is assuredly a collection of some splendid essays Sam has written over the last two decades in the alumni magazine of the University of Pennsylvania. But it is not just an exercise in vanity or a well-deserved display of his way with words and appetite for ideas. Something—something hard to get a handle on—holds these essays together.

That is, I guess, where I come in. I've been at Penn for most of the last half-century. I graduated in 1961, came back to teach in 1965, and have been here ever since. Woodland Avenue still ran through the campus when I was a freshman, and trolleys still ran along it. Zavelle's pathetic little place was the only bookstore on campus, and Horn and Hardart's was the best restaurant west of the Schuylkill.

In fact, I've "been" at Penn a good deal longer than half a century. My father graduated from Wharton in 1927 and from the law school three years later. By the time I got to be six or seven, he and my mom got another season ticket and let me come with them to Penn football games. We had the same seats every year: East stands, lower level, a little more than halfway up, a little to the right of the goalposts. Those were the days, my friend. Skippy Minisi, Eddie Bell, Reds Bagnell, and Chuck Bednarik. Notre Dame and Michigan. Army when Army was Blanchard and Davis. Penn State when it was the ambitious little upstart and Penn the powerhouse with nothing to gain by defeating the kids in the funny blue and white uniforms. And, almost every game, 78,000 people in the stands, squeezed tush to tush on those hard benches. The toughest sports ticket in town.

So I go a long way back, and I've never really gone away. I've followed *The Pennsylvania Gazette* over the years, sometimes closely, sometimes not. Last, but probably not least, I'm a historian with more than a passing interest in matters pertaining to Penn and higher education. I suspect it's some combination of those elements that prompted Sam to ask me to write this foreword. He knew I'd have some thoughts about what holds these portraits together.

That is, I suspect, where you come in. You are probably a Penn alum, or a Penn parent, or a Penn student. Or connected to one, or more than one. Whether or not you go back as far as I do, you too go back. You have your own notions of the university and your own experience of it. You will bring those notions and that experience to this collection. They will shape the spirit in which you read these stories, and they should. This is your university as much as mine. You too will figure out what of Penn pervades these pieces or abides in this bricolage.

I find myself thinking of the three dentists who await you. They are a remarkable trio. Quite possibly, an unparalleled trio. Could another profession produce three men as different, one from another, as Doc Holliday, Zane Grey, and Thomas Evans? Two of them icons of our culture to this day: Doc Holliday the legendary gunfighter at the OK Corral, Zane Grey the prince of the pulp western. The third a byword in his own time: Thomas Evans the confidant of royalty, the dentist of derring-do, next only to P. T. Barnum the most celebrated American in the world in the nineteenth century.

Could any three accountants compare? Any three butchers, bakers, or candlestick makers? Any three doctors, lawyers, or Indian chiefs?

Could their connection to Penn be just an accident? Could the confluence at almost the same historical moment of the three men—one who gave up the profession altogether, one who brought its practice to the highest pitch, and one who once confessed that his nervous edginess abated only when he was in a gunfight or doing dental work—be mere coincidence? Or did it have something to do with Penn or reveal something about Penn?

Let me propose that it did.

Penn is one of the oldest schools in the land. Indeed, it is the very oldest—the very first—nonsectarian college in the country and, for all I know, in the world. Yet tradition does not rest heavily upon it. It does not impose an identity on its students or its graduates. It does not imprint itself on them in any obvious way. To be a Harvard man, or a Vassar woman, or a Princetonian, is to activate expectations and stereotypes. To be from Penn is not so charged.

There is something disconcerting in this. It used to find expression in sweatshirts embossed "Not Penn State." It still turns up in T-shirts emblazoned "Puck Frinceton."

But there is something liberating in it too. The world of Penn people is wider. They don't have to conform or rebel. Penn puts them in the way of a lot of brilliant people and then leaves them to their own devices. It does not define them, and it never has defined them. It has always been a more diverse, diffuse place. Its students have always gone their own way—have always *had* to go their own way—have always had to *find* their own way—while they were here and after they left.

So there was always room at Penn for the sort of people who would be dentists or pulp novelists or gunslingers. Penn has always been an elite institution, but it has never been comfortable with hierarchy. Its founder, Ben Franklin, was an implacable foe of hierarchy and of its age-old markers, Latin and Greek. He conceived a college leveled by language. All its instruction was to have been in English. Latin and Greek were not even to have been taught, let alone to be the languages of teaching, as they were at every other college in the colonies. So far as Franklin could see, the classics were only credentials for the upper crust. He did not want a society with a crust.

As Sam explains in his fascinating piece on Provost William Smith, the college that Franklin founded did not keep faith with him. But the university that grew from that college did embrace a dental school, where students learned to work with their hands in people's mouths. Harvard, Yale, and Princeton would not have lowered themselves. It did establish a business school, where students learned about making money. To this day, Princeton does not have one, and Harvard and Yale have theirs only on the graduate level, so as not to soil their undergraduates. When I was a young professor, Penn did have a school of allied medical professions that (I think) taught physical and occupational therapy. It still does have schools that teach social work, veterinary medicine, nursing, and education, and it puts them on a par with the liberal arts and the learned professions.

And of course it did admit large numbers of Jews at a time when Harvard, Yale, Princeton, and most other elite institutions set savage anti-Semitic quotas. It did admit large numbers of women at a time when, except for Cornell, every other school in what would later become the Ivy League either excluded them altogether or segregated them in a college of another name, so as not to sully the Brown, Columbia, or Harvard degree.

Penn was, despite itself, a cosmopolitan place. Or, at any rate, it was not as provincial a place as its so-called peer institutions. And in that regard it was like the city in which it sat.

In the eighteenth century and into the nineteenth, Philadelphia was America's largest and richest city, and its cultural capital besides. Even in the early twentieth century, it was still the nation's premier industrial center, and second only to New York as an intellectual center.

The city is not a leading character in these pieces. But it plays a supporting role, sometimes an important one, and nowhere more than in Sam's brilliant evocation of the sixty-year friendship of William Carlos Williams and Ezra Pound, which began when they started their studies at Penn in 1902.

That friendship was another one of those unlikely—almost inconceivable—conjunctions. The literary critic Philip Rahv argued that all American literature could be divided between the refined and the willfully primitive, the palefaces and the redskins as he called them. Pound was the most influential American paleface poet of the twentieth century and Williams the most influential redskin. And they met at Penn in their teens and maintained a warm, responsive regard for each other to the day Williams died.

They never took a class together. Their interests converged in poetry, in theater, in fencing, and especially in the observatory where the astronomer's daughter was the adolescent Hilda Doolittle, who would soon take to calling herself H.D. and establish herself as an important modern poet in her own right. They both had an eye for her and spent more time at the observatory in Upper Darby than they did on astronomy.

At Penn, neither Pound nor Williams set himself on the path to poetic prominence that each would find within a decade of departing. Neither discovered his poetic voice. Neither found a mentor to guide him or a sponsor to support him while he searched for it. Penn was not a place that provided patronage to favored protégés any more than it demanded discipleship of them. Pound and Williams both had to find their own way. But each had learned enough in his years at Penn to pay the dues of a world-shifting originality.

Noam Chomsky, the subject of another of the scintillating portraits that await you, also arrived at his transformative breakthroughs on his own. But Chomsky, acclaimed as the foremost intellectual in the English-speaking world in a recent survey, did learn from the man who guided both his undergraduate and graduate studies at Penn, the great linguist Zellig Harris.

Chomsky's tale, as Sam relates it, may be the most revealing of all the stories Sam tells. In many ways, it is not about Penn at all.

Chomsky came to Harris not so much through his studies at Penn as through the circles in which he and Harris both traveled in Philadelphia radical politics and in the Philadelphia Jewish community. Penn and the Philadelphia elite have never been incestuously interwoven, in the way in which, say, Harvard and the Boston elite have been. They couldn't be, because there was never a unified elite in Philadelphia as there was in Boston. From the seventeenth century to the present, the city's tradition of tolerance and pluralism promoted a multiplicity of discordant elites. The difference was no small part of the reason that Ben Franklin left Boston and never went back.

Nonetheless, as Franklin found in the eighteenth century, the boundaries between the city's diverse elites were not impassable. There were relations, fortuities, and serendipities. There were patterns, even if those patterns were not coercive.

As Sam makes clear, Chomsky couldn't have become Chomsky without Harris. But Harris wouldn't have been at Penn if Penn had been a more traditional place with a larger stake in the fixed hierarchy of the liberal arts and their long-standing role in conferring gentility. Penn had been willing to establish a department of linguistics when its peers would not contaminate the curriculum with such an innovation, and it had been willing to appoint a Russian-born Jew as the department's chair when its peers would not hire Jewish faculty at all.

And still Chomsky would not have met Harris without the Jewish connection that had to do with Philadelphia, not with Penn. It would be too much to say that there was a synergy between the city and the university. The connections were never systemic. Neither town nor gown was organized coherently enough for that. But the connections were possible, and they were the more apt to be truly innovative for their less patterned quality. (There is another essay still to be written on the stunning succession of African American novelists who have come out of Penn in recent years. I'd love to see Sam take up that topic.)

This collection is full of these tantalizing conjunctions and juxtapositions, and of their irresistible reverberations.

Take Sam's adjacent essays on Chomsky and Scott Nearing, the greatest intellectual of our time and a man who might have been one of the greatest of his. Each was amply aware that wide acceptance could not be his lot. To do his work, each needed the patronage of those he criticized. In his work, each kicked men of money and power in the teeth. But Chomsky was able to do his work within the academy in no small measure because Nearing was kicked out of the academy.

Sam's account of the Scott Nearing case is a revelation. If you think you know the case, as I thought I did, you may have some surprises in store. If you don't know anything about it, you will learn the little that I knew—that Penn's firing of a brilliant young instructor with radical political and economic views led to the establishment of an unprecedented principle of academic freedom across America—and a lot more besides. You may even find the story more inspiring than sordid. Even at its most shameful, Penn turns out to have been a place of a fair degree of decency and an odd sort of grace.

Do not misunderstand. Sam's narrative is not an exercise in exculpation. He doesn't do cover-ups. Like the *Gazette* for which he writes, he simply covers the story. The chips fall where they fall. There is no shortage of duplicity and sanctimony in his tale of the trustees who fired Nearing. Indeed, their immorality—and their cowardice in hiding behind their corporate anonymity to the very end—makes me cringe to have spent so much of my life associated with a place once governed by such men.

But their craven mendacity and their naked avidity for control also provoked some of the strongest, most eloquent arguments you are likely to encounter anywhere. Professors who loathed what Nearing said, and what he stood for, grasped what was at stake and enunciated principles of free speech before those principles even existed in any embodied institutional form. Students who came from families of the very privilege Nearing assailed gave him standing ovations for his assaults on their privilege, moved no more by his rhetorical panache than by their own ethical instinct.

As far back as the first decades of the twentieth century, those professors understood that a university could not be governed by the trustees who governed it and still be in any authentic sense a university, and they protested the actions of their governors. Those students understood that Nearing made them think, and they cheered him for it. The articulation of our modern ideals of academic freedom took form in the Nearing case. They took form in colleges and universities across the country, not just at Penn. But Penn faculty and students formulated them first and most feelingly, in the crucible of their own immediate experience. Literally hundreds, perhaps thousands, of them spoke up and acted out. Learning that they did made me as proud to be a part of this university as the fourteen trustees who fired Scott Nearing make me ashamed.

Of course, the larger part of this book is not about the Penn people who made headlines and history. You will find profiles of great men, like Leon Higginbotham, and of major figures, like Robert Strausz-Hupé. But they are here as much for their human interest as for their historical significance. Sam is not trying to chronicle the history of the university. He is exploring the realm where the personal, the historical, and the intellectual intersect. He has an extraordinary gift for getting inside people and their ideas, and for evoking the atmosphere of this particular grove of academe.

Some of Sam's sketches are surely of professors with whom you studied. They include men and women of no great consequence beyond their classrooms, their scholarship, and the professional meetings they attend. But their modest stories are the lifeblood that courses through this institution and in many ways the truest history of the place after all.

Penn is lustred by the great scholars who have studied and taught here. But it would not exist without the quirky dedication and the quixotic commitment of the ones whose names count for little beyond the campus. They are the lifers, the ones my son loved to call the ivy-covered professors, and Sam catches them and implies their indispensability as no one else ever has.

Most of these savants have been my colleagues, one way and another. But I have learned about them all in these essays, and especially about a few of them whose ethics always made me queasy. Those, I confess, I'd mistrusted and kept my distance from. Sam went to them, not because his moral standards are lower than mine but because his appetite for life is larger. A writer can't be as picky as a professor about the company he keeps. Fastidiousness impoverishes him. You will be the richer for Sam's richness of spirit and avidity for the human comedy.

Even if you do not come at these character pieces with the curiosity that comes of having had a class with their subjects, you will learn from them and, I'd bet, love them. Not because my colleagues are lovable—most of them are not—but because Sam's artistry and his integrity alike are so exceptional.

Again and again, he gets the revealing twinkle, the telling word, the giveaway gesture. In almost every portrait, he rises to some remarkable image, like the one of Martin Seligman's "high forehead and receding hairline" giving "the odd impression that his brain has blasted the follicles right out of the front end of his dome."

But it is not just Sam's acuity in observation. It is not just his scrupulousness in catching his subjects warts and all: his fearlessness in calling them on things they'd rather not recall, his consistency in giving their detractors a fair hearing, his refusal to confine them in simplistic polarities and dualisms, his capacity to catch intriguing complexities.

It is also his extraordinary gift for appreciation. Not in the sense of alumni-magazine-puff-piece appreciation but in the much more powerful sense of understanding what to appreciate. It is striking how well Sam's essays stand the test of time. Even as he wrote, he saw that his subjects were more intriguing than they were cracked up to be in contemporary polemic. Their edges were actually less hard and more blurry, and their significances were deeper, than either their friends or their enemies saw. But Sam saw, and you will see with him. You could not ask for a better guide.

—Dr. Michael Zuckerman, professor of history.

Author's Note &
Acknowledgements

It took me a while to figure out that there might be a book lurking in the stories I've written for *The Pennsylvania Gazette* over the last 15 years. Not that I ever doubted the star quality of the University's cast of characters, living or dead. Any troupe that includes the likes of Ben Franklin, Noam Chomsky, Ezra Pound, Leon Higginbotham, Zane Grey, Kathleen Hall Jamieson, William Carlos Williams, Alan Kors, Thomas Evans, Martin Seligman, and Robert Strausz-Hupé—to name just a few—has the potential for pretty amazing theater.

But it's one thing to write about them individually in a bi-monthly magazine; it's another thing to gather those portraits into a book and imply some sort of historical coherence. Over time, though, as I found more—and still more—outsized characters to write about, a rough narrative began to take shape. By telling their collective stories, I hoped I might be able to cast a bit of light on the institution itself.

The articles I chose were written between 1991 and 2004, spanning two editorial regimes and most of my time at the *Gazette*. A few are essentially un-retouched, but most received at least a minor tune-up, and a couple got extreme makeovers. (In the interest of readability, I dropped the abbreviated school/class system of letters and numbers that we use to identify alumni, though I kept most of the formal titles used for faculty and administrators.)

For the most part, and for sound reasons involving my sanity, I resisted the temptation to update the faculty profiles. But I did add a postscript to the piece on Robert Strausz-Hupé. He had asked me to help him write the second volume of his autobiography a year or two after my *Gazette* profile appeared, and while we were never able to work that out, I spent quite a few enjoyable

---

hours in his study drinking Sri Lankan tea, listening to his remarkable reminiscences and geopolitical assessments, and sometimes taking notes. He died in February 2002, a week before his 99th birthday. I miss him still, despite—or maybe because of—our very different worldviews.

Two of the other profiled faculty members are no longer with us. The legendary Leon Higginbotham reached the heavenly bench in 1998, five years after leaving Penn for Harvard (though he did stay on as a trustee). The brilliantly eccentric Paul Korshin succumbed to complications of lymphoma last year. I doubt that anyone who met either man will ever forget him.

I did not go to Penn myself, though I am the son of an alumnus, Edward W. Hughes, who graduated from the Wharton School in 1937 and died, too soon, in 1976. He didn't talk much about his time at Penn in that commuter-school era, but a few years ago, when I cleaned out our family's house in Pocopson, Pennsylvania, I took a closer look at the silver loving cup that had been in his room for more than half a century. The inscription revealed that it had been awarded to him his senior year as the "outstanding undergraduate of the ETA chapter of Delta Phi." That may not carry the weight of a Spoon or Cane or Bowl, but it suggests that he made at least a brief ripple on the surface of the Bio Pond during his time at Penn. Among the many regrets I have of people and things he never got to know (especially his two wonderful grandsons), I'm sorry he wasn't able to see the astonishing resurgence of his alma mater. Or this book—which also would have pleased my mother, Margaret Hughes, who was not only my most loyal reader but certainly one of the most perceptive. She passed away in November, a loss I am still coming to grips with.

I was steered to Penn by Alan Halpern, who graduated from the College in 1947 and went on to become the Godfather of Philadelphia journalism. (He even mumbled like Brando.) Alan was a gentle and benevolent Don, though he carried a stiletto made of words, and when he made me offers I couldn't refuse, they usually involved a terrific magazine. One was the *Gazette*, since he served for some years on the alumni publications committee that oversaw it, and often nudged writers in its direction. A year or so ago, when I was having second thoughts about this book, he strongly encouraged me to go ahead with it. He died this past December, but his mark on journalism—and on scores of ink-stained wretches—is indelible.

Tony Lyle hired me in the spring of 1991, and though I wouldn't accuse him of being an easy man to work for, he had an amazing instinct for a good story and was generous with praise when he got one. Marshall Ledger, who served for six months as the *Gazette*'s interim editor, pointed me toward the Provost Smith papers, and continues to be a source of wise counsel and friendship. John Prendergast, who took over in 1996, has edited with a steady

---

18

hand and a clear eye, and provided the kind of productive atmosphere and freedom to pursue a story that most writers only dream about. The rest of my colleagues at the *Gazette*—Cathy Gontarek (who did the terrific cover design for this book), Susan Frith, Peter Ivory, and Linda Caiazzo—have been as collegial and good-humored a group as I could ask for. Bob Alig, the dynamic director of Alumni Relations and supportive publisher of the *Gazette*, gave some timely and much-appreciated encouragement to the idea of this book. Thanks also to Mark Lloyd, director of the University Archives and Records Center, for letting me use the wonderful illustration by Ronald Searle, which first appeared on the cover of the April 1997 *Gazette.*

Too many others to name individually, across campus and beyond, have provided kindness, friendship, humor, and wisdom. You know who you are, I hope. But I will single out history professor Mike Zuckerman, who, in writing the fine and evocative foreword, proved himself to be a generous mensch as well as a brilliant scholar.

I may not get goose-bumps when I hear "The Red and the Blue." But I am proud to be associated with this fascinating university, and grateful for the forum it has provided me to tell these stories—as well as for the freedom to pursue them wherever they led me.

ORIGINS

Dueling Quills:
The Provost Smith Papers

Benjamin Franklin & Provost William Smith

(First published in April 1997 as
"Your Most Obedient Servant: The Provost Smith Papers.")

The ink has been dry for more than two centuries, and the paper
has brittled and turned a murky tea color. But the edgy indignation
practically quivers on the page:

> *An eminent Dissenter called on me and let me know that Dr. Franklin
> took uncommon Pains to misrepresent our academy . . . ; saying that it was
> a narrow bigotted Institution, got into the Hands of the Proprietary Party
> as an engine of Government; that the Dissenters had no Chance in it (tho'
> God knows all the Masters but myself are of that Persuasion) . . . ; that we
> have no occasion to beg; & that my zeal proceeds from a fear of its sinking
> and my losing my Livelyhood. But alas! who can believe this . . . .*

Well, quite a few people could, actually. The author of those sentiments,
dated 14 September 1762, was the Reverend William Smith, an Anglican
priest, provost of the College of Philadelphia, and a man admired more for his
considerable talents than for his moral character. The recipient was another
Anglican clergyman: the Reverend Richard Peters, secretary of the Provincial
Land Office and president of the College's trustees.

The subject, of course, was Benjamin Franklin, who—having picked Smith to head the academy that would eventually become the University of Pennsylvania—had been surreptitiously dumped as president of the trustees and replaced by Peters. He was thus rendered administratively impotent in the college he had founded. For that and other reasons, wrote Smith, "the old Rancor is still brooding at the Heart of this Man."

That Smith and Franklin came to detest each other is not news to historians of colonial Pennsylvania, though it has not been overly emphasized in the official chronicles of the University. But if history can be viewed as a series of portraits drawn from forensic evidence, then that letter of Smith's—and the scores of other documents that make up the Provost Smith Papers recently acquired by Penn—has just the sort of scarred bones and crowned teeth that can help sharpen the fuzzy composites of the key players in the College's first quarter-century.

"Smith is absolutely crucial to the early history of the colony, and absolutely at the center of the early history of the University," says Dr. Michael Zuckerman, professor of history. "Anything that thickens the information up, whether it's stunningly new or just confirms what we have, is still valuable because it takes us out of the realm of raw speculation."

"The central role of William Smith in colonial Pennsylvania politics has not been a fully explored aspect of the University's official history," says Mark Lloyd, director of the University Archives and Records Center and the man responsible for buying the papers. "When that role of Smith is placed in its context, the University's own history is significantly different."

The papers consist of more than 350 documents, mostly letters from and to Smith, but also a miscellany of court orders (Smith was once imprisoned by the Pennsylvania Assembly on libel charges), honorary degrees, poems, and the like, many pertaining to the fledgling College.

"Pray do not mix private and Academy business in one Letter," Peters tells Smith in December 1762, after the provost has committed yet another epistolary indiscretion. Fortunately for us, Smith ignored his advice.

"Smith was such a brilliant writer," says Lloyd, "and so candid in his communications with his patron, Thomas Penn, that the papers reveal a clarity of his motivations and intentions which we would today think of as very confidential. The content of these papers—not only from Smith to Penn but from Penn to Smith—is rarely captured in writing in our era of multiple, immediate communication. The kinds of things that are in these letters we now say in person or over the telephone—or some of us, nowadays, in e-mail."

It would take a couple of centuries for the papers to make their way back to the University. In 1779, the American Revolutionaries—one of whom was

Franklin—forced Smith out of the provostship of the College, changing its name to the University of the State of Pennsylvania and reorganizing its charter to something closer to Franklin's original non-sectarian vision. Though Smith regained control of the College in 1789, he would lose it once and for all in 1791, at which point the institution finally shortened its name to the University of Pennsylvania. And when he left, he took his personal and professional papers with him.

After Smith died in 1803, the papers passed on to his descendants, one of whom—his great-grandson, Horace Wemyss Smith—drew on them in the process of writing a very sympathetic biography. Though they were available to scholars at the Historical Society of Pennsylvania, the papers remained in private hands until 1992, and none of the University's authorized histories made use of them. In his recent *Benjamin Franklin, Politician: The Mask and the Man*, Dr. Francis Jennings noted that when he first examined the Smith papers at the Historical Society back in the sixties, they were not even catalogued "because of fear that the owning family might retrieve them."

"I confess that I don't feel very fond of William Smith after reading those letters," says Dr. Robert Middlekauff, professor of history at the University of California at Berkeley, who read them in the course of writing his recent book *Benjamin Franklin and His Enemies*. "He was not a popular man among a lot of people. But this doesn't mean he wasn't important; he was. It doesn't mean that his papers weren't important; they certainly were, and are."

"I think it's very important for Penn to have these papers, since Smith was the most important figure in the early days of the College, and has not been very adequately written up," agrees Dr. Richard Dunn, emeritus professor of history. "There has not been a very good biography of him. These could give a much more inside picture as to what Mr. Smith was up to."

I am still in my confinement, and (what is worse) with but little Prospect of a Speedy Release . . . . I know I need say nothing to press you to expedite my Complaint and Appeal. Your Love of Liberty and Law will induce you to do this.

Smith wrote that letter to Thomas Penn on 12 March 1758 from the Market Street "gaol," where he had been tossed by the Pennsylvania Assembly on politically motivated charges of libel. Penn was the proprietor of Pennsylvania, and while his love of liberty is open to debate, he did indeed help Smith in his fight with the Assembly. Eventually the charges were overturned by a ruling from the British Privy Council, though not before Smith had taught a number of classes from his cell, with the full approval of the trustees.

Pennsylvania had two sources of political power in those days. The first was the proprietors—the Penn family—whose charter gave them ownership of virtually the entire province. Not only could they distribute land through the Provincial Land Office as a means of rewarding the faithful; they also appointed the governor and the judges. While Thomas Penn may have been William Penn's son, he had been married in the Anglican Church, was living in London, and had effectively repudiated the politics and the religious ethos of his father. He and Smith, observes Middlekauff, were "tied to one another by interest, politics, and what became a passionate hatred of Benjamin Franklin."

Opposing the Proprietary Party in the popularly elected Assembly was a faction known as the Quaker Party, led by Franklin. Franklin was not a Quaker, and he had his share of disagreements with the "stiffrumps," as he sometimes called the more unyielding members, but he did respect their principles and their religious tolerance. He did not respect Thomas Penn, or most of the men who worked for him. After a confrontation with Penn in 1757, Franklin wrote: "I was astonished to see him thus meanly give up his Father's Character and conceived at that moment a more cordial and thorough Contempt for him than I ever before felt for any Man living—a Contempt that I cannot express in Words."

Some heated issues were simmering in colonial Pennsylvania: the French and Indian War, religious factionalism, and the problems of assimilating large numbers of German-speaking settlers. Then there was the tricky matter of molding young minds, which led to the founding of the Academy of Philadelphia in 1749 and its evolution to the degree-granting College of Philadelphia in 1755. (The official founding date of the University, 1740, might be said to commemorate a gleam in the eye, not a birth.)

If Franklin was its founder, Thomas Penn was its funder, and the talented, charismatic Smith—who had impressed Franklin with his notions of education in *A General Idea of the College of Mirania* in 1753—seemed the perfect choice to head the Academy. In Jennings's view, the Academy was "founded as competition for the Quaker [Penn Charter] school," and under Smith, "it was soon to give clear signals that Quakers were unwelcome in it."

Smith's attitude toward education can be seen in a 1753 letter regarding the education of the Germans in the province:

> *Liberty is the most dangerous of all weapons, in the hands of those who know not the use & value of it. Those who are in most cases free to speak and act as they please, had need be well instructed how to speak and act.*

Franklin and Penn were also fearful of the Germans in Pennsylvania, both for their unpredictable foreignness and for the possibility that they would ally themselves with the French. All three favored creating a series of schools to educate and Anglify the Germans. (Education for the Germans, wrote Smith, "must be calculated rather to make good subjects than what is called good scholars.") They also proposed a German-language newspaper, though in a letter from Penn to Smith, dated 24 October 1755, Penn reveals his growing distrust of Franklin:

> *I am very well pleased to hear the Dutch press is like to meet with Success. I wish it could have been under any direction but that of Mr. Franklin, however. I hope the Society and their Agents will be very watchfull that nothing is printed in it which may encourage the Licencious spirit that has been with so much application raised, to subvert all Government and dispose the unthinking multitude to throw off their Allegiances.*

At the vortex of Pennsylvania politics was the question of defending the province against the often-horrific Indian attacks—and paying for it. The Quakers, who dominated the Assembly, did not believe in armed defense. Thomas Penn, who did believe in it, did not want his lands to be taxed to pay for it. Franklin, exasperated by both sides, organized a delivery of wagons and horses to General Edward Braddock; he also led a hotly-worded attempt to tax all lands, including those owned by the proprietors. The Penn-appointed governor vetoed that bill, but as that same letter shows, Penn himself saw Franklin as a source of treacherous hostility:

> *I am astonished at Mr. Franklin's telling you he was my Friend; after the Report and the two last messages from the Assembly, can any man believe other than that he would destroy my family at once was it in his power; I say this supposing he was the drawer of those papers as I hear from all hands he was; a man might have made most of the Arguments, and have kept to truth, but he must be a weak and a wicked one, to show rancour, malice, draw false conclusions, and even related things that never were . . . . [H]e has the opposition to Government at heart and . . . will be satisfied with nothing but a subversion of all Government . . . .*

Penn concluded by saying that he would be "much obliged" for "any early intelligence"—in other words, for Smith to become his informer on Franklin and the Assembly. This, by all accounts, Smith was ready, able, and willing to do. Jennings, who acknowledges that the Smith papers helped him flesh out Smith as a "clandestine agent," says bluntly: "Penn had hired Smith to be his personal CIA—and Smith performed that capacity very enthusiastically."

Smith didn't just provide information. In May 1755, he wrote a fiery anonymous tract titled *A Brief State of the Province of Pennsylvania*, which Middlekauff describes as a "full-throated attack on the Assembly and the Quakers." It proposed, among other things, that Parliament enact a law that would disenfranchise all the province's Germans ("ignorant, proud, stubborn Clowns" who voted "in Shoals" for Quaker Party candidates) and would require all members of the Assembly to swear an oath of allegiance to the Crown—effectively disenfranchising the Quakers, whose beliefs forbade such oaths. In another tract, *A Brief View of the Province of Pennsylvania for the Year 1755*, Smith labeled the Quakers "Enemies to their Country."

Those tracts infuriated the Assembly, and probably contributed to Smith's prison stint two years later. But Penn was clearly pleased with Smith's work, and on 15 February 1756 wrote coyly to him:

> *There has lately appeared a pamphlet giving an account of the conduct of Pennsylvanians—very judiciously wrote and published at a most proper time, the author I think we are all obliged to . . . .*

Penn then asked Smith to inform him whether Franklin, then deputy postmaster general for the colonies, *looks upon the post office as a valuable thing, and such as he would not willingly loose, if he does I throw it out to you whether there may not be a time when you can ask him how he can reconcile such a republican conduct, in one of the Kings Servants . . . .*

He concluded by praising Smith for his ability to *silently do what good you can, that method may render you of great service, tho I see by newspapers, they suspect you, and call you names, according to this very decent method of proceeding.*

In January 1755, Smith drafted a new charter that would transform the Academy into a degree-granting College, and was promptly named its provost. The charter stipulated that trustees, faculty, and officers all had to "swear in blood-curdling terms to uphold King George II against all rebels, and also to deny under oath the Roman Catholic doctrine of transubstantiation," according to Jennings. "If Franklin had qualms, they did not appear; he was elected to the showy and toothless post of president . . . ."

But in the spring of 1756, while Franklin was away in Virginia, Smith "conspired with Peters to strip Franklin of the presidency of the College," in the words of Lloyd. In a letter to his friend and scientific collaborator Ebenezer Kinnersley, Franklin wrote: "Before I left Philadelphia, everything to be done in the Academy was privately preconcerted in a Cabal without my Knowledge or Participation, and accordingly carried into Execution. The Schemes of Public Parties made it seem requisite to lessen my Influence wherever it could be lessened. The Trustees had reap'd the full Advantage of my Head, Hands, Heart and Purse, in getting through the first Difficulties of the Design, and when they thought they could do without me, they laid me aside."

By then Smith had become, in Middlekauff's words, a "figure of sensationalism, an important leader in education and in the Anglican Church in Philadelphia, a journalist skilled in more than invective, though that was his specialty, and the proprietor's agent." In doing so, he had also "identified himself unwittingly as the enemy of popular government in Pennsylvania." All of which would have lasting implications for the College.

Sometime in the mid-18th century, a wasp lays its eggs on an oak leaf. The leaf responds by creating a bubble-like capsule, within which is a dark, tannic tissue known as gall. Take a bucket of gall, mix it with rusty nails, and you've got something called iron-gall ink—tough, indelible, and perfect for an 18th-century character-assassination.

Not everything is as durable as that ink, though. When Lloyd learned that the Smith papers were being sold at auction, he convinced the University to buy—for just under $40,000—all but a few of the most valuable letters. But the papers were in even worse condition than Lloyd had thought.

"We discovered they were so fragile that they could not be used without threat of harsh deterioration," he says. "The paper, when it gets brittle, will break off in your hand. So now we had the Smith papers, but we were forced to require scholars to use the microfilm. In 1995, I began a campaign to conserve the papers." (He got some help from friends and colleagues of Michel Huber, who had just retired as secretary of the General Alumni Society and suggested that they give money to the Archives in lieu of a retirement gift.)

Lloyd took them to the Conservation Center for Art and Historic Artifacts in Center City Philadelphia, and on a rainy morning we drive over and watch as the staff washes and de-acidifies the old letters, applies patches of wheat-starch paste and hand-made Japanese paper to the tears and fragments, and sews some of the letters by hand into folders.

One letter is particularly eye-catching. It's dated 14 August 1762, and in it, Smith—then in London—tells Richard Peters:

> *Dr. Franklin is gone from hence to embark at Portsmouth, but in what Temper I cannot say. He & I were not in the best Terms, nor the worst. He heard when down at Oxford of a Letter I had sent three years ago there to prevent his having a Degree, which he took in great Dudgeon; tho' as we stood then, and his doing all he could to support the Assembly in oppression & prevent my obtaining Redress, he could not expect that I could say anything in his Favour. At Mr. Strahan's desire, we met at his House & had the matter of the Letter over, but explaining did not mend the matter much on either side.*

Franklin's "dudgeon" seems understandable. Smith's letter to the president of St. John's College at the University of Oxford suggested that Oxford not go ahead with its plan to give Franklin an honorary degree—on the grounds that his famous electrical experiments, which he had conducted with Ebenezer Kinnersley, were mostly Kinnersley's doing, not Franklin's. Kinnersley himself openly defended Franklin on the plagiarism charges, and one Oxford professor concluded that Smith—who had received an honorary degree from Oxford himself—was "extremely unworthy of the Honour he has received from our University." After the meeting at William Strahan's house, according to Carl van Doren's biography of Franklin, "Smith agreed that he had been misinformed and rancorous and promised to write another letter withdrawing his charges. He did not write it, but spread the news in London and Oxford that Franklin had lost many of his friends in Philadelphia."

"I made that man my Enemy by doing him too much kindness," Franklin would later write of Smith. "'Tis the honestest way of acquiring an Enemy. And, since 'tis convenient to have at least one Enemy, who by his readiness to revile one on all occasions may make one careful of one's conduct, I shall keep him an Enemy for that purpose."

Smith did have an important institutional admirer, though: the Anglican Church. One of the papers in the collection is a "Representation" by the Archbishop of Canterbury and five bishops, dated 12 March 1759, that beats the drum loudly for Smith:

> *That during all the late Disturbances in America, he has shown himself a most faithful subject to his [Majesty's] Government, taking every opportunity to excite the People to the Defence of their inestimable Possessions, and to discourage that pernicious Doctrine too prevalent there,*

viz: *"That it is unlawfull for Christian men to wear Weapons and serve*
in the Wars" . . .

That last line was an unsubtle swipe at the Quakers.

While in England, Smith raised some 6,000 pounds for the College. He was aided by the archbishop, who got him an audience with King George III—who, in turn, issued a royal brief authorizing Smith to collect a special offering from every parish of the Church of England. But he still had to contend with the likes of Franklin undercutting his efforts, as this letter to Peters, dated 2 October 1762, shows:

> *I fear I was too hasty in believing Franklin's Professions for our*
> *College. Soon after I wrote you last, I had occasion to be with one Mr.*
> *Hanna, a very benevolent & wealthy Gentleman of Barbadoes, into whose*
> *Hand I put one of the Cases for our College. Calling sometime afterwards,*
> *he told me he had enquired about the College of some Gentlemen from*
> *Philadelphia & was informed it was "an instrument of Dissenssion"—I*
> *replied that I believed that Intelligence must have been thru a very partial*
> *Channel . . . & begged he would take his Account from some other Persons*
> *I then named. He said he could not take that Trouble, & then gave me*
> *25 [pounds] intimating that it was not near so much as he intended, &*
> *that he did not give it freely . . . . I soon found that Mr. Hanna had his*
> *Information from an intimate Friend of his Mr. T. Allen, who had it from*
> *young Franklin, who is continually after Mrs. Downs, Allen's Sister in*
> *Law. This I discovered by the Help of a Lady.*

According to Lloyd, Smith then spread the word that "young Franklin"— Ben's son William—was illegitimate. Tit for tat.

Meanwhile, back at the College, Richard Peters was agonizing over the conduct of the faculty, who were embroiled in a nasty series of "squabbles," and in May 1763, he confessed to Smith:

> *Indeed at times I am dispirited myself and with all my upright*
> *Intentions I am prompted almost to despair of doing Good. Everybody*
> *here is in a Scramble for wealth and power . . . .*

And because of the lack of qualified candidates, he added, *I blush to tell you we have not one Church Tutor in all the Academy.* That was a potentially embarrassing situation for a school now openly beholden to the Anglican

Church, and three months later, it nearly destroyed Smith's fundraising tour, as he recounted to Peters on 23 August 1763.

The archbishop, he wrote:

> read to me a letter from a certain too zealous & officious Clergyman of our Church, residing not a Days Journey from Philadelphia, . . . bringing the most grievous Charges against our College, that the Presbyterians had all the Advantage of it; [that at the recent Commencement the lone Anglican graduate] was used ill on account of his Religion & denied a Tutor's Place, to make way for a raw Scotch Irish Presbyterian from the back woods; that I had left 14 Presbyterian, Baptist etc. Masters, & not a Churchman in the College; that all the late Elections for Trustees had gone for Dyssenters; that our honorary Degrees were prostituted to serve Dyssenters; [including] one who had formerly been a Leather Breeches Maker . . . . I was luckily able by a letter of yours I had about me, regretting that you could meet with no Church Tutors, to shew that our Situation rose from Necessity, not Choice . . . .

Smith also knew how to raise funds on his own behalf, as this letter of 4 June 1763 to Richard Peters shows:

> It will absolutely be impossible, on my Return, to subsist on 250 [pounds] your money . . . . Many Things lie at my Feet, which I could have here for Asking—But I do not once think of them, lest that should have been thought the chief Object of my Voyage thither. Yet still something must be done . . . .

By 10 August 1764, Penn was informing Smith that the trustees were increasing his salary by 100 pounds. But all that Anglican money and fundraising aid did not come without strings attached, and in that same letter Penn said he was *greatly pleased to find you so much approve of what you call the fundamental Article in answer to the Letter Signed by the Archbishop, Dr. Chandler and myself* . . . .

That "fundamental Article" was nothing less than a change of the College's charter to one effectively guaranteeing an Anglican majority on the board of trustees. From then on, the College would be wide open to charges of religious favoritism.

Strangely enough, Franklin was then staking his political capital on a campaign to persuade the British Government to take Pennsylvania away from the Penn family and govern it as a Crown Province. "The truth was that he wanted to hurt Penn more than anything else," writes Middlekauff. "He said—and believed—that he wanted a royal government for his province. More than that, however, he wanted to take the province away from Thomas Penn." That he would make the attempt a decade before the Revolution is more than just an irony. It was also one reason that he lost his elected seat in the Assembly in 1764, since most Pennsylvanians were even more leery of royal government than they were of Thomas Penn—and they signed petitions in droves to prove it.

On 15 February 1765 Penn told Smith that the news of Franklin's defeat had given him "great joy," and added: *you have acted with great spirit in opposition to the republican measures of the faction, and to undeceive the misled populace and bring them to a right understanding; your pen has been of great use and we thank you in particular for your zeal in the petition and giving us timely intelligence.*

By the time Franklin finally abandoned his bid to gain royal government for Pennsylvania in 1768, the Quaker Party's power had faded; and by 1770, Franklin—whose experiences with the British Government had helped to radicalize him—had cast his lot with the rising faction known as the Presbyterian Party. And Pennsylvania found itself on the road to revolution.

M ark Lloyd is sitting in the offices of *The Pennsylvania Gazette*, talking about Smith's alliance with Thomas Penn and the Anglican Church and its repercussions for the College. He has thought and written a good deal about this stuff, and he speaks slowly and deliberately, making sure the subtleties of his argument don't get lost.

"It seems to me that Smith advanced the interests of the College of Philadelphia in the most politically shrewd manner available to him," he says, "but that path isolated him, the trustees, and the College from the mainstream of American political thought by the mid-1770s. Rather than following the inspiration of Franklin's *Proposals for the Education of Youth in Pensilvania*, Smith made the College of Philadelphia largely a replica of Old World higher education. My view is that from his appointment at Penn in 1754 forward, Smith steadily beat a path toward the most traditional, most conservative English educational precedent—precisely because that was where he could find the strength necessary to sustain the institution."

But the Revolution would change all that, and after the occupying British army withdrew from Philadelphia in 1779, the Assembly, having closed the College for the previous academic year, established a committee to look into its "present State." They concluded that it was rotten. The College's administration and trustees "now stand attainted as Traitors"; they have "an Evident Hostility to the present Government and Constitution of this State, and . . . Enmity to the common Cause"; and the "fair and original Plan of equal Privileges to all Denominations hath not been fully adhered to."

That November, the College was re-chartered as the University of the State of Pennsylvania, and the senior ministers of Philadelphia's Episcopal, Presbyterian, Baptist, Lutheran, German Reformed, and Roman Catholic churches were appointed as *ex officio* trustees—a "triumph of religious tolerance," in the words of Lloyd. Smith was removed from office and replaced by the Reverend John Ewing, a Presbyterian professor. And Benjamin Franklin, one suspects, was a very satisfied man.

The political winds would shift again after the Revolution, though, and in 1789, after some angry petitioning by Smith, the Assembly passed an act allowing the College of Philadelphia to reopen, headed by Smith. Philadelphia was unable to support two institutions of higher learning, however, and in 1791 the Assembly merged the College and the University of the State of Pennsylvania into the University of Pennsylvania—with Ewing as provost. Smith, who by then had already founded the school in Maryland that became Washington College, was now consigned to the University's history.

Franklin died in 1790, and at a memorial service put on by the American Philosophical Society the following year, a eulogy was delivered by none other than the society's secretary, William Smith. It was a long, flowery, and surprisingly laudatory speech, though it did allude to the antagonism between himself and Franklin during "the unhappy divisions and disputes . . . in the provincial politics of Pennsylvania." The debates of that day "have been read and admired as among the most masterly compositions of the kind which our language afford," he assured his audience, but "he who now addresses you was too much an actor in the scene to be fit for the discussion of it."

After the eulogy, according to Horace Wemyss Smith's biography, Smith asked his young daughter Rebecca how she liked his speech.

"Oh, papa," she replied, "it *was* beautiful, very beautiful, indeed; only . . . I don't think you believed more than one-tenth part of what you said of old Ben lightning-rod. Did you?" At that point, his great-grandson noted, Smith, "without either affirming or denying, laughed heartily."

SWASHBUCKLING
DENTISTS

CROWNS AND CONFIDENCES

THOMAS EVANS

(First published in November/December 1999.)

How well I remember Dr. Evans, who was our family dentist. He had a black beard. Many tales of his "successes" were whispered, perhaps fostered by himself—be that as it may, he was certainly attracted by beauty . . . It seemed somehow symbolic of the fashionable Second Empire that for the first time in history a dentist had succeeded in achieving an establishment comparable to [that of] a prince.—Baroness Agnes de Stoeckl, *When Men Had Time.*

It sometimes happens that when the crowned heads of Europe wish to communicate with one another without any responsibility they send for Evans to fix their teeth. As you are not likely to send so far for a dentist, I need only add that the messages of this sort, which he bears, are always communicated to him by word of mouth and in the presence of no witnesses.—Letter from John Bigelow, American Consul-General in Paris, to William Seward, U.S. Secretary of State, November 21, 1862.

Some professions, by their very nature, suggest glamour, intrigue, adventure. Dentistry, with all due respect, is not one of them. Which makes the achievements of Dr. Thomas Evans—the West Philadelphia native who funded the dental institute and museum that bears his name

---

(and which merged, after his death, with Penn's School of Dentistry)—all the more remarkable.

Consider: Having moved from Pennsylvania to Paris in 1847 without even speaking French, he became the dentist of choice and the trusted friend of a glittering array of kings, princes, empresses, grand duchesses, czars, sultans and other potentates. (A visit from Evans, wrote Baroness de Stoeckl, was a "profound honour," since he chose his patients "as a King chooses his Ministers.") He became the court-appointed surgeon-dentist and confidant of the Emperor Napoleon III and his wife, the Empress Eugénie, and he probably saved the latter's life at the fall of the Second Empire when he helped her escape from the Parisian mob to England. (Evans also helped save the life of Germany's Crown Prince Frederick long enough for him to reign for 99 days as Emperor Frederick III by fashioning a silver tracheotomy cannula for the prince's cancerous throat, allowing him to breathe.)

Although he spent most of his life in France, and lived in many ways like a Frenchman—*Le Gaulois* opined that Evans "had a thoroughly Parisian look about him and could inspire our instinctive friendship"—he remained a loyal American citizen. He was largely responsible for convincing Napoleon III not to recognize the Confederacy, thus keeping France firmly on the sidelines of the American Civil War. "I have a feeling that in many ways he saw himself as a successor to Benjamin Franklin, serving as an American in Paris," says Dr. D. Walter Cohen, former dean of the dental school. "He really was a Renaissance person." And, like Franklin, he valued both the useful and the ornamental.

Evans was a highly skilled and innovative dentist—in addition to his deft touch with gold-foil fillings, he was the first to use vulcanite rubber as a base for dentures (turning down a franchise offered him by Charles Goodyear); he also introduced nitrous oxide as an anesthetic to Europe. In a time when teeth were a source of unalloyed misery—and in a country where the dental arts were the province of quacks—his talents were bankable. But the fact that so many important men and women trusted him was due to his reassuring chair-side manner, his engaging conversation—and his discretion. He once described himself as "my patients' father confessor," and he liked to say that: "Ears hear, but they as mouth must often close."

Highly sensitive to human suffering, he introduced a light, ventilated, American-style ambulance and field hospital to the French, which saved many lives during the Franco-Prussian War of 1870-71. ("It is the dream of every French soldier, if he is wounded, to be taken to this ambulance," wrote Henry Labouchere, Paris correspondent for the London *Daily News.*)

For such contributions he was made a Commander of the Legion of Honor, the first American to enter the ranks of that organization.

Along the way, he became the publisher of the *American Register*, an English-language newspaper in Paris; organized the American Charitable Association of Paris to aid indigent American citizens; helped found the first American community church in Paris; and gave 100,000 francs to the Lafayette Home for young American women who came to Paris to study art.

As the Second Empire gave way to the Third Republic, "Handsome Tom" took on a beautiful mistress, Méry Laurent, who inspired so many artists and writers—including Edouard Manet and the poet Stéphane Mallarmé—that one wag appreciatively dubbed her "*toute la lyre*," the lyre in question being that of Orpheus. While acquiring mistresses may not rank among life's loftiest achievements, this one did indirectly lead to an art collection that *Le Figaro* hyperbolically described as "one of the most important and best collections of paintings which exists." It included several by Manet himself, three of which would resurface in the dental school's storage warehouse nearly 80 years after Evans' death—thus providing the foundation of the school's current endowment.

A few of the nearly 200 medals, ribbons, and other gaudy baubles he received from his royal clients still hang in a glass case at the entrance to the dental-school library. The carriage that Evans used to smuggle the Empress Eugénie out of Paris has been rescued from a shed at the New Bolton Center by Dr. James F. Galbally Jr., associate dean of the dental school, and taken to the Blérancourt Museum near Paris as a symbol of Franco-American friendship. The Manets are hanging in museums in Boston, Pittsburgh and Philadelphia. Evans' letters and papers are in the Department of Special Collections in Van Pelt Library and the dental-school library. The jewels—diamond necklaces, ruby-studded snuffboxes, brooches and rings and stickpins, inventoried at more than $1 million after his death—are in museums and private hands. By such remains can we identify the man.

F rom a very early age, Evans had an unusual sense of destiny. The boy who grew up in a Quaker household near what is now 37th and Chestnut streets saw his name "on a silver plate or perhaps a brass one—Thomas W. Evans, Dentist," he later wrote. "At night I dreamed of this plate on the door, of people coming to have their teeth filled, new ones made for them . . . and even in those childish days I thought perhaps I might some day be called Doctor . . . ."

His father tried to steer him toward a career as a lawyer, but finally gave in and let the sure-handed Tom become apprenticed to a silver- and goldsmith named Joseph Warner. There he became adept at manipulating metals; picked the brains of any dentists who came into Warner's shop; and read whatever books on dentistry he could get his hands on. His first patients were sheep and dogs and cattle, whose teeth he would drill and then fill with a tin-foil amalgam. Later, some trusting two-legged souls allowed him to plug their cavities.

In 1843, having attended lectures at Jefferson Medical College and studied with a leading Philadelphia dentist, he earned a certificate permitting him to practice the "art and mystery of dentistry." After practicing briefly in Baltimore, he hung out his shingle in Lancaster, Pennsylvania, and began making a name for himself with the new technique of gold-foil fillings.

Evans' motto—"gold, only gold"—was a wise one, says Dr. Milton B. Asbell, author of *A Century of Dentistry: A History of the University of Pennsylvania School of Dental Medicine 1878-1978*. Gold, he explains, "adhered to all surfaces of the tooth; it didn't decay; and when you were finished you could polish it and it looked like a piece of jewelry." Evans didn't invent the technique—which involves taking paper-thin sheets of gold, rolling them into tiny balls and then hammering them into a cavity, where they coalesce into each other—but his expertise with it brought him his fame and much of his fortune.

In 1847, he won the "First Premium" for his gold-foil fillings at the Franklin Institute's exhibition of arts and manufacture. The exhibit caught the eye of a Philadelphia physician named John C. Clark, who recommended him to Dr. Cyrus Starr Brewster, an American dentist in Paris whose clients included King Louis Philippe and his court. That November the 24-year-old dentist and his wife, Agnes, arrived by steamer in France.

A few months later, the Revolution of 1848 sent Louis Philippe, the "Citizen King," packing. By the end of that year, Prince Louis Napoleon—Napoleon Bonaparte's nephew—had gone from exiled pretender to president of the French Republic. A *coup d'etat* in 1851 paved the way for him to become Emperor Napoleon III.

By then he was already a patient of Evans, who had responded to an urgent summons to relieve a howling toothache the year before. Evans, filling in for Brewster (who was either traveling or ill), had handled the prince's molar with gentle efficiency. As he was leaving, Louis Napoleon said: "You are a young fellow, but clever. I like you." It was, to borrow from another Paris-loving American, the beginning of a beautiful friendship.

Each had a good deal to offer the other. Evans provided relief from frequent agony (the emperor, he wrote, had "extremely delicate teeth" and was "more than usually sensitive to pain") as well as his agreeable company and keen observations. Louis Napoleon could offer the enormous prestige of his imperial patronage—not to mention inside information about his plans to rebuild Paris, which enabled Evans to buy up strategically situated real estate and then sell it, at very handsome profits.

The emperor, who was enlightened enough to value talent and character over pedigree, "had an excellent opinion of dentists in general," wrote Evans, "and saw no reason why they should not be as proud of their specialty as the practitioners of any branch of medicine or surgery."

It was a good time to be an American dentist, armed with a good knowledge of anatomy and the latest scientific advancements. In the wake of the French Revolution, the profession had regressed to a medieval level, its status discernible from the old French proverb, "To lie like a dentist."

"Physicians and surgeons considered the care of the teeth as unworthy of their attention and science," wrote Evans, and as a result, "extractions were left to be performed by mountebanks at street corners, or fakirs at fairs, where the howls of the victims were drowned by the beating of drums, the clash of cymbals and the laughter and applause of the delighted and admiring crowd." Dentists, he added pointedly, were "expected to enter the house by the back-stairs," and he admitted that the occasional barb at his profession "sometimes left a sting." After a few years, Evans' reputation had reached a level where, if his wealthy patients did not treat him with respect, he politely sent them elsewhere. The effects of that, he noted, were "wonderful."

When Louis Napoleon began casting about for a wife, he entrusted Evans with the task of sounding out Princess Caroline Stephanie of Sweden while he tended to the royal bicuspids. Evans carried out his mission well—the first of many diplomacies—but in the end Napoleon married the Spanish Countess of Teba, Eugénie-Marie de Montijo de Guzman, in 1853. Evans, who had been filling her cavities, too, was naturally invited to the wedding, and later that year he was formally appointed "Surgeon Dentist to the Emperor," with a status comparable to that of the court physicians.

When Evans was about to depart for a visit to the United States in 1854, the emperor invited him to the Palace St.-Cloud, receiving him in the empress's antechamber. He then brought out the five-pointed star of the Legion of Honor, and pinned it on Evans' jacket.

"We want you to go home a knight," said Louis Napoleon, at which point Eugénie entered the room, saying that she wanted "to be the first to congratulate the Chevalier."

"I hope your friends in America," the emperor added, "will understand how much you are appreciated by us."

A summer day in 1864. The emperor's private study at Compiègne. Louis Napoleon is in an unusually somber mood. The American Civil War is going badly again, he reminds Evans; General J.A. Early's army is advancing on Washington; and he would not be at all surprised to be awakened some day soon by the news that the capital has been captured. He informs Evans that he is being pressured by England to recognize the Confederacy as the only way to bring about the end of the war, and acknowledges that he is strongly considering doing so.

Such a move would be devastating to the Union, and Evans, the only pro-Northern voice to have Louis Napoleon's ear, knows that he has to make a strong case. The war, he tells the emperor, is "certainly approaching an end"; the resources of the South are almost exhausted; and with nearly a million seasoned soldiers in the field, the military power of the North is "irresistible." Becoming "warm," as he later put it, and "quite carried away by my subject," he pleads for, in his own words, "hands off and to wait a little longer," since recognizing the Confederacy "would only cause much more blood to flow."

At that moment a hidden door opens in the wall. The eight-year-old prince imperial, known as Lou-Lou, enters the room. Evans goes for the heart. "For this boy's sake you cannot act," he says, putting his arm around Lou-Lou. "He is to succeed you, and the people of my country would visit it upon his head, if you had helped to destroy our great and happy Union."

Before the emperor has a chance to respond, Evans offers to take the next steamer to the United States and assess the military and political situation for himself, then report back. Louis Napoleon, with a hint of amusement, gives him his blessing and agrees to hold off on a decision until he receives Evans' report.

In Washington, the mood is glum, both for the prospects of ending the war and for President Lincoln's reelection. Evans meets with a "rather gloomy and dispirited" Seward and a guardedly optimistic Lincoln, who according to Evans is "much pleased" with the self-appointed mission. "Well, I guess we shall be able to pull through; it may take some time," Lincoln concludes. "But we shall succeed, *I think*." He and Seward suggest that Evans visit General Ulysses S. Grant, and provide him with a special pass and introductions.

Nightfall at City Point, Virginia., where the Army of the Potomac is laying siege to Richmond and Petersburg. A large campfire keeps the mosquitoes somewhat at bay. Grant lights a cigar, throws his leg over the arm of his chair and begins to talk.

It is the first of several personal meetings. Grant is frank and open with Evans, allowing him to take notes about his military strategy and discussing his correspondence with General William Tecumseh Sherman, which will lead to the famous march through Georgia. Grant is "very positive about the final result of the war," writes Evans, who is impressed with the general's military bearing. Together, they ride toward Richmond, at times drawing near enough to see the Confederate pickets; occasionally a shot whistles over their heads. (Grant will later write to his wife suggesting that they send one of their sons to France to be educated under Evans' auspices, and after his presidency will be entertained by Evans in Paris.)

Back in Washington, the mood is increasingly optimistic, and Evans concludes that the end of the war is "not far distant." He writes a letter detailing his observations to Louis Napoleon—who decides not to recognize the Confederacy, after all. The emperor later tells Evans that as soon as he read of Sherman's proposed plan to cut to the sea through Georgia, he saw by his maps that it was the "beginning of the end."

Evans was not an overly modest man, but any suspicions that he might have exaggerated his own influence with Louis Napoleon were, according to Seward, "entirely removed during our civil war . . . The execution of the trust by the doctor was in all respects moderate and becoming."

T he *Grand Prix d'Honneur* from the Paris Exposition of 1867: Where is it now? It was awarded to Evans—or, more properly, to the U.S. Sanitary Commission—for his exhibit of hospital tents, railroad hospital cars, surgical instruments and the like. Evans had already seen firsthand the gruesome results of modern warfare during the Crimean War and the French-Italian conflict of 1859, and his visit to Grant's headquarters allowed him to study a subject close to his heart: "provisions made for the care of the sick and wounded." That, and the two months he spent in Philadelphia afterwards gathering information about the latest developments in hygiene, led to a book detailing the work of the sanitary commission (a volunteer citizens' association that supplemented the work of the Army Medical Bureau). It was followed by another book, *Sanitary Institutions During the Austro-Prussian-Italian Conflict* of 1866. Both would impress important readers in Europe, and would, despite resistance from bureaucracies, lead to changes in the treatment of wounded soldiers.

With the help of Dr. Edward Crane, his friend and literary editor, Evans assembled, at his own expense, the various inventions that had saved tens of thousands of lives during the Civil War, and had them shipped to the Paris Exposition. The *Grand Prix d'Honneur* was presented by the emperor, and Evans himself received a special prize for his design of a light, well-ventilated "flying ambulance." One ranking physician from the French Army wrote that the various articles of the exhibition "all bear the stamp of the enlightened patriotism and the importance which the Americans attach to the preservation of human life and the alleviation of the inevitable evils of war."

When the Exposition ended, Evans quietly stored the materials on land near his own property for possible future use. Three years later, on the eve of the Franco-Prussian War, he would be elected president of the newly formed American International Sanitary Committee. During the grim siege of Paris, the American Ambulance, as the collection was called, would save many lives. By then, Evans would be involved in another, more personal mission of mercy.

The Franco-Prussian War was a bloody, humiliating disaster for France, as Evans had predicted, and it cost the emperor his crown. Louis Napoleon was taken prisoner by Germany following a disastrous battle at Sedan, and when the news reached Paris, the same people who had been shouting *"Vive la guerre!"* responded by tearing the Napoleonic eagles off the wrought-iron fences outside the Tuileries and shouting "Down with the Empire!" and "Death to the Spanish Woman!" General Louis Trochu, the military governor of Paris who had pledged to defend Eugénie to the death, locked himself in the Louvre until things quieted down.

It was not a good time to be the empress regent, who knew that her husband was a prisoner of war but did not know whether her 14-year-old Lou-Lou, a soldier in the French Army, was dead or alive. When Eugénie—accompanied by an attendant, Madame Lebreton—finally fled the Tuileries, she turned instinctively to Evans' mansion, Bella Rosa, on the Avenue de l'Imperatrice.

"The evil days have come," she told him, "and I am left alone." Evans did not hesitate to help her, even though he knew that the revolutionaries might well seize his property—or himself—in retaliation.

He began by persuading the exhausted empress to get some sleep and wait until the next morning, when he would take her by carriage, in disguise, to the coastal town of Deauville, where his wife was on holiday. Some members of the palace staff, anticipating the worst, had obtained several travel documents, including a British passport issued to "C.W. Campbell, M.D." and his patient, "Mrs. Burslem." Crane became Dr. Campbell; the empress became his patient; Evans would be her brother; and Madame Lebreton, her nurse.

At 5 o' clock the next morning, Evans, Crane, the empress and Madame Lebreton stepped into his brown, four-seated carriage and set off for the coast. When they passed through the Porte Maillot, Evans casually blocked the view of the empress with his body and a newspaper, and told the sentry that he and his friends were going for a drive in the country.

The journey took about a day and a half, and though it was tiring and uncomfortable—and occasionally unnerving—they made Deauville without serious mishap. Evans spent money liberally on rooms and fresh horses and carriages, and had to think quickly on a number of occasions. In the town of Lisieux, the story goes, a policeman was abusing a man in the street, whereupon Eugénie loudly announced that she was the empress and that the man must be let go. Evans gestured with his finger that the poor woman was off her nut, and the passers-by laughed and went on their way.

At her hotel in Deauville, Agnes Evans was astonished to see her "dear Tom," who looked faint and "deadly pale with great tears on his cheeks." He told her: "I have the empress to save—she must be hidden in your room until we can get her out of the country." He and Crane then found a British sailing yacht and asked the owner, Sir John Burgoyne, if he would take them across the channel to England. Burgoyne first refused, then, at Evans' and Crane's urging, put the question to his wife, who shamed him into agreeing.

"It is a great responsibility that you are asking me to assume," Burgoyne told him. "Perhaps," Evans replied; "but the greater the responsibility, the greater the honor."

The honor almost killed them. A terrific gale blew up, and nearly sank the ship. But after a harrowing night, they anchored in Ryde, on the Isle of Wight, and checked into a hotel, whereupon Evans discovered from a newspaper that the prince imperial was in Hastings, a short distance away. Evans then engineered the reunion, which must have been almost as touching as his rather ripe prose suggests: "The tears of joy flowed abundantly, and her lips murmured words of thanks to Heaven . . ."

The emperor, released by Prussia the following year, joined Eugénie at the mansion near London that Evans had helped her find. He died there two years later. Lou-Lou was killed in 1879 by Zulu warriors during a guerrilla war in South Africa. The only one who could identify the decomposed and mutilated body was Evans, who knew where the gold-foil fillings would be. The empress lived sadly on for many years, occasionally visited by Evans, who wrote *The Fall of the Second French Empire: Fragments of My Memoirs* to refute the "calumnies" that had been written about the imperial couple. Even his enemies would concede that he had remained loyal to the Second Empire, long after there was anything in it for him. But he adapted pretty well to the Third Republic, too.

She was tall, with an exquisite tea-rose complexion, blue eyes, and fair hair with hints of red, a laughing beauty with arched eyebrows and a wide-eyed gaze that gave her a bewitching expression of surprise. Her mouth was sensual, her bosom formidable, and she excited artists, especially Manet . . . .—Gerald Carson, *The Dentist and the Empress.*

One night in the spring of 1872, a beautiful actress named Marie Laurent appeared in an operetta titled *Le Roi Carotte*. After the performance, a basket brimming with white roses was handed to her. Attached was the card of *Thomas W. Evans, Dentist.*

"He carried her off into the warm April night in a handsome carriage," wrote Carson, "he a whiskered fiftyish gentleman with courtly manners, to see a show and later sip champagne in a cabaret." The next year, at the Chatelet theater, "the dancers parted, and Marie made her spectacular nude leap out of the silver shell."

Her name was later anglicized to Méry, and she enjoyed a "stable, orderly, almost bourgeois relationship" with Evans that lasted for a quarter of a century, despite the presence of the devoted Mrs. Evans at Bella Rosa. He gave her a monthly allowance of 5,000 francs, later raised it to 10,000, and provided her with an apartment on the Rue de Rome as well as a summer cottage at 9 Boulevard Lannes.

In return, along with her charms, Laurent introduced Evans to a wide circle of artists and writers, who were her friends and sometimes her lovers. Because of her salon in the apartment he was bankrolling, Evans became a rather discriminating art collector, buying paintings by Manet and James McNeill Whistler, among others. He indulged himself in the occasional literary enterprise, writing an introduction to the English version of *The Memoirs of Heinrich Heine*. Mallarmé, in love with Laurent but willing to accommodate her wealthy American benefactor, was kind enough to call Evans' essay a "subtle aesthetic piece of analysis." He also accompanied Evans and Laurent on a 10-day trip to the spa at Royat, and included Evans on a list of close friends who were to receive a copy of his latest book.

For Manet, Laurent was a favorite model, a faithful friend and quite possibly a lover. He painted her as the moody personification of "Autumn" in 1881, though as his health declined, he turned increasingly to still-lifes with flowers, two of which would be bought by Evans. For many years after his death in 1883, Laurent would place the first lilacs of the season on his grave.

"Flowers in a Crystal Vase," painted in 1882, is inscribed: "to my friend Dr. Evans, Manet," though the relationship was probably based mostly on their mutual friends, especially Laurent. She was a kind soul and a stimulating conversationalist as well as a beauty, and she appears to have been about as faithful to Evans as he was to Mrs. Evans. One night he caught her sneaking off to meet Manet after she had pleaded a migraine, though it only took a few days of sulking and stroking for him to get over it.

"In her own inconstant way," suggests Carson, "Méry Laurent was very much attached to the doctor." Laurent herself once said that leaving Evans "would be a wicked thing to do." So, she added: "I content myself with deceiving him."

W alter Cohen is holding forth in his office in Center City Philadelphia, wearing one of those baby-blue smocks that dentists use to shield their shirts from spray and spittle. On a wall facing his desk hangs a framed copy of "Flowers in a Crystal Vase," its colors slightly brighter than the original's. Cohen, the chancellor emeritus of Medical College of Pennsylvania-Hahnemann University, still keeps up his periodontal practice, and is kind enough to squeeze in an interview about Evans between patients.

Back in the late 1940s, when he was a student at Penn's dental school, the Evans Museum was open once a year, on Alumni Day. He still remembers visiting it as a junior and seeing "this beautiful writing table" that the czar of Russia had given to Evans, inlaid with photographs of Nicholas, Alexandra, and their children. The whole museum, for that matter, was filled with the extravagant mementos of Evans' life: paintings and jewelry, medals and tea services and snuffboxes—even Evans' carriage.

But in the late 1950s, under the late Dean Lester W. Burket, the school needed space for classrooms, and the museum was turned into the admissions emergency clinic. Its contents were cleared out. Some things went to the Smithsonian Institution in Washington; some were put in storage warehouses. Others ended up in dumpsters.

"When they cleared out the museum, things were thrown in the trash that people picked up," says Cohen. "Faculty members told me that sketches, the death mask of Verdi, I think—things that were significant were just tossed out. That was traumatic. I'm glad I wasn't part of that."

But Cohen could not forget that table. When he became dean in 1972, he and a curator from the Philadelphia Museum of Art drove up to a warehouse in North Philadelphia, where the remains of the Evans collection were stored. They finally found the czar's gift, which was badly warped.

Then, says Cohen: "I saw this lovely painting of a flower in a brioche, and it was signed 'Manet.' And I said, 'Look at this!'"

The curator reminded him that some of the paintings in the Evans collection were not considered authentic, and Cohen acknowledged the possibility that the "Manet" was among them. But he liked it, so he took it back and hung it in his office, where it remained for several years, along with another "fake" Manet they had found, a lithograph titled "Polichinelle."

The school, he decided, should take a detailed inventory of what remained of the Evans collection, with the idea of selling off its contents to form an endowment. They called in Christie's, the auction house, whose consultants went through the collection.

"When they came to my office, they said, 'What's this?'" he recalls. "I said, 'It's signed "Manet," but I've been told it's a fake.'" Christie's agreed, and valued it at $400.

In 1979, Dr. Paul Todd Makler, now curator of the University's art collection, became a special assistant to President Martin Meyerson and recommended that an inventory of Penn's entire art collection be taken. One of his first stops was the dental school, where he saw the painting of the brioche hanging behind a secretary's desk. "I didn't think it should sit there," he says, "so I took it off the wall and brought it back on the trolley car to my home and said to my wife, 'Look! We have a Manet!' And then we started to look into the matter."

Makler took it first to the Philadelphia Museum of Art, whose curator of French Impressionism did not think it authentic. Makler, unconvinced, then called an old friend: Anne Coffin Hanson, professor of art history at Yale University and author of *Manet and the Modern Tradition*. The painting "looked good" to her, recalls Makler, whereupon she went back and read the 1897 *notaire*'s list of Evans' possessions when he died, and discovered that the dentist had indeed owned a number of paintings by Manet. One was an oil of a brioche, which Manet had mentioned in his expense book ("Evans, 1880, brioche . . . 500 [francs]"). Another was the lithograph of Polichinelle, "with the autograph signature of the artist." Another was a "marine view." Then there was one of flowers in a crystal vase—which, after another search of that North Philadelphia warehouse, was found, unframed, in a box of miscellaneous items. It was inscribed, "*a mon ami le Dr Evans, Manet.*" Hanson would later write up the story in an article for *Art in America* titled "A Tale of Two Manets."

By then, a sympathetic judge had agreed to let the school "de-accession" its collection, and in 1983 the "Still Life with Brioche" and "Flowers in a Crystal Vase" were auctioned off for $2.1 million. "Brioche" now hangs in the Carnegie Museum of Art in Pittsburgh; "Flowers" is at the Museum of Fine Arts in Boston. The "Polichinelle" lithograph went to the Philadelphia Museum of Art.

But the third oil painting by Manet, the "marine view" ("Beach, Low Tide") that had hung in Evans' operating office in Paris, was unaccounted for—until Cohen mentioned it to one of his dental patients: the late Violette DeMazia, curator of the Barnes Foundation in Merion, Pennsylvania. She knew exactly where it was: in the Rockefeller collection in New York. The lawyer who settled Evans' estate, she said, took it in lieu of a fee.

W hen Charles C. Harrison, provost of the University, sailed to France in June 1897, he intended to talk to Evans about a possible legacy. That impending visit, notes Milton Asbell in his history of the dental school, was a "stimulus" to Evans, who reacted by "setting down in black and white very definite plans concerning the distribution of his wealth."

But Harrison and Evans never got to have that talk. Agnes Evans died shortly before Harrison arrived. Evans immediately sailed for America, intending to bury her in Woodlands Cemetery in West Philadelphia. Harrison headed back to the United States, but he missed him on this side of the Atlantic, too. (According to Carson, Evans did have a "congenial meeting" with Harrison's predecessor, Dr. William Pepper, since Evans was then trying to convince French universities to recognize American college degrees.) And in November—almost exactly half a century after arriving in France—Evans died suddenly at Bella Rosa.

He was buried in the mausoleum he had built for his family in Woodlands Cemetery, which is marked by a 150-foot, Washington Monument-like monolith that cost upwards of $100,000 in 1897 dollars. It still casts the longest shadow in the neighborhood.

T om and Agnes Evans had no children. The closest he came to a dental heir was a former playmate of Lou-Lou's at the Tuileries named Arthur C. Hugenschmidt—who, at Evans' urging, attended Penn's new School of Dentistry, then gradually took over Evans' practice, which he carried on, with considerable flair, for half a century. (One of his patients was Dr. Robert Strausz-Hupé, the subject of "Smoke and Steel.") Evans had less luck with his nephew John Henry Evans, whom he had brought from Philadelphia to work as an apprentice in his office. The younger Evans so infuriated his Uncle Tom with his pretensions to nobility (and for swiping some of his patients and using the famous name *Evans* on a line of dental products) that the elder Evans tried—unsuccessfully—to have him deported.

He also pointedly cut him out of his will, "for reasons as well known to the said John Henry Evans as to me."

Many thought that Evans would leave his fortune—some $5 million in 1897 dollars—to the city of Paris, or for a museum there that would display his art collection and royal gifts. But when the will was opened, it provided for a museum and a dental school—"not inferior to any already established"—on his family's property at 40th and Spruce streets in Philadelphia.

Evans' relatives—16 of them, led by the said John Henry Evans—tried to overturn the will, on the grounds that he had left the money to the Thomas W. Evans Museum and Dental Institute, which did not actually exist at the time of his death. Years of legal wrangling followed. So did millions of dollars—not to mention a Manet—in lawyers' fees. By the time the dust settled, the Philadelphia-based Thomas W. Evans Museum and Dental Institute Society was left with about $1.75 million—a goodly sum in those days, but not enough to build *and* staff the kind of facility Evans had envisioned. The University had a keen interest in the outcome, but since it could not afford to look *too* interested, Harrison advised Dr. Edward C. Kirk, dean of the dental school, to "leave it severely alone."

Finally, in 1912, a compromise was announced: the new institution would be called the "Thomas W. Evans Museum and Dental Institute School of Dentistry University of Pennsylvania," and its board would be made up of trustees of both organizations. In May, 1913, the cornerstone for the handsome collegiate Gothic building was laid, amid much hoopla and praise for Evans. Among the well-wishers was the former Empress Eugénie, then 87 years old, who sent a letter congratulating Kirk on the "realization of the generous idea" of her late friend and protector.

"I am reminded of his sincerity," she wrote, "the proof of which he gave me in the darkest hours of my life."

E vans' life inspired several books, many magazine and newspaper articles, and a number of doctoral theses, including Anthony Branch's unpublished "Dr. Thomas W. Evans: American Dentist in Paris 1847-1897," a copy of which is in the dental school's library. But his story is one for the movies, really, and when Walter Cohen was dean of the dental school, he went so far as to pitch the film rights to *Masterpiece Theatre* and a few Hollywood producers. There was some interest, he recalls, but there was also one small catch.

The character of Evans, he was told, could not be a dentist.

DENTIST OF THE PURPLE SAGE

ZANE GREY

(First published in March/April 2004.)

Consider the plight of our fictional hero, Ken Ward, a freshman at an Eastern university suspiciously similar to Penn in the 1890s:

He has already started a near-riot for refusing to give up his seat in a lecture hall to a sophomore. Worse, the sophomore he slugged to start the melee turned out to be not only class president but captain of the varsity baseball team, which Ward had been hoping to join.

Now he is a marked man, and on a cold winter afternoon, he hurries from class and finds himself face-to-face with a tall, bronze-haired sophomore.

"Boys, here's that slugging Freshie!" yelled the Soph. "We've got him now."

Ward takes off, pursued by a dozen bloodthirsty sophomores. He turns first toward the university's "magnificent club-house" (a dead ringer for Houston Hall), but finally heads for College Hall—which turns out to be crawling with the enemy.

Ken was heavy and fast on his feet, and with fear lending him wings he made a run through College Hall that would have been a delight to the football coach . . . He knocked them right and left, and many a surprised Soph he tumbled over.

Fleeing the building, his tormentors hot on his trail, he runs toward a distant avenue and finally clambers up a high, icy stairway that leads up to the sidewalk. Enter Fate, in the form of two boys carrying a bushel basket of potatoes. A "daring inspiration" flashes through our hero's mind, and he grabs the basket from the boys. What follows sounds like something out of a pulp-fiction Western, transplanted to an Eastern university:

The bronze-headed Soph was half-way up the steps. His followers, twelve or more, were climbing after him. Then a line of others stretched all the way to College Hall.

With a grim certainty of his mastery of the situation Ken threw a huge potato at his leading pursuer. Fair and square on the bronze head it struck with a sharp crack. Like a tenpin the Soph went down . . . Deliberately Ken fired the heavy missiles. They struck with sodden thuds against the bodies of the struggling sophomores . . . Then two more started up abreast. The first Ken hit over the eye with a very small potato, which popped like an explosive bullet and flew into bits . . . Ken landed on the second fellow in the pit of the stomach with a very large potato. There was a sound as of a suddenly struck bass-drum. The Soph crumpled up over the railing, slid down, and fell among his comrades, effectually blocking the stairway . . .

"Dodge, you Indian!" yelled Ken, as he threw. And seldom it was that dodging was of any use.

—From *The Young Pitcher,* by Zane Grey.

B efore Zane Grey was a pulp-Western superstar, he was a dentist, and before he was a dentist he was a pretty fair ballplayer—good enough to turn down several professional offers in order to come to Penn on what amounted to a baseball scholarship. His name was Pearl Zane Gray back then (he would later change the spelling to *Grey),* and his live arm and strong bat lustered his wobbly career as a dental student.

The Young Pitcher, one of several baseball books he churned out, is highly autobiographical—the potato-pitching scene really happened—and undoubtedly the best-selling novel ever set on the Penn campus, thinly disguised though it was. It paints a lively portrait of *fin de siècle* Penn, and of baseball in its raw, still-evolving youth. (Aficionados of the game today would get a kick out of such pitching terms as "jump ball," "drop ball," and "in curve.")

It is not a prose masterpiece; nothing that Zane Grey wrote was. But it's bursting with Horatio Alger pluck, befitting a man who started with nothing and, through hard work, a little luck, and a passion for his subject matter became the most commercially successful writer of his era.

By the time *The Young Pitcher* was published in 1911, Grey had achieved enough success that he could drop dentistry, which he had been reluctantly practicing in Manhattan. He was living in Lackawaxen, Pennsylvania, on the Delaware River, where he spent his days writing and fishing—not necessarily in that order. The year before, he had published *The Heritage of the Desert*, his first Western novel, whose hero is a consumptive Easterner headed west in search of a new life and a better climate for his TB. (One wonders if he had in mind the story of his fellow Philadelphia-trained dentist, Doc Holliday.)

The Heritage of the Desert would tap a rich vein in the American psyche, and the novel he was already working on, *Riders of the Purple Sage*, would hit a mother lode. And they were just the start. By the time Grey died in 1939, his main publisher, Harpers, had hailed him as the "greatest selling author of all time," and estimated that his books had sold more than 17 million copies, notes Thomas Pauly in *Zane Grey: His Life, His Adventures, His Women*. Altogether, he churned out some 90 books, two-thirds of them Westerns, and the manuscripts kept trickling out of his estate for years after death stopped his hand. (His *George Washington, Frontiersman*, wasn't published until 1994.) An astonishing 110 movies have been made from his novels, while *Zane Grey Theatre*, hosted by Dick Powell, brought Grey's spirit to prime-time from 1956-1962.

Yet his success as a writer came in spite of a glaring lack of craft.

"[A]lmost any passage in any one of Zane Grey's books makes it cruelly obvious that the man failed to master even the most basic unit of his craft: the prose sentence," writes Larry McMurtry in an essay titled "Pulpmaster." "It's not evident from the prose that Zane Grey even noticed sentences—he was scribbling them off too fast . . ." Try this, from *The Heritage of the Desert*:

> *For an instant Hare's brain reeled, and Mescal's broken murmurings were meaningless. Then his faculties grew steady and acute; he held the girl as if he intended never to let her go. Mescal clung to him with a wildness that gave him anxiety for her reason; there was something almost fierce in the tension of her arms, in the blind groping for his face.*
>
> *"Mescal! It's Jack, safe and well," he said. "Let me look at you."*
>
> *At the sound of his voice all her rigid strength changed to a yielding weakness . . .*

But if it's easy to snicker at him for being a Writer of the Purple Prose, it's also missing the point. The fact that his "cactus opera" (to borrow *The New Yorker*'s phrase) often erupts in breathless bursts of melodrama doesn't mean it has no merit; just that its merits are somewhat artless. Grey was an outdoorsman, not a craftsman; he seldom bothered to rework his rough drafts, preferring to let his wife, Dolly, take care of that unpleasantness while he went off and fished. (After he and his family moved to California, he became one of the world's great sport-fishermen, sailing around the globe and setting records for everything from bluefin tuna to tiger shark.) When Dolly didn't make over his work, editors often rejected it.

For all his lack of craft, Grey seems to have been in touch with something primal—a sort of arch-storyteller whose soap-operatic tales resonated with the public in a way that more sophisticated literature wouldn't. He was also wildly in love with his subject matter, and had the constitution and the desire to channel rivers of words—more than nine million of them, by one estimate—onto the page. Perhaps, as Larry McMurtry suggests, "it will soon be discovered that there is even a gene for pulp fiction—or, if not a whole gene, at least an errant particle that induces in its victims a kind of lifelong, low-grade logorrhea."

The same defiant energies that made Pearl Gray take on bullying sophomores would lead Zane Grey to imagine the mythic West in book after book after book. His timing was perfect. Another Pennsylvanian, Owen Wister, had already helped create that mythos in *The Virginian*, published in 1902. Grey seized it and galloped with it across the plains, deserts, and mountains of the West.

"Novels by Zane Grey crystallized a set of symbols for the American West in the minds of his millions of readers," wrote Kevin S. Blake in a *Geographical Review* essay titled "Zane Grey and Images of the American West." "He infused the frontier myth with vivid imagery of a sublime and beautiful landscape inhabited by heroic cowboys, deadly gunmen, polygamous Mormons, and noble Indians. He also localized the myth in and along the southern margin of the Colorado Plateau, so that this landscape became the quintessential West. By extending his version into the 1930s, Grey encouraged the belief that the Wild West persisted well into the twentieth century."

His effect on the nation's self-image can be gleaned from a 1952 "Talk of the Town" item in *The New Yorker*. The State Department had "just asked Mrs. Grey's permission to translate 'Riders of the Purple Sage' into Annamese," the magazine noted, "so that it can be distributed in Indo-China for propaganda purposes."

It was sheer human glory in the deed of a fearless man. It was hot, primitive instinct to live—to fight . . . Venters lifted his rifle and pulled the trigger twice.

The first flush, the raging of Venters's wrath, passed, to leave him in sullen, almost cold possession of his will. It was a deadly mood, utterly foreign to his nature, engendered, fostered, and released by the wild passions of wild men in a wild country . . .

Yes, the border was a bloody place. But life had always been bloody.
Men were blood-spillers . . . On sea, on land, everywhere—shooting,
stabbing, cursing, clashing, fighting men!

—Zane Grey, *Riders of the Purple Sage.*

It might be stretching things to say that the sophomore Class of 1895 helped transform Pearl Gray, a penniless, girly-named dental student from Ohio, into Zane Grey, the driven creator of manly Western tales adored by millions. Then again, it might not. True, the Sophs were just a product of the world around them, acting out their bullying rituals like every other sophomore class of that era. (A decade later, some Sophs from the Class of 1904 would toss a recalcitrant freshman named Ezra Pound into the Lily Pond, as the Bio Pond was then called.) And Gray might well have become a successful, high-testosterone writer had he never encountered a member of that hated breed. But if you were looking for a defining moment in the young man's psychic growth, the temptation to zoom in on that first trial by fire is irresistible.

It began when he attended an anatomy lecture in an amphitheater—presumably in the building now called Logan Hall—and made the mistake of sitting in a row traditionally reserved for upperclassmen. A big, blond, "husky-voiced sophomore" got to his feet and roared: "Watch me throw Freshie out!"

Freshie may have been scared, but he wasn't budging. When the sophomore tried to pull him away, Pearl gave him a violent shove that sent him backward over a row of seats into the midst of his classmates.

Here's how biographer Frank Gruber, drawing on Grey's unfinished, unpublished autobiography, put it: "Pandemonium broke out. The sophomores rose en masse to get to Pearl, and the freshmen spilled down from their heights to rescue their champion. The amphitheater became a scene of riot, and when it was over Pearl was stark naked, except for one sock. His clothing had been torn from him, including his shoes."

Compare that with the more detailed, fictional version in *The Young Pitcher*:

> *"Hang, Freshie!" bellowed a freshman from the topmost row. It was*
> *acceptance of the challenge, the battle-cry flung down to the Sophs. A roar*
> *rose from the pit. The freshmen, outnumbering the sophomores, drowned*
> *the roar in a hoarser one . . .*
>
> *Ken thrilled in all his being. The freshmen were with him! . . . [H]e*
> *clenched his fingers into the bench, vowing he would hang there until hauled*

away . . . Suddenly Ken let go his hold, pushed one fellow violently, then swung his fists . . .

Like climbing, tumbling apes the two classes spilled themselves up and down the benches, and those nearest Ken laid hold of him, pulling him in opposite directions . . .

His clothes were torn to tatters in a twinkling; they were soon torn completely off, leaving only his shoes and socks . . . There was one more prolonged, straining struggle, then Ken was pulled away from the sophomores . . . [I]t was first blood for the freshman class.

One of his fellow classmen lent him an overcoat to hide his nakedness. Ken Ward was a hero now. So, in real life, was Pearl Gray.

F or a while, anyway. Despite his athletic prowess, Gray was never a Big Man On Campus, and his years at Penn were not all sunshine. (His unpublished autobiography ends during the summer between his freshman and sophomore years, notes Pauly—just before Gray was arrested on a paternity charge based on a complaint by a young lady in Ohio.) He was something of a loner, a trait magnified by the fact that he didn't drink—though he did learn to play poker at Penn, which would serve him well on some of his Western sojourns. His main non-athletic sanctuary was the new Frank Furness-designed library, even if he didn't go there for the books. "I seldom read anything," he later acknowledged; "there I seemed to escape from the turmoil of college, and from myself."

His approach to his dental studies was similarly lackadaisical. Mechanical and operative dentistry were a "trial"; he didn't care for anatomy and physiology; he found chemistry difficult and the chemistry professor, Dr. Wormly, "crabby and austere." (In *The Young Pitcher*, Wormly's counterpart is nicknamed *Crab.*) The only thing he really liked was histology (microscopic anatomy) and its professor, Robert "Bobby" Formad.

To make matters worse, the University decreed that a student had to pass his first year's examinations before he could play on a team—which meant that Gray had to take his exams two months before everybody else.

That he survived may have had something to do with a tolerant attitude toward athletes. "He went before Old Pop Wormly in chemistry, who asked Pearl a few simple questions," writes Gruber. "Pearl had to guess at the answers." Wormly then asked him about baseball, knowing nothing about the game himself. "When Pearl finished, Wormly drawled, 'Well, Mr. Gray,

you know a good deal more about baseball than you do about chemistry.'"
He gave Gray a passing grade.

Gray did even worse in some other courses, but his hide was saved by
Professor Formad, who dispensed with the exam and gave him a 99. "You
are one of the best students in histology I have ever had," he told Gray. That
grade raised his average enough for him to stay on at Penn.

Equally important, it allowed Gray to play for the varsity, and according
to his unpublished memoir, he made the team that wintry day when he
decimated his sophomore tormentors with potatoes. After that battle, it
seems, he went back to his rented room in West Philadelphia, wondering if
he would be expelled or arrested, when a "short, derby-hatted man with a
huge cigar in his mouth" showed up at his door and gave Gray the once-over.
Here is Gruber's account, based on that unfinished memoir:

> *"Where'd you get the whip?" he demanded.*
> *Pearl could only stare at him.*
> *The little man chuckled. "Pearl Gray, I know all about you. I've had
> a report about your pitching in Ohio from one of our alumni scouts. I'm
> Arthur Irwin of the Philadelphia National League team, but I'm also the
> varsity baseball coach at the university. Now, keep it under your hat, but
> that potato stunt of yours has made you a member of the Pennsylvania
> varsity!"*

Actually, Arthur Irwin—whom Gray affectionately fictionalized as "Worry
Arthurs" in *The Young Pitcher*, and to whom he dedicated one of his other baseball
books—didn't start managing the Phillies until 1894, Gray's sophomore year.
(Two years later, Irwin became manager of the New York Giants—whom
Penn beat in an exhibition game.) And one has to wonder if Zane Grey didn't
embroider the facts a little about the reason for his ascension to the varsity.

Pearl Gray soon had another thing to worry about. Before his first season,
the National League changed the distance between the pitcher's mound and
home plate from 50 feet to 60, and the college teams had to follow the new
rule. Gray, who had spent years practicing his curveball for the old dimensions,
suddenly couldn't get one over the plate.

Since he could still hit, he was put in the outfield. There may be some
clues about his fielding prowess in *The Young Pitcher*. During a particularly
ugly loss, outfielder Ken Ward "ran around like a chicken with its head off,"
in the words of an opposing player, and was finally benched. But the young
team's plucky performance inspired a rousing speech to the undergraduates
on "college spirit" from the university's fictional President Halstead. After

a token warning about the fate that might befall a student who "slights his studies for athletic glory," the president scolded the upperclassmen for not supporting the team, and concluded by singling out a certain outfielder:

> *"That young fellow Ward—what torture that inning of successive hard hits to his territory! . . . Every attempt he made was a failure—that is, failure from the point of view of properly fielding the ball. But, gentlemen, that day was not a failure for young Ward. It was a grand success . . . the most splendid effort ever made on Grant Field. For it was made against defeat, fear, ridicule. It was elimination of self."*

Chances are, President Halstead's real-life Penn counterpart, Charles C. Harrison, never singled out Pearl Gray for such treacly praise. But Gray didn't want for glory. In the last game of his senior season, he came to bat against the University of Virginia with two outs in the bottom of the ninth, a man on second, and Penn down a run. A professor shouted: "Gray, the honor of the University of Pennsylvania rests with you!"

Gray responded with a home run.

"The crowd covered him with roses," writes Gruber, "and the papers called him the real-life Frank Merriwell, the popular fiction character who always came up to bat in the last half of the ninth and won the game."

The memory of that triumph probably helped sustain him during the next decade, during which he moved to New York, practiced dentistry, and tried to crack the publishing world. Years later, he would tell interviewers that a wealthy dental patient had offered to lend him the money to publish his first book—*Betty Zane*, a Revolutionary War-era novel based on one of his ancestors. What he didn't say was that the patient was one Lina Elise Roth, better known as Dolly, whom he had been courting for three years. Dolly paid the cost of self-publishing *Betty Zane* in 1903, and in 1907, two years after they married, she used the last of her inheritance to underwrite his first solo trip to the West.

That trip grew out of a talk by one J. C. "Buffalo" Jones, a former buffalo hunter who was attempting to breed "cattalo"—a hybrid of buffalo and cattle—on his ranch near the Grand Canyon. Grey heard him speak at the Campfire Club in New York, and while most of the audience hooted at his implausible-sounding adventure stories, Grey believed him. He proposed to accompany Jones out West and write a book about his work. Jones agreed, and the planning commenced—until Grey saw how much the trip would cost, at which point he realized he couldn't afford it. But Dolly, who was sharp enough to describe her husband's more overblown passages as "periods of retardation," also had the vision to see his potential.

"I've got a hunch that this trip to the West will be the turning point in your career," she told him.

The trip—during which he rode into the wilderness with some tough-minded Mormons, shot a mountain lion, and drank in the landscape—sparked a lifelong obsession with the West. It also yielded *The Last of the Plainsmen*, whose scope was considerably broader than Buffalo Jones' cattalo experiments.

There was only one problem. "I do not see anything in this to convince me you can write either narrative or fiction," a Harper Brothers editor named Ripley Hitchcock told Grey after reading *The Last of the Plainsmen*. A dozen other publishers also rejected it. Even when the Outing Publishing Company agreed to print the book, it didn't pay him anything for it.

But Grey, bless his stubborn soul, kept at it, and just two years after his humiliating rejection, he asked Hitchcock to read his new book, a sprawling Western novel titled *The Heritage of the Desert*.

Hitchcock read it, and summoned Grey to New York.

"You've done it," Hitchcock told him. "You've made me eat my words. It's a fine novel, and here's the proof of it." With that, he handed the writer a contract.

Seven years later, Grey would return to Philadelphia in order to receive an honorary Master of Letters degree from Provost Edgar Fahs Smith. The citation poured praise upon the dental-school alumnus, noting that his "travels and adventures, since graduation from the University, have been vividly portrayed in fascinating and instructive volumes of fiction."

Instructive is a particularly nice word to describe Grey's novels. One wonders if Zane would have used it to describe Pearl's treatment at the hands of the Sophs—or the message he sent back with those potatoes.

Have Drill, Will Travel

Doc Holliday

(First published in March/April 2004.)

He was an unlikely gunslinger: a slight, well-dressed, rather delicate-looking man, with piercing blue eyes set in a head "a phrenologist would delight in examining," as one Colorado newspaperman put it in May 1882. "He is well educated," the Pueblo *Daily Chieftain*'s reporter continued, "and his conversation shows him to be a man of considerable culture."

A few days later, a reporter from the Denver *Republican* also admitted to being "very much surprised at Holliday's appearance, which is as different as could be from the generally conceived idea of a killer." Holliday's hands were "small and soft like a woman's," he added, "but the work they have done is anything but womanly. The slender forefinger which has dealt the cards has dealt death to many a rustler . . ."

Both those articles were written some seven months after the shootout at the OK Corral in Tombstone, Arizona Territory, which burned the legend of Doc Holliday into the national memory. Not all the papers were so respectful, however. Holliday was then wanted for murder in Arizona, and the *Rocky Mountain News* referred to him as the "notorious" leader of "the infamous Earp gang of thugs, murderers, and desperadoes."

He could have easily gone down in history as a big-time villain, a small-time thug, or nothing. To become a legend by killing people, you need to be in the right place at the right time. It also helps to have the chroniclers—most of them, anyway—on your side.

F or Penn to claim Doc Holliday as an alumnus is really not much of a stretch. True, he attended the Pennsylvania College of Dental Surgery (PCDS) rather than the University itself, but the PCDS was more or less absorbed into Penn's School of Dental Medicine in the years after Holliday earned his DDS degree in 1872. (Penn's Department of Dentistry, which soon became the School of Dental Medicine, was founded in 1878.) One of Holliday's professors, Dr. James Truman, later became the dental school's dean; his students would include one Pearl Zane Gray.

When Holliday arrived in Philadelphia from Georgia in the fall of 1870, the PCDS was located at 10th and Arch streets, though he probably spent some time in West Philadelphia, since clinical lectures at Blockley Hospital were open to all students. According to Dr. Frank Heynick, author of *Doc Holliday, DDS*, the college's two-year curriculum was "unsurpassed for its day and age," and Holliday, who wrote his thesis on "Diseases of the Teeth," graduated near the top of his class. He spent eight months at the dental practice of a preceptor, Dr. Lucien Frank of Valdosta, Georgia, Holliday's hometown. A gold molar crown that he reportedly made for a six-year-old girl in 1871 was still intact when she died in 1967 at age 102.

In the summer of 1872, he began practicing his trade in Atlanta, but was plagued by a persistent, debilitating cough. A doctor diagnosed it as tuberculosis, which had already killed Holliday's mother and stepbrother. If he wanted to live a little longer, the doctor said, he should head out to the drier, healthier West.

"There, by one of those singular transformations that nobody can understand," noted the Leadville (Colorado) *Daily Democrat* in 1884, "he became widely known as a desperate man."

H e settled first in Dallas, and "shared top prize in several categories of dental craftsmanship at the annual North Texas Fair," according to Heynick. "But [his] persistent coughing made patients shy away from him. And his fatalism about his disease together with a certain love of risk and liquor led him to spend more and more nights in the gambling halls."

One of those gambling halls, in Dallas, was the site of his first shootout, on New Year's Day, 1875. He apparently wasn't much of a shot then; nobody was hit. For the next five years he drifted about the West, from Texas to Kansas to New Mexico, sometimes practicing dentistry, often dealing cards—and getting into increasingly deadly dust-ups.

During that time he met the other characters in his brief, two-act drama: the Hungarian-born Mary Katherine Haroney, better known as Big Nose Kate, a part-time prostitute and sometime girlfriend. Wyatt Earp, saloon-keeper, gambler, and part-time lawman; and his brothers, Virgil and Morgan. Bat Masterson, gambler and lawman. Various cowboys and cattle-rustlers, some good, some bad, most somewhere in between.

It was a dissolute, flash-point life, and one suited to Holliday's brand of nervous energy. He once told Wyatt Earp that his edginess abated only when he was in a gunfight or doing dental work. (Now *that's* a pathology.) Earp didn't leave us any words about Holliday's dental artistry, but he did describe him as "the most skillful gambler, and the nerviest, fastest, deadliest man with a six-gun I ever saw."

Holliday didn't limit himself to a six-shooter. In Fort Griffin, Texas, he stabbed a recalcitrant gambler named Ed Bailey to death with a knife. (After he was arrested for murder, the story goes, he was held in a hotel room—until Big Nose Kate set a fire in the hotel as a diversion, then used a pistol to persuade the reigning deputy to let him go.) And when he got to Tombstone, he showed himself to be pretty lethal with a shotgun, too.

The brief, murderous gunfight near the OK Corral, which took place on October 26, 1881, became a defining moment in the national psyche. The story is usually told from the point of view of the Earps and Holliday, with clearly drawn Good Guys (them) and Bad Guys (the cattle-rustling cowboys). The reality was more complicated. If it happened today, it would be written off as a turf-war, fueled by trash-talking and booze.

When it was over, three cowboys—Billy Clanton, Frank McClaury, and Tom McClaury—were dead, and Holliday, Virgil Earp (Tombstone's city marshal), and Morgan Earp were wounded. Holliday and the Earps were arraigned on homicide charges, but Judge Wells Spicer ruled that they had acted lawfully, if not very wisely.

Five months later, friends of the dead cowboys shot and killed Morgan Earp while he was playing pool. Wyatt and Holliday led a "vendetta posse" across Arizona, killing one of those friends in Tucson. Holliday fled to New Mexico and then to Denver, where a "crank" named Perry Mallen identified himself as a sheriff and stuck two pistols under his nose. He demanded that Holliday be returned to Arizona, where a murder warrant had been issued for his arrest by Sheriff John Behan.

"If I am taken back to Arizona, that is the last of Holliday," the dentist told the Denver *Republican*. "We hunted the rustlers, and they all hate us. John Behan, Sheriff of Cochise County, is one of the gang, and a deadly enemy of mine, who would give any money to have me killed." Holliday traced their feud to the fact that he had once told Behan, in front of a crowd, that the sheriff was "gambling with money which I had given his woman."

In the end, Holliday avoided extradition through some clever legal maneuvering and some influential friends. "The results of their efforts," noted the *Republican*, "led to the coining of a new word in Colorado— 'Hollidaying.'"

Two years later he shot another man in Leadville, but it appears to have been in self-defense, and Holliday was released. After that, his only arrests were for vagrancy.

By 1887, Holliday's luck was running out and his health was failing fast. He headed to Glenwood Springs, a health resort along the Colorado River famous for its therapeutic hot springs.

"To help finance the treatment, he hung up his dentist's shingle for the last time," writes Heynick. Unfortunately, sulphurous hot springs were *not* what the doctor ordered for tuberculosis, and soon Holliday slipped into a coma at the Hotel Glenwood, supposedly coming out of it long enough to ask for a glass of whisky, which he drank with some satisfaction. According to that version of history, his last words were: "This is funny." Some attributed that remark to the fact that he realized he was going to die without his boots on, despite his prediction to the contrary.

Holliday gave up the ghost on November 8, 1887, at the age of 36. His remains are thought to be buried somewhere in the Linwood Cemetery, though no one knows exactly where.

After his death, a number of newspapers published lengthy eulogies. Among those quoted by the Denver *Republican* was Holliday's attorney, one Colonel Deweese, who allowed that the good dentist would "just as lief kill a man as not," adding: "All he looked out for usually was to have the law on his side.

"I said to him one day, 'Doctor, don't your conscience ever trouble you?' 'No,' he replied, with that peculiar cough of his, 'I coughed that up with my lungs long ago.'"

FRIENDSHIPS

Moderns in the Quad

Ezra Pound & William Carlos Williams

(First published in April 1998.)

An April evening, 1903. The gloaming of an era. High up in Philadelphia's Academy of Music, a handsome, olive-skinned medical student sits by himself, taking in the scene before him with dark, calmly observant eyes. Far below, on stage, a Greek chorus of 15 "captive maidens" sways in a circular dance, singing. It's the University's production of *Iphigenia Among the Taurians*, and every detail, from the maidens' gowns to the scenery, has been carefully interpreted from antiquity by the Department of Greek. The entire *play* is in Greek, for that matter, and while the program does contain an English-prose translation for hoi polloi, a reviewer would claim that "a more select and cultivated audience never crowded the Academy."

The medical student, William Carlos Williams, is focusing on one of the maidens—who is actually his good friend Ezra Weston Loomis Pound, then a 17-year-old sophomore. Pound and his fellow chorus girls have spent months rehearsing their movements and honing their Greek, but although *The Pennsylvanian*'s reviewer concludes that they went through their dances with "care and some grace," Williams is not quite so reverent. Almost half a century later, he would recall in his *Autobiography* that Pound "tore" at his "great blond wig" as he "waved his arms about and heaved his massive breasts in ecstacies of extreme emotion." Now that's entertainment.

67

B efore they began reinventing poetry in earnest, long before they became famous and infamous as the Saint and the Sinner of modern American verse, Williams and Pound were students and close friends at Penn. It was a stormy relationship that would last for 60 years, surviving not just their divergent poetic worldviews but also their very different personalities—not to mention Pound's later political ravings and ugly bouts of anti-Semitism, his aborted trial for treason and 13-year confinement in St. Elizabeth's mental hospital.

"Dear Assen Poop," begins one letter from Williams. "You're too damned thickheaded to know you're asleep—and have been from the beginning." Pound, for his part, once called Williams "stupider than a mud-duck" for publicly attacking his work. "I could never take him as a steady diet," Williams wrote later. "He was often brilliant but an ass. But I never (so long as I kept away) got tired of him, or, for a fact, ceased to love him . . ." The affection, and the respect, ran deeper than the rancor.

They met at a time when the old roadmaps for literature and art were about to be torn up and redrawn. And though both borrowed extensively from older writers—Pound especially seized on medieval Provencal and Italian as his poetic models, and drew deeply from the ancient Greek, Latin, and Chinese—they figured out dynamic ways to "make it new."

"If you have Pound and Williams at the same place at a very formative time in their careers—there's no parallel for that," says Dr. Hugh Kenner, author of *The Pound Era* and many other books and articles on modern poetry. "Between them, they define a good deal of modernism."

Not that the were doing anything very modern at Penn. Pound was mostly writing overblown troubadour-style verse in those days—"I think of him as a sort of American pre-Raphaelite poet then," says Dr. Jean-Michel Rabaté, professor of English—while Williams was trying to emulate Keats, and losing something in the emulation. Both knew they wanted to write great poetry; neither had figured out how to do it. And they didn't get any encouragement from the faculty.

But they did get unique—if very different—educations at Penn that would greatly influence the style and content of their writing. And they influenced each other, sometimes profoundly. ("Before meeting Pound," Williams once said, "is like B.C. and A.D.") Their relationship, along their romantically entangled friendship with another young poet—Hilda Doolittle, the striking daughter of a Penn astronomy professor who would become better known as H.D.—would soon have a catalytic effect on poetry.

"It is true that not a whole lot of modern poetry was getting written at Penn," says Jane Penner, a graduate student writing her dissertation on

Williams. "Even Pound was doing pretty derivative stuff at that point. What was crucial was that network of friendships. For a long time, modernism was taught as something created by isolated individuals. In fact, a more productive idea of modernism was the idea of the group and the network of friendships. And in that sense, Penn becomes very crucial as a background for modernism."

"They were not modernists when they were at the University," adds Dr. Emily Wallace, former professor of English at Penn and author of numerous articles on Williams, Pound, and H.D. "But they were embarking on that endeavor, without quite knowing what road they would take."

We can thank a young pianist named Morrison Van Cleve for introducing them in the fall of 1902. Williams, a freshman, had recently moved into 303 Brooks, on the south side of what was then known as the Triangle, overlooking Hamilton Walk. One night he heard piano music coming from the room next door, and after listening for a while, he picked up his violin and riffed on the chords cascading through the wall. A few minutes later, Van Cleve knocked on the door and introduced himself. At some point in the conversation, Williams mentioned that what he was really interested in was poetry. Van Cleve replied that he knew an eccentric fellow who also liked to write, and that the two of them should meet. He returned with Pound, a 16-year-old sophomore with green eyes and reddish-gold hair who had recently moved onto the ground floor of the new Memorial Tower Arch. "It took just one look," Williams later recalled, "and I knew he was it!"

"I was fascinated by the man," he later wrote of Pound. "He was the livest, most intelligent and unexplainable thing I'd ever seen, and the most fun—except for his often painful self-consciousness and his coughing laugh . . . And he had, at bottom, an inexhaustible patience, an infinite depth of human imagination and sympathy. Vicious, catty at times, neglectful, if he trusted you not to mind, but warm and devoted . . ."

Unlike most of Pound's classmates, who found him insufferable, Williams was able to see through the masks to the artist. Which is not to say that he always approved of his friend's behavior. Pound's heavy-handed attempt to pick up a younger girl on Chestnut Street, for example, appalled Williams, who in those days might be described as a lusty, tormented Boy Scout.

Pound's "early rekolektn" of Williams, recounted in one of his highly idiosyncratic letters, "is you in a room on the South side of the triangle, and me sayin come on nowt, and you deciding on gawd an righteousness and the pursuit of labour in the form of Dr. Gumbo's treatise on the lesions of the bungbone, or some other therapeutic compilation."

Their educations at Penn were as different as their personalities. Williams had come straight to the School of Medicine from the Horace Mann School in New York, having decided to support himself financially—and help humanity—by becoming a doctor.

"I was in the Medical School without academic degree, studying physics, chemistry, anatomy, physiology, pathology," he wrote in his autobiography. "I watched Ezra—by direct effect—suffering the thrusts of his professors. That was the difference between us."

Williams' literary education at Penn consisted mainly of sneak-reading Keats and Victor Hugo between anatomy courses—and whatever he learned from Pound, a compulsive polymath and "village explainer," in Gertrude Stein's memorable phrase. "Ezra, even then, used to assault me (as he still does) for my lack of education and reading," sighed Williams. "He would say that I should become more acquainted with the differential calculus—like himself, of course. I'd reply that a course in comparative anatomy wouldn't at all harm him, if it came to that."

Along with offering a precise, scientific approach to the realities of the human body, Williams' medical education had a lasting effect on his poetry and prose.

"The writing Williams did in Penn courses consisted mostly of case histories, a not-uninteresting discipline," notes Kenner in an essay titled "Poets at the Blackboard." "The case history is dense, it is cryptic, it is crisp, and it is factual. That is not a bad way to be writing day in, day out if God is determined to drive Keats from your mind." In fact, Kenner adds, most of Williams' work "can be gathered under those two rubrics: the Case History (see 'To Elsie'), the Comparative Anatomy."

"The fact that Williams was a medical student connected him to things, to 'no ideas but in things,'" notes Emily Wallace. "That's what a medical doctor had to work with, and that's a major factor in modernism—the exact tone, the precise color."

His medical training also kept him grounded in a way that his precocious friend was not. At Penn, "I used to argue with Pound," Williams later recalled. "I'd say 'bread' and he'd say 'caviar.' It was a sort of simplification of our positions. Once, in 1912 I think it was, in a letter (we were still carrying on our argument) he wrote, 'all right, bread.' But I guess he went back to caviar."

Pound, Williams acknowledged, "was always far more precocious than I and had gone madly on, even to Yeats—who passed through Philadelphia and read to the Penn students in 1903. I did not hear him."

By then Pound had already decided he would devote his life to art, though he hoped to support himself by teaching in the academy. It was not to be, and his experiences at Penn would darkly color his view of American universities.

"All the U. of P. or . . . any other god damn American college does or will do for a man of letters is to ask him to go away without breaking the silence," he wrote in a letter to Penn's Alumni Secretary in 1929. And yet:

"For all Pound's anti-university rhetoric, he is very much a university product," points out Gail McDonald in *Learning to be Modern: Pound, Eliot, and the American University.* "The texts and languages he studied at Hamilton and Pennsylvania provided material for poetry throughout his life, and the limitations of Germanic educational methods gave him a foil against which to define his poetic identity." One could also argue that it was at Penn that he taught himself to be abstruse and allusive, a quality that would provide abundant grist for the mills of scholars—as witnessed by the staggering number of Pound-related books in Van Pelt Library.

As a freshman in the College, Pound was required to take English composition, public speaking, algebra, German grammar, American Colonial history, principles of government in the United States, and Latin. That curriculum is in itself "a scenario for long stretches of the *Cantos,*" points out Kenner in his essay. In fact, he says, "we may remark on its likeness to an extended elective curriculum and reflect that there is more to college than the freshman year."

Blackboards, with their cryptic, half-erased fragments of esoterica, were just beginning to function as a sort of modern palimpsest, and may have helped inspire the modernist technique of fusing seemingly disparate subjects, argues Kenner. The reason there are ideograms and hieroglyphics in the *Cantos,* and "a reproduction of a neon sign with the word *SODA* and some asterisks around it on a page of an early poem by Williams . . . can be traced to that sort of connoisseurship—the connoisseurship of the enigmatic, emblematic sign, the sort of thing that is left on a blackboard by somebody else."

Dr. Felix Schelling, a brilliant Elizabethan scholar with a distinctly Victorian sensibility, was chairman of the English department, and Dr. Hugo Rennert was a one-man Department of Romance Languages. Though Pound respected the abilities of both men, he later clashed bitterly with Schelling, and once referred to Rennert as a "natural worm."

There were a few professors Pound openly liked and admired. He remembered Dean Child, who taught him Chaucer, as "an ideal companion for the young barbarian" and a "man with real love of letters & true flair." He apparently enjoyed Walton Brooks McDaniel, who taught him Latin and later said that he had been "challenged by Pound's exuberance and brilliance." And when Herman Ames, a history professor, died in 1936, Pound wrote to Ames' colleague Roy Nichols expressing his regret that Ames never had the "minor entertainment of knowing that his patiences and indulgences of 30 years ago hadn't been wholly wasted on one of his most cantankerous pupils."

Others were not so indulgent. One of his freshman instructors "remembered him as being abrupt, wanting recognition, and disliked by 'teachers and classmates for what seemed like unnecessary eccentricities,'" notes John Tytell in *Ezra Pound: The Solitary Volcano*. "He played the smart aleck in class, but he could also be oversensitive and emotional: once he defended a poem under attack in class, read it aloud, and was overcome by his own tears."

After two undistinguished years as an undergraduate, during which he was the butt of more than a few practical jokes, Pound transferred to Hamilton—either because he wasn't doing that well at Penn or because his father didn't care for the company he was keeping or because he wanted to study languages not available at the University. He blossomed intellectually at Hamilton, gaining the respect and friendship of several professors. But after four years of "learning to be a college man," he told a friend, "it seems to be the only thing I can do." The choice was between graduate work and "an insane asylum," he added, "although maybe that isn't so very different."

Say it: No ideas but in things! (Williams, *Paterson*)
The natural object is always the perfect symbol. (Pound)

They were obsessed with *things*, those two. (Though Pound, during his Penn days, was somewhat more mystical in his verse.) What things, I wonder, might they have taken from their University days?

Start with a pocket guide to the stars: both Pound and Williams made regular visits to the Flower Astronomical Observatory in then-bucolic Upper Darby, where the real attraction was Hilda Doolittle, then a student at Friends Central. Her father was Dr. Charles Doolittle, the Flower Professor of Astronomy at Penn, who seldom "focused upon anything nearer, literally, than the moon," according to Williams.

"Ezra was wonderfully in love with her and I thought exaggerated her beauty ridiculously," he noted. "To me she was just a good guy and I enjoyed, uncomfortably, being with her." There were times when Williams regarded her as something more than just a good guy, though, which earned him some "dirty looks" from Pound.

For Williams, I also think of Thomas Eakins' *The Agnew Clinic*, which he passed every time he entered the Medical Laboratories Building. (He was also a contributing art editor of the *Scope*, the medical school's yearbook, which used that painting as the frontispiece.) Skunk cabbage, since he wrote an ode on that pungent spring swamp-plant for Hilda Doolittle. (Bad move:

"She listened incredulously and then burst into a guffaw, catching her breath the way only Hilda could—almost hysterical," Williams recalled in *I Wanted to Write a Poem*. "I never tried it with her again.") Prunes, since it was over a bowl of that sweet fruit that he met another important modernist-to-be, the painter Charles Demuth, at a boarding house at 3615 Locust Street. A stethoscope, for listening and diagnosing, since as Kenner points out, "A surprising number of his poems were based on conversations, sometimes with patients." A scalpel, for dissecting. ("Surely the similarity between the positions in which one holds a pen and a scalpel was not lost on Williams," writes Hugh Crawford, author of *Modernism, Medicine, and William Carlos Williams*. "Neither was the importance of reading the body.") Williams himself recalled "falling in love" with the corpse of a light-skinned black woman, naked on a medical-school dissecting table.

So much depends upon a wild, white beard, the one he wore as Polonius in the Mask & Wig production of *Mr. Hamlet of Denmark*. When the Wiggers took their show to Washington, Williams ad-libbed a reference to President Theodore Roosevelt—"Has your Majesty been moose hunting?"—that brought down the house.

I pause at the last item—a nightshirt—but somehow I think he would agree that it belongs on this list. One night when he had visited Hilda Doolittle in Upper Darby and missed the last trolley back to campus, she invited him to sleep on the couch downstairs—whereupon, while wearing one of her father's nightshirts, Williams proceeded to have an embarrassingly, um, amorous dream.

For Pound, Jean-Michel Rabaté suggests a maple bud, since the poet always had a deep, almost mystical attachment to trees. He and Doolittle—whom he called "Dryad," a wood nymph—spent passionate moments in the tree-house of a maple in her Upper Darby yard, and one of the poems in *Hilda's Book*, his first, hand-bound collection of poems, includes the lines:

Nathless I have been a tree amid the wood
And many new things understood
That were rank folly to my head before.

Rabaté also suggests a coin, since Pound's father was an assayer at the U.S. Mint in Philadelphia, and Pound had a long (and often crackpot) interest in monetary matters. I would add to that a big tin watch, which he was remembered for taking out and winding, very deliberately, in the back of one of his classes. A pair of bright-red socks, since his "loudness in half-hose" was one reason that a group of sophomores threw him into the Lily

Pond (as the Bio Pond was then called) one spring day in 1902, giving him a coat of mud and the nickname "Lily" Pound.

Take a football, and tell him to go deep: Pound enjoyed watching games at Franklin Field, even serving as an usher for a while. A few years later, when he was living in London, he would compare his delight in meeting famous writers and hearing stories about them with the "sort of thrill that I used to have in hearing of the deeds of T. Truxtun Hare; the sort that future freshmen will have in hearing how 'Mike' Bennett stopped Weeks."

Hand both poets fencing foils, and watch out. Pound once said that he learned more from Signor Terrone, the Penn fencing instructor, than anybody else at the University, but Terrone found him too impulsive, and unlike Williams, Pound was never good enough to make the varsity team. One afternoon at his parents' house in Wyncote, Pound plucked a couple of walking canes from the umbrella stand and challenged Williams to be *en garde*. After a few easily parried thrusts, Williams recalled, Pound suddenly "came plunging wildly in without restraint, and hit me with the point of the cane above my right eye to fairly lay me out." In a letter three decades later, Williams fumed: "I could have shoved the stick through his mouth and out at his ass hole if it had been important enough to do so . . ." Paul Mariani, author of *William Carlos Williams: A New World Naked*, suggests that the incident may have been touched off by Pound not liking "the sense of covert rivalry he was smelling" in Williams' attitude toward Doolittle.

Six years after that incident, Pound would dedicate a book of poems to Williams. It was titled *Ripostes*.

> *Ezra Pound would come to my room to read me his poems, the very early ones, some of those in* A Lume Spento. *It was a painful experience. For it was often impossible to hear the lines the way he read them, and of all things in the world the last I should have wanted to do would have been to hurt him—no matter how empty I myself might have felt, and worthless, as a critic. But I listened; that's all he wanted, I imagine, from anyone. His voice would trail off in the final lines of many of the lyrics until they were inaudible—from his intensity.* (Williams, *Autobiography*.)

"What matters ultimately is the poetry that was written," says Jean-Michel Rabaté. "I don't think Williams would have written what he wrote without Pound. Pound learned from Williams, but more on the human plan." Old Ez also appreciated Bill's fluency in French and Spanish, not to mention "as a very good friend, a very good ear, a good listener, and so on." But at that time, Rabaté notes, "Williams' own poetic models were too romantic for Pound. Pound was writing a sonnet a day and then destroying them. He had this notion that one could train for the big work. And I'm not sure whether Williams had this idea."

While Williams was "a little stuck" at the level of a Keats-wannabe—"a direct outpouring, gushing of the heart," in Rabaté's words—"he saw in Pound somebody who had the same impulse but was already training himself in the technique. This idea of training oneself—this was the idea that somehow pushed Williams forward.

"It's technically what they learned from each other that's really amazing," Rabaté adds, citing Pound's early work as an example. "There was this notebook that he wrote for Hilda Doolittle—*Hilda's Book*. It's very bad. Very very very bad. What's surprising is how fast he matured to write the first of the *Personae* poems by 1909. That was just a few years later. Completely different, having mastered a lot."

"From a literary standpoint," writes Crawford, "Williams's desire for clear vision and articulation can best be traced to the early influence of Ezra Pound, whose famous rules for Imagism include 'Direct treatment of the "thing" whether subjective or objective,' and 'To use absolutely no word that does not contribute to the presentation.'"

"Pound gave me the original lesson," Williams told an interviewer in the late 1950s. "Never use two words where one will do."

A nother spring evening, this one in 1905. Williams, now a junior, sits at a desk in his room at 318 Joseph Leidy Hall, overlooking the Lily Pond. He has just returned from a weekend visit to the Pound family home in Wyncote, just north of Philadelphia, and is recounting the visit in a letter to his mother.

> *After supper Pound and I went to his room where we had a long talk on subjects that I love yet have not time to study and which he is making a life work of. That is literature, and the drama and the classics, also a little philosophy. He, Pound, is a fine fellow; he is the essence of optimism and has a cast-iron faith that is something to admire . . . But not one person in a thousand likes him, and a great many people detest him and why? Because he is so darned full of conceits and affectation. He is really a brilliant talker and thinker but delights in making himself just exactly what he is not: a laughing boor. His friends must be all patience in order to find him out and even then you must not let him know it, for he will*

immediately put on some artificial mood and be really unbearable. It is too bad, for he loves to be liked, yet there is some quality in him which makes him too proud to try to please people . . . He is afraid of being taken in if he trusts his really tender heart to mercies of a cruel crowd and so keeps it hidden and trusts no one.

It's a remarkable portrait of one artist as a young man by another, and helps explain why Williams would stick with his difficult friend for the rest of his life. "Williams was very careful in drawing conclusions," says Emily Wallace, "and he had been a friend of Pound's since 1902. So by the time he wrote that letter, he had had a lot of time to diagnose the patient."

Some six months after that visit, Pound began his graduate work at Penn, intending to earn his Ph.D. and then to teach. In retrospect, it seems inevitable that something would go wrong. Though nobody doubted his intelligence, Pound was temperamentally unsuited to be a member of any college faculty but his own. And the strong emphasis on linguistics and historical studies was probably stifling to someone with his cast of mind.

"Pound—and Williams, too—found these approaches intolerant of the creative imagination, a situation which may in fact have persisted into later decades," notes Dr. Daniel Hoffman, the poet and Felix E. Schelling Professor Emeritus of English, who edited a collection of essays titled *Ezra Pound and William Carlos Williams: The University of Pennsylvania Conference Papers.* "And so one must conclude that it was fortunate for modern American poetry that they both enrolled at Penn. Because they were both contrarian from the word *go*."

Pound didn't help his own cause when he circulated verses caricaturing certain professors. He also managed to flunk a course in the history of literary criticism taught by Josiah Penniman, who later became provost of the University. The irony of that failure is jaw-dropping, given that Pound's literary criticism is now considered among the most perceptive of the 20th century. "So far as I know I was the only student who was making any attempt to understand the subject of literary criticism," he wrote later, "and the only student with any interest in the subject."

Pound's academic advisor was Felix Schelling, who considered him a poseur, and later said as much in a review of the early *Cantos.* "If I am unlike other people, how is it a pose, isn't it merely common honesty?" responded Pound in a letter. "There are twelve or more [volumes of poetry and criticism] to prove some slight biological variant between me and the other ex-Penn '05 or ex-seminarists. Isn't it nearly time that one allowed me the honesty of never having pretended the contrary?" (In that same letter, Pound apologized for having once contended in class that George Bernard Shaw was greater than Shakespeare.)

Yet "Pound actually learned a lot from the way English was taught then at Penn," says Rabaté. "I've got a little book published in 1917 by Professor Schelling, and in it one can see a sort of pre-Eliotan approach to the English tradition . . . Swinburne is his model, so he's very Victorian in matters of taste, but one can see this very wide range of interests—and also a comparative spirit, having to do with Italian poetry and so on."

Pound was actually "the first to be totally interdisciplinary" in his approach to literature, adds Rabaté, who notes that "a lot of what the University is today would correspond to what Pound had in mind." A decade after he left Penn, Pound wrote Schelling to propose a fellowship for poets and other creative types, who would be able to attend lectures and classes across the University without the usual course requirements or exams. Schelling acknowledged that it was an "interesting" idea. But that was as far as it got.

While Schelling may have been Pound's graduate advisor, the young scholar-poet took more courses in the Romance languages with Hugo Rennert than anything else. He told a friend that he studied Spanish when he woke, Provencal after breakfast, Latin in the middle of the day, French in the late afternoon, and Italian after dinner. He was particularly enamored of Rennert's course in Provencal, later alluding to it in Canto XX:

> *And that year I went up to Freiburg,*
> *And Rennert had said: "Nobody, no, nobody,*
> *Knows anything about Provencal . . .*

Pound received his M.A. in 1906, and some of the work he did for it would appear four years later in his book *The Spirit of Romance*. He was also made a Harrison Fellow in Romanics, a plum appointment that paid for his tuition and provided a $500 stipend, which he used to travel to Spain as part of a thesis on the role of the *gracioso* in the plays of Lope de Vega. Normally, the Harrison Fellowship was for two years, followed by a part-time teaching appointment at the University. But in the spring of 1907, Pound was informed that his fellowship was not being renewed. He had "spatted with nearly everybody," he admitted to a friend. And he had failed to impress his professors with his work ethic.

"I remember him as . . . absolutely evading all work to such an extent that I recall saying to him, 'Mr. Pound, you are either a humbug or a genius,'" Schelling told a colleague in 1920, when Pound submitted an expanded version of *The Spirit of Romance* in lieu of a doctoral dissertation. The request was turned down, as was another, similar one in 1932—which led to a bitter exchange between the two men, ending with Pound's plaintive growl: "Damn it all, I never did dislike you."

Some have argued that their contentious relationship may have ultimately helped Pound's work. "To be a Prometheus requires a Titan against whom to rebel," suggests Hoffman. "Pound may well have been lucky in his antagonist."

"It is unsurprising that Pound and Williams should have left Penn feeling they had been taught trivially, much of the time, by people they could respect only intermittently," writes Hugh Kenner. "That was a natural consequence of not becoming some teacher's apprentice . . . Seeing what they became, though, they were well taught. It is hard to specify anything they should have been taught instead. Especially, it is doubtful that creative writing courses would have been a good idea. God help Williams if he'd been flypapered by such a course. And if Pound had been enrolled in one, God help the instructor."

In December 1909, the year Pound's *Personae* was published to wide acclaim, an alumni publication called *Old Penn* ran two articles about the recent graduate who was becoming the toast of London. It was arguably the only part of the University to extend him a friendly hand. "The remarkable reception in England to the poetry of Ezra Pound, a former student and Harrison Fellow in the University, gives sincere pleasure to his friends at Pennsylvania where his genius and scholarship were recognized in his student days," noted the article's author (probably the magazine's editor, George Nitzsche). "His work shows individuality, force and beauty and versatility of talent . . ."

The following week the magazine published two of his poems, "The Ballad of the Goodly Fere" and "And Thus in Nineveh," along with a photo borrowed from *The Evening Bulletin*. "We are jealous of the fact that England should have discovered and honored his genius rather than his own native America," that same author allowed, "but we are duly proud of him as a son of Pennsylvania."

Some nine years later, *Old Penn* would change its name to *The Pennsylvania Gazette*.

In recent years, a small, springtime celebration of Williams and his work has been held in the Ware College House library, which has a permanent exhibition of Williams memorabilia. Various students, faculty, and staff read their favorite poems or prose pieces, and through the window overlooking the Quad, the great old elm tree can be seen, swelling with new leaves.

It's a fine way to remember Williams, who in his later years was treated pretty well by the University. He received an honorary degree, gave a talk on campus, had a few poems published in the *General Magazine and Historical Chronicle*, and kept up a warm correspondence with English professor Sculley Bradley, whom he called "my best rooter" at Penn.

There is no celebration of Pound, even though he, not Williams, lived in the building now known as Ware, and even though Pound was easily the more influential of the two. (Without Pound, the critic George Steiner once said, "twentieth-century literature is inconceivable," and even his severest critics acknowledge the poet's enormous contributions to everyone from William Butler Yeats and T.S. Eliot to James Joyce and Ernest Hemingway.) Even before his wartime broadcasts, he was never invited back to Penn to teach, or to read; he never received an honorary degree. There is only one small literary prize in his name, for translation.

It's his own damn fault, of course—unless you accept the premise that he really was mentally ill, and thus not entirely responsible for his actions. Pound himself didn't buy that argument. A few years before his death, he told Allen Ginsberg: "At seventy, I realized that instead of being a lunatic, I was a moron." The admission might have brought a certain poignant satisfaction to his old friend Bill Williams, who had often told him pretty much the same thing. "Anything I've done has been an accident," Pound went on. "Any good has been spoiled by my intentions. The preoccupation with irrelevant and stupid things. And the worst mistake I made was that stupid, suburban prejudice of anti-Semitism."

For many people, the remorse was too little, too late. But still . . .

"It's a shame, really," says Rabaté, who hates Pound's wartime politics and prejudices as much as anyone. "The University has never really acknowledged Pound in any way. There is no plaque here, nothing like that. And I don't think there ever will be."

Williams died in 1963, after a long series of strokes. When the news reached Pound in Venice, he sent a telegram to Williams' wife, Florence. It read simply:

> *A magnificent fight he made of it for you. He bore with me sixty years, and I shall never find another poet friend like him.*

SPEECH!

NOAM CHOMSKY & ZELLIG HARRIS

(First published in July/August 2001.)

N *ot-not-not.* A hand raps lightly on the office door.

It's the universal grammar of Knuckle, a language that goes deeper than human speech. Dr. A. Noam Chomsky glances over his shoulder and emits an utterance to the rapper: "OK, just a minute," which turns out to mean something like, "Come back in five or 10 minutes and try again." Then he revs up his language module and the quiet torrent of words resumes, his discourse segueing effortlessly from the structure of cognitive systems to the degradation of classical liberalism to Eugene Debs and the crushing of the labor movement to Richard Nixon's dismantling of the Bretton Woods international economic system to the World Trade Organization's next meeting in Qatar to the totalitarian nature of corporations to—

NOT-NOT-NOT. The meaning of this second Knuckle discourse is clear even to someone who has never heard the dialect before. Chomsky again says that he'll be done in "just a minute," which this time I translate to mean, "I know this chowderhead is taking advantage of my generosity, but since he came all the way up from Philadelphia, let's cut him a little slack."

The knuckles belong to Bev Stohl, Chomsky's personable assistant and, um, temporal structuralist. She reigns supreme in the outer office of the Department of Linguistics and Philosophy at MIT, where Chomsky is the Institute Professor of Linguistics. Even legendary anarchists sometimes need a firm hand and a system to save them from their own discursive effusiveness.

A question: Given that he pretty much changed the course of linguistics and the cognitive sciences with his theory of a "language faculty" inherent in all humans, does it ever strike him as ironic that his own language faculty borders on the superhuman?

"No," he says mildly, twisting a small piece of paper in his fingers. "I don't particularly like speaking. It's one of those things which I never intended to do."

Hmm. That would explain the barely audible voice and the initial hesitancy to accept yet another interview request. (His schedule is booked months in advance, and he turns down several interview requests each day.) But it should not be taken to mean that he stumbled blindly into his second career as a public intellectual and high-profile dissident.

"I remember very well deciding whether to make that move," he says, pinpointing the decision to about 1960. "You can't get into these things casually. If you get involved, it's going to be very demanding, and more than a full-time life. You either do it seriously or you don't do it at all."

Chomsky, by any definition of the word, does it *seriously*. In Poland, some people assumed there were two Noam Chomskys: the seminal, prolific linguist and the seminal, prolific dissenter. The notion that one man could be both was apparently incomprehensible. Even now, this 72-year-old grandfather of four shows few signs of slowing down. Dr. Lila Gleitman, the Steven and Marcia Roth Professor of Psychology and professor of linguistics at Penn and an old friend of Chomsky's, may have figured out his secret. She thinks it's "unfair that he has 30-hour days and the rest of us only have 24-hour days."

Y ears ago, someone wrote in *The New York Times* that, "Judged in terms of the power, range, novelty and influence of his thought, Noam Chomsky is arguably the most important intellectual alive." The line is irresistible for anyone writing a story about him, though Chomsky himself—a frequent critic of the *Times* (and most other orthodox news media)—likes to point out that the next, less-quoted sentence is: "Since that's the case, how can he write such terrible things about American foreign policy?"

His own writing almost never appears on the op-ed page of the *Times* or other mainstream newspapers, which helps explain why so many people vaguely recall his name but know nothing else about him. This doesn't seem to bother him too much. Being relegated to the political margins is proof of his Propaganda Model—in which various "filters," most of them economic, ensure that the mass media play a propagandistic role.

"In the United States, what I say should be marginalized," he once said. "In fact, if I stopped being marginalized, I'd rethink what I'm doing."

And yet: according to a recent survey by the Institute for Scientific Information, only Marx, Lenin, Shakespeare, Aristotle, the Bible, Plato, and Freud are cited more often in academic journals than Chomsky, who edges out Hegel and Cicero. "He is staggering in his productivity," says Dr. Edward Herman, the emeritus professor of finance who has collaborated with Chomsky on books and essays about politics, including *Manufacturing Consent: The Political Economy of the Mass Media.* "He's also an incredibly generous man with his time."

Search Penn's on-line library catalogue under *author: chomsky noam* and no fewer than 98 titles appear. That includes a few duplications, as well as interview collections like *Keeping the Rabble in Line* (with David Barsamian), but it doesn't include biographical works like *Chomsky for Beginners* (whose cover depicts the donnish professor as a superhero, complete with a cape and a red *N* on his chest) or Robert Barsky's *Noam Chomsky: A Life of Dissent* (which can be downloaded off the Internet). Several massive websites devote themselves to his online output, including *Bad News: Noam Chomsky*, which modestly describes itself as "sort of a supplement to the far more essential *Noam Chomsky Archive.*" Various documentaries of his speeches and interviews are available on video, including *Manufacturing Consent: Noam Chomsky and the Media*, a two-part video documentary that chronicles Chomsky's efforts to impart some "intellectual self-defense" against what he sees as the power-serving manipulations of most news organizations.

Demonstrating a link between his linguistic theories and his political views is easier said than done. Some say that his generative-language theory emphasizes a common—and creative—human heritage, an honorable liberal notion. While he is politically a man of the left, I suggest, the notion of a genetic language faculty seems to run counter to the (usually) left-liberal view that environment, not heredity, is what most shapes humans.

"That has been assumed, but I don't think it makes any sense," he says quietly. "For one thing, the idea that your cognitive systems are biologically unstructured is just insane. The only question is why anybody believes it, since it's so obviously outlandish. And I certainly don't think it has anything to do with the left. In Cambridge in the 1950s, the few of us graduate students who did not accept the prevailing, largely behaviorist orthodoxy were all on the left. And the ones who most advocated it were people who were extremely reactionary. I don't draw any particular conclusions from that, just to point out it's not a left-right issue."

NOT-NOT-NOT. Three knuckle-strikes and you're out, I figure, and shut off my tape recorder. As we get to our feet and step through the door leading from his office, I mention ruefully that we got to about half the questions on my list. "You can always send me some more by e-mail," he says gently, and we shake hands goodbye. I take him up on his offer, which makes me part of the problem: some of his e-mails are almost 4,000 words long.

> *Noam Chomsky, in particular, says flatly and often that he has very little concern for language in and of itself; never has, never will. His driving concern is with mental structure, and language is the most revealing tool he has for getting at the mind.*—Randy Harris, *The Linguistic Wars.*

It's been more than 40 years since Chomsky first kicked open the door of linguistics with his theory of generative grammar and a human language faculty. Most of his work since then has essentially been refining and deepening that theory. (He now refers to the language faculty as the "I-language," *I* standing for *internal, individual,* and *intentional.*) And yet he remains the 800-pound gorilla in linguistics, the one whose work every student has to deal with, and whose dominance in the field is often compared to the relative dominance of people like Einstein and Freud.

"Doing linguistics for the last 40 years is a matter of agreeing or disagreeing with Chomsky—contributing to that program, or trying to contribute from a slightly different perspective," says Lila Gleitman. "But he won't go away. He set the agenda; he was a great technical contributor; and he was a great empirical contributor. So at many, many levels, he just dominated the field and pervaded the field."

"He has transformed not just linguistics but the whole of cognitive psychology," says Anthony Kroch, professor and chair of linguistics. "He hasn't done it alone, and it will take a while for people to understand what was happening."

Kroch, who received his doctorate from Chomsky's department at MIT in the early '70s but was not interested in becoming an acolyte, later performed an analysis of historical syntax in 16th-century English. He thought the data he was using would pose a challenge to Chomsky's generative paradigm—until he analyzed it.

"The work I did in the early '80s made me appreciate in a personal way what an impressive thinker Chomsky was, because I had started out to prove him wrong, and I had succeeded in proving him right—or at least the data made more sense if I believed him than if I disbelieved him. And that's convincing in a way that no amount of just listening to somebody else could possibly be."

Was Chomsky pleased with Kroch's findings, I wonder, or was he indifferent because he knew he was right to begin with? "I think the latter," Kroch answers quickly. "You could say, 'Well, arrogant son of a bitch,' and so on. But remember what Einstein said when people went and measured the perturbations in the orbit of Mercury, and somebody asked him, 'What would you have said if it had come out the other way?' Einstein said, 'I would have said that they made an error.' That sounds very arrogant, but once you know something really deeply, you sort of *know* it. And I think Chomsky had reason to think that he had really got hold of something."

T he young man who would become arguably the most influential intellectual ever to graduate from Penn nearly dropped out his sophomore year. By then it was 1947, and Chomsky was commuting from his parents' house in the East Oak Lane section of Philadelphia and teaching Hebrew School on the side. His father, Dr. William Chomsky, was the head of the Hebrew School system in Philadelphia, and a respected Semitic philologist who wrote a book on medieval Hebrew grammar.

In his spare time, Noam was running youth groups, "all involved in affairs of what was then Palestine." He was a Zionist in those days, though it was a leftist stream of Zionism, one whose bi-nationalist outlook would be considered anti-Zionist today. (Chomsky then, as now, opposed the creation of a Jewish state in Palestine, believing that it would carve up the territory and marginalize its Arab population.)

The idea of moving to Palestine and joining a kibbutz was becoming more and more alluring—especially since he found himself "very disillusioned" by courses that had looked exciting in the Penn catalogue, but weren't.

"I was about ready to quit," he recalls. "That's when I met Harris."

That would be the late Dr. Zellig Harris, the Russian-born linguist who founded and chaired the linguistics department at Penn (first in the nation), and whose books included *Methods in Structural Linguistics*, *Mathematical Structures of Language*, and *Papers in Structural and Transformational Linguistics*. Although his family and Chomsky's knew each other slightly as part of the same Philadelphia Jewish community, it wasn't until they began to talk at Penn—drawn together not by linguistics but by politics—that the neurological sparks began to fly.

"The primary teacher of Noam was Zellig Harris," says Dr. Henry Hiz, emeritus professor of linguistics, who also taught Chomsky at Penn. "It's very difficult to describe the profound influence Harris had on him—and on me, too."

"Zellig was a primary influence on Noam, perhaps *the* primary influence back then," agrees Carol Chomsky, who went by Carol Schatz until she and Noam were married in 1949. (See "The Way They Were—And Are.") "Noam admired him enormously, and I think it's fair to say that Zellig was responsible, in so many different ways, for the direction that Noam's intellectual life took then and later."

The relationship between Harris and Chomsky appears to have been a complicated one. The two later parted ways, and while Chomsky downplays that and attributes it mostly to his own growing political activism during the 1960s, he also mentions "Zellig's lack of interest in my work, which dates back to the late '40s, when I was an undergraduate"—adding that "it was never of the slightest concern to me—never thought about it twice, in fact; seemed entirely natural, for whatever reason."

He has acknowledged Harris's influence on him, both personally and professionally.

"My formal introduction to the field of linguistics was in 1947, when Zellig Harris gave me the proofs of his *Methods in Structural Linguistics* to read," noted Chomsky in the 1975 introduction to his own early work, *The Logical Structure of Linguistic Theory* (a chunk of which served as his 1955 Ph.D. dissertation for Harris). "I found it very intriguing and, after some stimulating discussions with Harris, decided to major in linguistics as an undergraduate" at Penn.

Harris, says Chomsky now, "was a very impressive person in many respects, and one of the things that he was very much involved in at the time and attracted me instantly was the socialist, bi-nationalist ideas about then-Palestine. He was a leading figure in a group called Avukah, which was sort of a left-Zionist, anarchist, socialist group of young Jewish intellectuals. The core interest was Palestine, but it was broader than that.

"He never wrote much," Chomsky adds, "but he was a very powerful personality, and he was very interested in encouraging young people to do things."

Along with teaching him a "tremendous amount" about political matters, Chomsky recalls, Harris "just kind of suggested that I might want to sit in on some of his courses. I did, and I got excited about that." So much for dropping out.

"In retrospect, I'm pretty sure he was trying to encourage me to get back in," says Chomsky. "I started taking, at his suggestion, graduate courses in philosophy and math."

Those included graduate-level philosophy courses with the late Dr. Nelson Goodman, and graduate-level mathematics with the late Dr. Nathan Fine. He also studied Arabic with Dr. Giorgio Levi Della Vida, whom he has described as an "antifascist exile from Italy who was a marvelous person as well as an outstanding scholar." And, of course, he took linguistics courses with Harris, though according to Chomsky, they usually didn't meet in classrooms.

"There used to be a Horn & Hardart's right past 34th Street on Woodland Avenue," he recalls, "and we'd often meet in the upstairs, or in his apartment in Princeton. His wife was a mathematician; she was working with Einstein."

Despite the linguistics courses, most of which were with Harris, Chomsky says he "never studied linguistics in a conventional or formal manner" at Penn. "The fact of the matter is I have no professional training or credentials. I could never get admitted to this department [at MIT]. It's kind of a well-known fact in the field; it's not a secret. I had a very idiosyncratic background, and was interested in other things."

"Chomsky's education reflected Harris's interests closely," writes Randy Harris in *The Linguistic Wars*. "It involved work in philosophy, logic, and mathematics well beyond the normal training for a linguist. He read more deeply in epistemology, an area where speculation about the great Bloomfieldian taboo, mental structure, is not only legitimate, but inescapable." The reference is to Leonard Bloomfield, the linguist who dominated the field in the 1920s, '30s, and '40s, and whose approach is now considered highly methodical, empirical, and behaviorist.

Henry Hiz was a visiting lecturer at Penn in 1951, and among the students in his advanced class in logic and linguistics was Chomsky, then a graduate student. "He was very aggressive," recalls Hiz; "not only listening but commenting about my lectures. He was very good. And we talked outside my class a lot. I was very impressed."

Chomsky's undergraduate honors thesis, which drew somewhat on his father's work in Hebrew, was titled "Morphophonemics of Modern Hebrew." He later revised and expanded it for his master's thesis, completed in 1951. That thesis "set the stage for some of his later work," writes Barsky, his biographer, and "is taken to be the first example of modern generative grammar."

That thesis didn't have much impact at Penn, Chomsky suggests. "As far as I can recall, Henry Hoenigswald was the only faculty member who ever looked at my undergraduate or M.A. thesis, and no one (to my knowledge) looked at anything I did later." (Hoenigswald, now emeritus professor of linguistics, says he "didn't really know [Chomsky] very well," though he does recall that he was "very brilliant at all times.")

It was the U.S. Army that prompted him to get his Penn Ph.D., which he "never expected" to receive. In April 1955, having spent most of the past four years pursuing his own edgy interests as a Harvard Junior Fellow (for which he was sponsored by Nelson Goodman), he got a draft notice.

"I was 1-A," Chomsky recalls. "I was going to be drafted right away. I figured I'd try to get myself a six-week deferment until the middle of June, so I applied for a Ph.D. I asked Harris and Goodman, who were still at Penn, if they would mind if I re-registered—I hadn't been registered at Penn in four years. I just handed in a chapter of what I was working on for a thesis, and they sent me some questions via mail, which I wrote inadequate answers to—that was my exams. I got a six-week deferment, and I got my Ph.D."

That dissertation, titled "Transformational Analysis," was actually a 175-page section of a massive work titled *The Logical Structure of Linguistic Theory*, which was so avant-garde that it wouldn't be published until 1975, and then only in part. "I was writing mostly for myself, because nobody was interested in this long thing," he says. "It was 500 pages, I guess. My wife and I ran it off on something called a hectograph. I don't know how it worked, but it turned everything purple. The whole room was purple. We just ran off 20 or 30 copies of this thing for friends."

The original copy of "Transformational Analysis"—typed in sober black ink and signed by Harris—is still in the Rare Book and Manuscript collection at Van Pelt Library. In his preface, Chomsky wrote that it was "carried out in close collaboration with Zellig Harris, to whom I am indebted for many of the fundamental underlying ideas." In addition to citing Harris's *Methods in Structural Linguistics* and an article in *Language*, "Transformational Analysis" was also informed by Henry Hiz's then-unpublished "Positional Algebras and Structural Linguistics." And in the opening pages, he stated that a linguistic grammar should answer such then-radical questions as: "How can a speaker generate new sentences?"

The Logical Structure of Linguistic Theory was "written for Chomskyan linguists when there was only one, Chomsky," notes Randy Harris. Another linguist, H. Allan Gleason, later recalled: "A few linguists found it very difficult; most found it quite impossible. A few thought some of the points were possibly interesting; most simply had no idea as to how it might relate to what they knew as linguistics." They would, soon enough.

Today, Chomsky says that if his hand had not been forced by the Army, his academic career might have ended. "Because I really had no specific intention of going on in academic work. I was fairly interested in what I was doing, but it wasn't a field. That's why I'm at MIT"—which in those days didn't even have an undergraduate linguistics department.

His appointment was in MIT's Research Laboratory of Electronics—the perfect spot for Chomsky, who says he didn't know the difference "between a radio and a toaster." (He also told the director that the machine-translation project to which he would be assigned had "no intellectual interest and was also pointless"—and got hired anyway.) But his research was open-ended and his appointment only partial, so in order to support his family he had to teach: German, French, philosophy, logic—and linguistics. "He taught *his* linguistics," writes Randy Harris, "and the lecture notes for this course became the answer to the rhetorical gulf between the audience for *Logical Structure* . . . and everyone else in the field."

Those notes were revised and published in 1957 as *Syntactic Structures*. Once again, Chomsky noted in the preface: "During the entire period of this research I have had the benefit of very frequent and lengthy conversations with Zellig S. Harris. So many of his ideas and suggestions are incorporated into the text below and in the research on which it is based that I will make no attempt to indicate them by special reference."

Syntactic Structures was "one of the masterpieces of linguistics," says Randy Harris in *The Linguistic Wars*. "Lucid, convincing, syntactically daring, the calm voice of reason calling from the edge of a semantic jungle Bloomfield had shooed his followers from, it spoke directly to the imagination and ambition of the entire field."

Chomsky, whom Harris describes as a "moody Hamlet" occupying center stage during the linguistic "border disputes," is not terribly impressed by the dramatization of his professional work.

"I never paid attention to the 'linguistic wars' fabricated by enthusiastic postmodernists," he says. "The stories are comical."

*N*im Chimpsky couldn't fathom the nuances of linguistics but Noam Chomsky *can.*

Semantically, there is a reason for that. Nim Chimpsky was a celebrated chimpanzee. A researcher tried to teach him to put together words (using signs) to make sentences that adhered to the rules of grammar. It didn't work. Chimps don't have the I-language.

The nuances of linguistics couldn't be fathomed by Nim Chimpsky but can be by Noam Chomsky.

This time, forget the meaning, the semantic significance. The two italicized statements about Nim and Noam are "transformationally" related sentences, meaning that they are syntactic variations with the same meaning.

Transformational grammar was developed not by Chomsky but by Zellig Harris. (Or: *Zellig Harris, not Chomsky, developed transformational grammar.*) Chomsky later wrote that when he "began to investigate generative syntax more seriously" in the late 1950s, he would "adapt for this purpose a new concept that had been developed by Zellig Harris and some of his students, namely, the concept of 'grammatical transformation.'" ("Generative" refers to the mental machinery for describing all of the infinite possibilities for sentences with a few "rules.") For Chomsky, transformational grammar was not an end but a beginning.

"Chomsky is a very original mind, and made out of Harrisian ideas many new ideas, new directions," points out Henry Hiz. "Harris was not writing about psychological matters; he was writing about formal properties of language. And Chomsky was writing that language was a mental process. And then, that it is the same throughout humanity. Languages therefore are different from each other externally only—internally they are the same."

For Harris, says Anthony Kroch, transformational grammar was an important tool for analyzing and working with the data. "Chomsky said, 'Don't think about the data; think about the knowledge that the person has that allows them to *produce* the data.' And that was mentalism—what's in the minds of people. Psychology at that time was behaviorist, and linguists, to the extent that they thought about psychology, were behaviorist."

In an epochal 1959 review of B. F. Skinner's *Verbal Behavior* in the journal *Language*, Chomsky demolished the thesis that all language is learned behavior, dismissing as "quite empty" the "claim that all verbal behavior is acquired and maintained in 'strength' through reinforcement." The fact that all normal children quickly acquire "essentially comparable grammars of great complexity," Chomsky wrote, "suggests that human beings are somehow specially designed to do this, with data-handling or 'hypothesis-formulating' ability of unknown character and complexity."

That was the essence of the Chomskyan revolution. The study of linguistic structure, he added, "may ultimately lead to some significant insights into this matter." He was right—though as usual, the devil would be in the details.

The brave new world into which Chomsky had led linguistics was an alien one for his former mentor.

"Harris was a behaviorist in his own way, and so for him this was heretical and wrong-headed," says Kroch. "And it looked like a big step backwards, because behaviorism was a kind of progress over the woolly-headed mentalism of the late-19th century. So from the point of view of 1950s psychology, it looked like Chomsky was saying, 'I want to go back.' But of course, it turns out that what Chomsky meant wasn't a step back but a step forward."

Around 1980, the efforts of Chomsky and others to show that the "apparent complexity and variety of language was only superficial" crystallized in what is known as the "Principles and Parameters" model. That model postulated "general principles of the language faculty and a finite array of options" or parameters, he says, and it constituted a "major break from a tradition of some 2,500 years."

Since the early 1980s, Chomsky started every linguistics class with the words: "Let's see how 'perfect' language might be." That attempt "always led into a maze of problems until about 10 years ago, when things seemed to me to begin to fall together," he recounts. "That's what came to be called the 'minimalist program.'"

All these programs and models about language—sparked by flashes of insight, rigorously tested, vigorously debated—have grudgingly yielded results that resonate far beyond linguistics.

"It is possible that in the study of the mind/brain we are approaching a situation that is comparable with the physical sciences in the seventeenth century," Chomsky told Randy Harris, "when the great scientific revolution took place that laid the basis for the extraordinary accomplishments of subsequent years and determined much of the course of civilization since."

Zellig Harris, who retired in 1980, died in 1992. Five years later, Chomsky was the featured speaker at a Penn-sponsored conference that celebrated Harris's posthumously published book, *The Transformation of Capitalist Society*, though his remarks focused not on Harris but on the problems caused by capitalism.

"It's true that I had no contact with Zellig after about 1964," says Chomsky. "Maybe a letter or two. Remember that by the early 1960s, I was head-over-heels involved in antiwar activities (as well as a host of other activist engagements)." As a result, he "rarely had any contact with people who were not similarly engaged."

While losing contact with Harris was difficult from a personal point of view, he acknowledges, "it was nothing unusual at the time. Same with just about everyone who wasn't involved in the activism that was taking over my life."

When Norman Mailer was arrested for crossing a police line at the 1967 anti-war demonstration in Washington, he found himself in a jail cell next to Chomsky, who had been nabbed on a similar charge. In *The Armies of the Night*, Mailer describes him as a "slim sharp-featured man with an ascetic expression, and an air of gentle but absolute moral integrity." After trying to think up an incisive question or two about linguistics for the "tightly packed conceptual coils of Chomsky's intellections," Mailer changed his tack and the two men "chatted mildly of the day, the arrests . . . and of when they would get out. Chomsky—by all odds a dedicated teacher—seemed uneasy at the thought of missing class on Monday."

Most of Chomsky's activism does not involve hobnobbing in jail cells with celebrities. A lot of it is lonely, dogged work: speaking out at churches and universities on U.S. policy in places like Iraq and Indonesia; giving interviews to small magazines and radio stations; and churning out truckloads of articles and books. He is a draw, certainly—one of the very few among political southpaws—but the market for cerebral left-anarchist moral scourges has never been bullish. What drives him is a sense of outrage and responsibility: the "responsibility of intellectuals to speak the truth and to expose lies," as he wrote back in 1967.

He's been at this for more than 60 years, having written his first political article—about the Spanish Civil War—when he was 10. "It was about the ominous nature of Barcelona falling after Austria and Czechoslovakia," he recalls, "and 'you know what this means.'" He still gets a fond look in his eyes when discussing the Catalonian anarchist movement, which was crushed by communists and fascists. "I was always on the side of the losers," he once said. (Given that he voted for Ralph Nader in the most recent presidential election, he still is.)

Chomsky's own anarchist views have deep philosophical roots—though given the misconceptions generated by the word *anarchist*, he often uses *libertarian socialist* instead. He cites Adam Smith and Wilhelm von Humboldt as two "founders of modern liberalism" who believed in "what was later called a kind of 'instinct for freedom.'" From those "fundamental rights" grounded in our nature, "many leading figures of classical liberalism drew very libertarian conclusions, which then fit into the anarchist tradition." And most of those classical liberals, he maintains, "would be appalled by what's called classical liberalism today."

In keeping with that "instinct for freedom," Chomsky encourages those dissatisfied with the American political system to organize themselves and get involved. "The dominant political philosophy with progressive groups is that people are stupid, ignorant, don't understand what's good for them," he argues. "'It would be improper to allow them to run their own affairs, so we just have to do that for them.'"

That outlook, he explains, "goes back to James Madison and the constitutional system, which is supposed to be not a democracy but what's called a *polyarchy* in the political-science literature—a system in which those who call themselves the 'responsible men' or the 'intelligent minority' or something, rule. The role of the population is to observe and agree once in a while, to lend their weight to one or another member of the dominant group, and then go home and do something else. The little secret that's not mentioned is that the 'responsible men' become responsible by serving external power."

In a democracy, Chomsky argues, propaganda plays the same role that violence plays in a dictatorship. Those who control and benefit from the political system preserve it by marginalizing alternative political views (like his); by selectively reporting on the actions and consequences of American foreign policy (virtually ignoring massacres in U.S.-supported Indonesia, for example, while focusing on similar crimes in "enemy" countries like Cambodia); and by creating political apathy among the general population.

That apathy is achieved by all sorts of devious means, ranging from campaign contributions that exclude all but the wealthy to an over-emphasis on sports and other frothy diversions by media conglomerates. Corporate mergers among news organizations, he notes, contribute to the narrow range of views and the general climate of propaganda. And while he has been searing in his criticism of the U.S. government, he is even more concerned about the alternative power structure—the "major corporate system"—now on the ascendant.

"A corporation is about as close to a totalitarian institution as anything humans have devised—unaccountable, secret, hierarchic," he says. "*That's* where the decisions ought to go, according to the prevailing ideology."

For those who find his worldview more suited to the *X-Files*, Chomsky would shrug and say that most Western intellectuals can't allow themselves to even acknowledge the propaganda model, let alone buck the system. His views get a better hearing in Europe and even Israel, despite his withering criticisms of the Israeli government. (In his view, the Israeli press is both more honest and more open to divergent viewpoints than its American counterpart.)

One can—and many people do—disagree with his flagellating approach, but his own moral code is one of almost unbearably high standards. To him, there is little moral value in criticizing the actions of one's official enemies, even if the criticism is factually correct.

"The moral significance of some human action is determined by its anticipated human consequences," he says. "That holds true for condemnation as well as any other action. Thus, Soviet commissars and Nazi propagandists bitterly condemned U.S. crimes, quite often accurately. What was the moral value of that condemnation? In fact, it was negative: these were acts of depravity, from a moral point of view."

"It's kind of impressive that he has really always criticized his own side of things," says Anthony Kroch. "He's Jewish and he criticizes Israel; he's American and he criticizes the American government. And people get really furious. But it's not like there's going to be a mass movement of people who are self-critical. Nationalism is pretty dangerous and murders people by the millions—and yet one guy who is consistently anti-nationalist gets everybody up in a lather."

At one point during our e-mail exchanges, I ask Chomsky what keeps him engaged.

"I'm often asked that, and never understand," he replied. "If you see a child being beaten to death in the streets, and try to do something about it, does someone have to ask you why you are engaged? The only sensible question is why I am so little engaged, and why many others choose to be even less engaged."

The last word goes to Carol Chomsky, who has been involved in her share of political activities over the years—and who, presumably, knows him better than anyone. I ask her if she ever disagrees with her husband about politics.

"Sometimes I do disagree," she replies. "Mostly I keep quiet about it, because one never wins an argument with Noam."

The Way They Were
(and Are)

Noam & Carol Chomsky

(First published in July/August 2001.)

When Dr. Carol Chomsky accompanies her husband on lecture tours, she often finds herself surrounded by "very young and breathless" women, who inevitably ask her the same question: "So what's it like to be married to *Noam Chomsky?*" Her response, which took her some time to work out: "I'll tell you one thing—it's never boring!"

A mixed compliment, perhaps, but no small achievement, given that she's known him since they were children and has been married to him for more than half a century.

Back in the old country—Philadelphia—she was known as Carol Schatz. Her family and Noam's belonged to the same synagogue.

"His mother was my Hebrew School teacher, and his father was the principal of the Hebrew School," she says in an e-mail interview. "Later, when I attended the Hebrew Teachers' College of Philadelphia (Gratz College), his father was one of the professors."

It's hardly surprising that it took some time before she became romantically interested in a boy she had known since she was five.

"When we were early teenagers, I viewed him as an overly intellectual, undersized, 'nerdy' sort of kid," she recalls. "In our early teens, he definitely wasn't somebody I would have wanted to date."

But by the time she was about 15, she found herself changing her mind. "We were heavily involved in Jewish cultural activities—Zionist youth groups (for Noam it was certainly not the standard 'Zionist' viewpoint), Hebrew-speaking groups, Hebrew-speaking summer camps, social activities. He knew more about these things than anyone else, and assumed a position of leadership. So he was very noticeable and admirable."

They began to date sometime in 1947—the year she began at Penn, and the year that a disillusioned Noam nearly dropped out. Her memories of the University are a little warmer than her husband's. "I loved it there," she says. "I found my interests; had many excellent, even wonderful professors; and looking back, received a quite satisfactory intellectual grounding."

But as for those first, heady years of college romance, well . . .

"My recollection is that Noam and I didn't see all that much of each other at Penn, simply because we were so busy," she says. "We were both working (teaching Hebrew School), and involved in so many things outside of school. Life was compartmentalized. You went to school during the day, did your homework, taught Hebrew School, and pursued the rest of your life in what time remained."

Somehow, they found the time to get married in 1949, when she was 19 and he had just turned 21. Did she, I wonder, have any idea what she was getting in for?

"I think I did know what I was getting in for, but found it exciting," she says. "One of his political 'mentors' took me aside and explained to me about his politics, the extent of his radicalism, and the dangers his views could come to pose over time. He wanted to make sure I was aware of how extreme Noam's views were and what that might mean for the future. So I guess you could say I did know, in a general and overall sort of way."

Two years after she graduated from Penn in 1951, the young couple moved to a kibbutz in the new country of Israel. While Noam was turned off by the "Stalinist" political leanings of the kibbutz, they both had some practical objections, too.

"The setup that we foresaw there would not have been personally acceptable," she explains. "I would have lived in the kibbutz of our choice, and Noam would have spent the week in the city at a university job, coming home on weekends. This didn't seem desirable to either of us. I think we never really regretted the decision not to return." They now live in the Boston suburb of Lexington.

In the 1960s, Noam's political activities were sufficiently intense that they decided that she should go back to graduate school to earn her doctorate. That way, if he were jailed for any length of time, she could support herself and their children, Aviva, Diane, and Harry. That never happened, though he has seen the inside of a jail. (See "Speech!")

She got her Ph.D. in linguistics at Harvard, and her work has been in language development and psycholinguistics. But don't jump to any conclusions. "It's a very different sort of 'linguistics' from Noam's pursuits," she says. "I always have to laugh when people talk about how interesting our dinner-table conversation must be since we're in the same field."

She taught for many years at the Harvard Graduate School of Education, in the Department of Reading and Language, and became involved in "educational issues of literacy and the like." She has since "moved into educational technology, and developed software for language and reading."

I wonder if she has any hopes or dreams of a quiet, disengaged retirement with Noam, now that he is in his seventies and a grandfather of four.

"I've given up on that one," she responds. "He'll never stop. Actually, it's probably a good thing for him. So I settle for water sports in the summers, an occasional hour of television during the long, dark winters, and endless discussions of the grandchildren's latest antics. Not too bad a deal."

CRISES

The Unmaking of a Radical

Scott Nearing

(First published in March/April 2002 as "An Affair to Remember.")

On the morning of June 16, 1915, Dr. Scott Nearing received a telephone call from his secretary at the Wharton School. She read him a short letter that had just arrived from Provost Edgar Fahs Smith:

> *My dear Mr. Nearing,*
> *As the term of your appointment as assistant professor of economics for 1914-15 is about to expire, I am directed by the trustees of the University of Pennsylvania to inform you that it will not be renewed.*
> *With best wishes, I am,*
> *Yours sincerely,*
> *Edgar Fahs Smith.*

The news came as a shock to the 31-year-old Nearing, who was the only assistant professor with a favorable faculty recommendation not to be rehired. But it was hardly a surprise. For several years he had, in effect, been standing on top of the academy hurling denunciations at the gods, and he had no intention of heading for shelter just because lightning was forking down and his mortarboard was made of copper.

His dismissal set off the worst moral and public-relations crisis of the University's history, one that would only be rivaled in recent years by the Water Buffalo incident. In both cases, the University acted as a lightning rod for highly charged political currents—some national, some unique to the academy. And in both, the tremendous public outcry and Penn's reluctant self-examination would lead to a healthy reassessment of its principles.

Nobody ever questioned Scott Nearing's brilliance or his oratorical skills. Having won a city scholarship to Penn after graduating at the top of his high-school class, he excelled as a student and on the University's debating team. In 1905, *Old Penn* (the *Gazette*'s predecessor) reported that Nearing had received a "prolonged ovation" for his "excellent rebuttal" to Columbia University's team in a debate about whether the Interstate Commerce Commission should be vested with authority. Nearing, who maintained that it should, pointed to several cases of "unjust discrimination" by the nation's railroads—which, he argued forcefully, clearly needed governmental oversight.

It was a characteristic assault on the powers-that-were. Although he was born into a wealthy coal-operating family in Morris Run, Pennsylvania, Nearing soon rejected most of the bulwarks of the era's capitalism.

The distribution of wealth, he wrote, was the "most difficult as well as the most interesting part of our science." While American society had reached the stage where its people had learned how to produce wealth, "as yet they have never learned to distribute it so as to satisfy all the interested parties."

In a time of seismic societal tremors, Nearing's worldview was built on a rock of moral conviction. He "saw his role not only as a social scientist investigating modern society but as a teacher working 'for the liberation of the individual soul,'" notes John Saltmarsh, author of *Scott Nearing: An Intellectual Biography*. "His economic analysis revealed that modern society was fragmenting and degenerating because of the failure of the dominant class to meet its social duty."

"If I am rich and you are poor," Nearing wrote, "both of us are corrupted by inequality."

He became an outspoken opponent of child labor and inherited wealth, and would champion women's rights and racial equality decades before either cause became popular. Yet with people he could be brutally insensitive and blunt—"an idiosyncratic ideologue from the word *go*," in the words of Dr. Daniel Hoffman, the poet and Felix E. Schelling Professor of English Emeritus, who knew Nearing in the last decades of his 100-year life. That ideology led to his joining—and his quick expulsion by—the Communist Party in the 1920s, and ultimately to a Spartan life as an organic farmer on the coast of Maine, where he became a kind of counter-cultural hero to the young. It also led him to conclude that the Albania of Enver Hoxha was a wonderful example of a planned economy.

As a Penn student, Nearing was profoundly influenced by Dr. Simon Nelson Patten, professor of economics. After hearing Patten's discussion on "Adam Smith and his reasoning concerning capital," Nearing realized that he had found a teacher who "suggested to us that the established order was not all that it might be." Patten, he later recalled, "spoke to his students constantly, not of the things that had passed, but of the things that were to be."

When Nearing began teaching, he soon became one of the "Wharton Eight," a group of faculty who believed that they "should make a contribution not only to our students and the University but also to the society at large," in Nearing's words. Patten described Nearing as one of Penn's "most effective men, a man of extraordinary ability, of superlative popularity and a man who, to my mind, exerted the greatest moral force for good in the University." He also noted that Nearing "had the largest class in the University—there were 400 in his class—and no one could have done his work better."

For Nearing, the role of a teacher was that of a "sentry—an outpost in the realm of ideas." Though some economists found his methods unscientific, he was a vigorous, prolific scholar. During his brief tenure at Penn he wrote *The Solution of the Child Labor Problem*; *The Super Race*; *Women and Social Progress* (with his first wife, Nellie, as co-author); *Financing the Wage Earner's Family*; *Social Religion*; *Social Sanity*; *Reducing the Cost of Living*; *Wages in the United States, 1908-10*; *Anthracite*; and *Income*.

He was highly regarded by his students, who would later sign petitions in droves protesting his dismissal. "Many of us do not agree with his economic theories, yet every one must admit that he is one of the few men who actually perform the service that the University expects of them," wrote a Wharton student named Jacques M. Schwab. "He makes the college men think. A professor who can do that is, in my opinion, worth his weight in gold."

I n his autobiographical book *The Making of a Radical*, Nearing recalled how Wharton Dean James T. Young called him into his office and said: "Mr. Nearing, if I were in your place I would do a little less public speaking about child labor." Nearing, who served as secretary of the Pennsylvania

Child Labor Committee, believed that the "child who is working is not developing intellectually, may be degraded morally, and is apt to be stunted physically." The low wages paid to workers, he argued, forced families to send their children into the factories and mines.

As Young's warning suggested, Nearing was making enemies. Prominent alumni had been complaining to the editor of the *Alumni Register*, Horace Mather Lippincott, who wrote that members of the teaching profession, especially those dealing with "economic, financial, statistical, or legal principles which underlay the practice of government, should carefully avoid a participation in exciting or controversial questions of the moment.

"Morally, the man who joins an institution thereby relinquishes his right to complete freedom of speech," the *Register* added, and he should resign rather than "embarrass the management of the institution."

Provost Smith, who was not keen on "academic people meddling in political questions," had already set the tone.

"Suppose, for illustration, that I, as a chemist, should discover that some slaughtering company was putting formalin in its sausage," Smith is reported to have said; "now surely that would be none of my business."

Nearing saw his role differently. "Either the teacher is a hireling of the established order, who is receiving a fee to act as its apologist or champion, or else the teacher is a servant of the community and as such is bound to take whatever stand the exigencies of his position demand."

In late 1913, three academic organizations—the American Economics Association, the American Sociological Society, and the American Political Science Association—adopted identical resolutions supporting the principles of "liberty of thought, freedom of speech, and security of tenure." That led to a Joint Committee on Academic Freedom, which in turn led to the American Association of University Professors (AAUP)—whose first members included Nearing, Patten, Young, and Roswell McCrea, the new Wharton dean. According to the Philadelphia *North American*, the "direct cause" for the resolutions was the "efforts of reactionary trustees of the University of Pennsylvania to inaugurate a systematic elimination of progressive teachers."

"I do not believe in muzzling any member of the faculty," responded Provost Smith. "I do believe, however, that no man may go too far."

Amid rumors that Nearing might be dismissed, McCrea said: "There is no question about the open hostility toward Dr. Nearing . . . on the part of certain interests."

Chief among those interests was, apparently, Joseph Grundy, a Bucks County wool manufacturer and politician who served as president of the Pennsylvania Manufacturers Association and later became a U.S. senator.

He strongly opposed any child-labor legislation, and had repeatedly crossed swords with Nearing. Given his prominence in the state legislature, which was approving increasingly large appropriations for the financially strapped University, Grundy was a force to be reckoned with.

Yet Nearing openly flirted with danger. In one of his economics classes devoted to the theory of consumption, he pinned a newspaper account of a lavish high-society dinner given by Mrs. E. T. Stotesbury of Philadelphia to the bulletin board and wrote the words *Sin and Social Salvation* on the blackboard. Not only was Stotesbury's husband a wealthy trustee of the University, but her son, the late James H. Cromwell, was a student—and was sitting in that class. It was an outrageous—even cruel—act, and it prompted a number of alumni to protest Nearing's "inquisitorial examinations into the social conditions surrounding the homes and families of the students." And yet, according to Saltmarsh, the students themselves (with the presumable exception of Cromwell), "broke into a prolonged ovation at the end of the class."

Although the trustees voted by a nine-to-five margin in 1914 to promote Nearing to assistant professor, they also sent copies of a new bylaw warning him and other assistant professors that their appointments were for one year only. One trustee explained that Nearing's promotion was intended to be "an appointment on probation."

If Nearing was concerned about his status, he didn't show it. He wrote a fiery open letter (printed in local newspapers) to a business-friendly evangelical minister named Billy Sunday, who was believed to have been brought to Philadelphia to help avert a transit strike. The "most sinister crimes against the ideals of Christ's religion are committed by the system of industry for profit," which paid "hideously low" wages, wrote Nearing—who then invited Samuel Gompers, president of the American Federation of Labor, to campus. When Provost Smith refused to allow the student Civic Club to use any University facilities for Gompers' address, the infuriated students formed a Free Speech Club and rented a hall off-campus—only to find that their posters announcing the lecture had been torn down. Nearing took his classes off-campus to hear the talk anyway.

A few months later he supported the re-formation of a campus chapter of the Intercollegiate Socialist Society. He also contributed articles to the *International Socialist Review* with titles like "The Parasitic Power of Property" and "The Impending Conflict."

In the late spring, Effingham B. Morris, a trustee and president of the Girard Trust Company, personally told Nearing that there would be "no eliminations from the University faculty." But, he added: "We will give you young fellows plenty of rope. You will hang yourselves."

The trustees tried to pull the lever as quietly as possible, waiting until the academic year had ended and the students and faculty had left campus. Knowing that Nearing hadn't a chance of finding a new job on such short notice, they voted to arrange payment of his salary for another year. But since that could be "construed only as an admission of the nefarious character of their actions," writes Saltmarsh, "they voted not to have the salary provision recorded in the minutes of their meeting."

"We 'young fellows' did not propose to be hanged without a tussle," wrote Nearing in his autobiography. He sent out some 1,500 letters "to the newspapers of Pennsylvania, the leading papers of the country, the press associations, associates in other universities, and to influential individuals all over the United States."

"From the outset the case was national news," he recalled. "Publicity was excellent and generally in our favor."

"Nearing Affair National Issue," was the *Philadelphia Public Ledger*'s front-page headline on June 20. "Colleges throughout Country Discuss its Effect on 'Free Speech.' Professors of Wide Repute Fear University Will Suffer."

Although some local members of the General Alumni Society issued a statement supporting the trustees' action, Penn's reputation did indeed suffer. *The New Republic* cast the trustees as "black reactionaries," adding: "The issues here are as vital as any in American life, because the Universities are coming more and more to focus the thought of the nation . . . They cannot do the work if they are governed by stupid rich men or stupid politicians." Many newspapers expressed similar sentiments, though not all. *The New York Times* sided with the University, saying that "there is altogether too much foolish babbling on the part of some professors."

When the fledgling AAUP took up Nearing's cause, it brought instant prestige and publicity. The organization's president, John Dewey, argued that if the governing boards of universities were to treat a professor as a "hired man," they would "drive from their institutions all men of ability and backbone, and retain to teach the youth of the country only weaklings in mind and character."

The day after Nearing was let go, Dr. Lightner Witmer, professor and chair of psychology, told Patten: "I don't give a damn for Nearing. He and I disagree on almost everything, but this is my fight. If they can do that to him they can do it to any of us. It is time to act." Witmer cancelled his vacation plans and spent the summer investigating and writing *The Nearing Case: The Limitations of Academic Freedom at the University of Pennsylvania by an Act of the Board of Trustees.*

Professor Felix E. Schelling, professor and chair of English—and, like Witmer, a political conservative—led a faculty movement to have the trustees' decision reversed. "Gentlemen," he noted tartly, "do not do such things." The Wharton faculty demanded that Nearing be rehired, and raised the equivalent of half a year's salary to assist him in his campaign.

Some 1,500 Penn students signed a petition protesting Nearing's dismissal. One unnamed professor reported "serious dissatisfaction and dissension within the university and without," adding that Penn had been "humiliated in the public view" and that "younger members of the faculty are shaken in their sense of security and allegiance to the university," while older professors "are perplexed and dissatisfied."

Amid concerns of an "impending exodus among the faculty," Nearing himself urged them to stay: "The University does not belong to the Trustees," he told colleagues; "it belongs to you, its teachers, and its students. That the Trustees have an essentially undemocratic power and have used it irresponsibly does not warrant you confirming them in it. You must think of your students and of the University's mission."

For months, Penn's administration and trustees tried to ignore the furor, making little attempt to explain their decision beyond the refrain that it was in the "best interests of the University." Finally, on October 2, 1915, the semester's first issue of *Old Penn* led off with "A Letter on the Nearing Case," subtitled: "A Letter from an Alumnus to His Fellow Alumni." The author was Dr. J. William White, a famously feisty Penn trustee and alumnus. The letter was 17 magazine pages long.

White vigorously denied that Nearing's dismissal "was part of a so-called plan to carry out a reactionary policy against free academic discussion and freedom of individual speech." Rather, he said, "soberminded, sensible persons had received from Dr. Nearing the strong impression that he advocated the ruthless redistribution of property, that he believed in the personal iniquity of those who lived on incomes derived even from their own savings, that he thought the alternative of work or starvation should be presented even to the old, the feeble, and the diseased."

While that impression may have been "misunderstood" by White's "senior friends," he acknowledged, "the fact that they had been given the opportunity to do so made me still more doubtful of his fitness to represent the University before the [people] as one of its chosen expounders of the principles of Economics." After repeated complaints, White said, he realized it was his "duty as a Trustee to consider whether his influence on the whole was helpful or prejudicial."

On October 16, *Old Penn*'s cover story was "A Statement of Principles by the Board of Trustees of the University." Noting that a university should help students "acquire knowledge of information heretofore gathered," investigate "every department of human knowledge without restriction," and publish the findings "both within and without the University," the trustees adopted "as an adequate expression of their views and purpose" a statement made by the rector of Aberdeen University in 1874: "Universities should be places in which thought is free from all fetters, and in which all sources of knowledge and all aids of learning should be accessible to all comers, without distinction of creed or country, riches or poverty."

But they still defended their action: "When an individual teacher's methods, language and temperament provoke continued and widespread criticism alike from parents of students and from the general public who know him only by his public utterances, the freedom of choice in selection of some other person is a right equally as inherent in the Board of Trustees . . . as is the right of freedom of opinion and thought, and teaching in the faculties. And this duty must be exercised for the good of the University as a whole."

"The Nearing case was at best a tissue of mistakes and misjudgments," wrote the late Edward Potts Cheyney, professor of history, in his *History of the University of Pennsylvania 1740-1940*. "It is not at all certain that Dr. Nearing should have been reappointed to a position in the University," he added, "but neither he nor any other teacher should be abruptly separated from it without notice or discussion. Teachers are appointees, not employees of the Board."

After the whole mess was over, Cheyney noted, Provost Smith persuaded the trustees to make a series of changes in the by-laws that provided "a more orderly procedure in short appointments and placed the responsibility for removals in the case of full professors, except for the very last step, on the Faculties, where it belonged." Since 1915, he added, there had been "no instance of removal without the approving judgment of the Faculty."

Nearing's career never recovered. Though he was hired the following year by Toledo University as professor of political science and dean of its College of Arts and Sciences, he soon sparked a furor by opposing American entry into the Great War—and by saying that "the phrase 'freedom and justice for all,' as recited by the innocent children," was "humbug." In March 1917, the Toledo trustees voted by a close margin to dismiss him.

That was the year of the Russian Revolution, and after Nearing joined the leftist People's Council for Democracy and Peace, a Justice Department infiltrator described him as "very popular and DANGEROUS for he is looked to as being very wise." He ran for Congress as the Socialist Party's candidate from New York in 1918—he was known affectionately as "the professor," and would often use a folding blackboard to make his points—but was defeated by Fiorello LaGuardia. That same year he was indicted for having written a pamphlet titled *The Great Madness*, which federal officials described as "clearly a violation of the Espionage Law, being a frank description of the war as a capitalist scheme." After he delivered a riveting closing argument on his own behalf, a jury found him not guilty—though it did find the American Socialist Society guilty of *publishing* the pamphlet.

Nearing joined the Communist Party in 1927, but lasted less than three years before simultaneously resigning and getting expelled for his "non-Marxian conceptions." It was, he noted, his "last institutional connection." From there, he went back to the land, first in Vermont, then in Maine—*Living the Good Life*, as he and his wife Helen put it.

I n the mid-1960s, Dan Hoffman and his wife Elizabeth bought an old farmhouse on Penobscot Bay in Maine, one cove over from the Nearings'.

"By now the Nearings with their 'good life' and their simplicity and their frugal back-to-the-land preachings were written up in the *Whole Earth Catalogue*," recalls Hoffman, "and summer after summer there'd be an endless parade of Volkswagen minibuses in various states of disintegration crammed with hippie-type kids looking for the Nearings. So they were really the center of a cult."

One year, Hoffman made a chair out of alder saplings, and along with fellow poet Phillip Booth brought it over to the Nearings'.

"I presented it to Scott, saying that this was the non-stipendiary chair of the Wharton School: the Nearing Chair," recalls Hoffman. "Now, he was a very dour-looking man, but he really broke into a smile. The next summer I went to call, and I didn't see it. So I asked Helen, 'What has Scott done with the chair?' And she said, 'Oh, well, during the winter he cut it up for firewood and burned it.'"

In 1966, Nearing attended a peace meeting in Bar Harbor. One of the speakers was Dr. Derk Bodde, professor of what was then called Oriental Studies at Penn. After the meeting ended, Nearing wrote, Bodde came to him and said: "We always mention you around the University as the guarantor of the high degree of academic freedom that we now enjoy. Whatever the intention of the trustees when they dismissed you, the furor raised over the case stood as a horrendous warning to the University not to let it happen again."

"My real regret is that I have been deprived of day-to-day contact with students in my chosen field," Nearing wrote in his autobiography, which was published in 1972. "I am not bitter, vindictive, nor resentful. I look upon the whole affair as part of the cold war which has played so large a role in the history of individuals in the past half century."

The University had changed a great deal by then. In 1973, on the recommendation of the faculty and then-President Martin Meyerson, the trustees—led by the late William Day—invited the Nearings down to Penn. At a dinner held at the old Faculty Club, Meyerson presented the 89-year-old Nearing with a resolution. It read:

> *In recognition of a singular career begun as a member of the Faculty of the Wharton School, and for adhering to a belief that to seek out and to teach the truth is life's highest aim, the Trustees have designated Scott Nearing as Honorary Emeritus Professor of Economics, effective April 25, 1973.*

According to Meyerson, Nearing was "very happy" with the honorific. He mulls over his choice of words for a moment, then amends it: "I think he was overjoyed."

The Nearings, he adds, expressed a desire that the University take over their house in Maine after their death—"keep the library there and use it as a kind of retreat for students to come up and use it in the summer." For practical reasons, that didn't work out. The hand-built house and property instead became the Good Life Center: "Advancing Helen and Scott Nearing's commitment to social justice and simple living," in the words of its website. But the request itself made it clear that the old warrior had finally accepted the peace pipe.

After the dinner at the Faculty Club, Nearing aired some of his political views, which were as far-left as they had ever been. "Helen was thinking that he was coming off as more of a socialist than he or she wanted him to be," recalls Meyerson with a wry smile. "Finally she said, 'Careful now. They may take your new professorship away!'"

Through a Glass Darkly

Stephen Glass

(First published in November/December 1998.)

"I have to get this off my chest," wrote Stephen Glass. "I have a confession to make. During my tenure as Executive Editor of this newspaper, I have allowed a grave omission to occur."

A tantalizing lead for his farewell "Enemy of the People" column in *The Daily Pennsylvanian*. Reading it today, one wonders: What awful sin was this now-infamous alumnus going to cough up? Could it be that—even back then—he had spun quotes and characters from whole cloth and was about to admit it?

Well, not exactly. The "grave omission" was that he hadn't publicly praised his own staff, the scores of students who worked under him, "laboring to all hours in the night in their idealistic quest for truth, justice, and the American way." A little fulsome, maybe, but a nice gesture. No wonder his staff adored him.

As that farewell column continued, Glass began spinning an image that is somewhat more remarkable in hindsight than it was at the time: that of a looking glass, a mirror of the University itself, which the *DP*'s staffers "slave in this office for hours on end to construct." And it was that mirror's reflection, he wrote, "that allows members of the University to be self-critical and strive for excellence."

Then there was this: "This mirror is not and should not be 'nice.' Rather, this reflection is more useful when the glass is pure—emphasizing each wrinkle and each scar. Only by seeing our true self will we ever improve."

"It is a quiet, brutal war," says a Hard at the University of Pennsylvania, who asked that his name not be used since many of his colleagues are Sensors. "For [Sensors, successories] is a church, and these posters are the idols. They have to convert you to it."

—From "Writing on the Wall,"
by Stephen Glass, in the March 24, 1997, *New Republic.*

You might not have known about the bitter nationwide struggle between the Sensors—fanatical followers of uplifting messages known as "successories"—and the Hards, described as non-believing "academics and irritated employees." And even though it was being fought out right here at Penn, among other places, you were in good company. Outside of Stephen Glass's mind, it seems, most of those warriors didn't exist.

"There's no way of verifying whether that's an honest quote or not," says Tyce Palmaffy, an editorial assistant at *The New Republic*, about the Hard line from Penn. "It's anonymous. But some of the material was definitely made up, and that one is indicative of his process of deceit."

By now, a good portion of the Western world has heard about Glass, the shooting star who was found to have pulled off one of the most amazing journalistic con jobs in history. He was unmasked in May, confronted with incontrovertible evidence that he had been fabricating quotes and people and organizations in his stories, submitting notes from nonexistent interviews to fact-checkers, even constructing a faux website to throw off the reporters and editors who were closing in on him. At age 25, he was fired from his job as associate editor of *The New Republic*, and his freelance contracts with *George, Rolling Stone,* and *Harper's* were cancelled. Today, readers hoping to find the fabricated stories at *The New Republic*'s website are met with an apology and an explanation of why those stories—more than two dozen of them—are no longer there. ("Mr. Glass's work was dishonest in any medium—paper or electronic—and here in cyberspace, just as in the magazine, we regret its publication.") Now there are websites with titles like *A Tissue of Lies: the Stephen Glass Index* cataloguing his inventions as well as the media commentary—of which there have been truckloads, including lengthy features in recent issues of *Vanity Fair* and *Philadelphia* magazine by *DP* alums Buzz Bissinger and Sabrina Rubin.

So what happened? What could have transformed the likeable, talented, high-minded young editor who was constantly asking people "Are you mad at me?" into a spinner of mendacious and increasingly whacked-out yarns about churches whose members believed that George Bush was the reincarnation of Christ and shopping-mall Santas whose fear of child-molestation suits led to a Union of Concerned Santas and Easter Bunnies? Not to mention less amusing brands of plagiarism and invention, one of which prompted *George* editor John F. Kennedy Jr. to send a letter to President Bill Clinton's legal advisor, Vernon Jordan, apologizing for a Glass-spun quote about Jordan's sexual preferences.

Theories abound, many of them plausible, some of them fascinating, all of them insufficient. In the end, no one really knows what happened except Glass himself, now a reclusive law student at Georgetown University, where he recently qualified for the Law Review, but for "personal reasons" declined to participate. And so far, he has maintained a deafening silence.

"Stephen I don't think is going to be able to talk to you, for a couple of reasons," said his Washington attorney, Gerson Zweifach. "One is that it's much too soon for him to feel comfortable speaking publicly about this. The other is that there are some pending legal matters that make it much more complicated for him to discuss the events of the last year." (Glass is being sued by the anti-drug group DARE over one of his *New Republic* pieces.)

It's a sad story; a tragedy, really. Having led the *DP* through turbulent waters with high-profile panache and gone on to become a rising star in the high-octane world of Washington journalism, he was seen as a success story and even a role model; his fall stunned his former colleagues and friends at the *DP* and throughout the University. For most, the natural inclination to conduct caustic post-mortems was tempered by a real sadness and desire to defend him—and to make it clear to outsiders that what happened recently had no bearing on his work at the *DP*.

"If you talk to anyone who was there at the same time as him, I don't think you'll find anyone at the paper who questioned his ethics or integrity at all," says Charlie Ornstein, who worked under Glass as a reporter and later became executive editor himself. "To the contrary, among the people who he trained and supervised, there was a real sense of admiration and a real sense that he was trying to instill values. And I think that was part of the reason everyone is so surprised."

"When this thing first broke," says *Philadelphia* magazine editor Eliot Kaplan, "I was hoping that he would hold a press conference and say, 'I've been secretly doing a book on how easy it is to fool the mainstream press, and now my book will be out next year.' But that didn't happen.

"I feel very badly for him," adds Kaplan, who had tried to hire Glass on more than one occasion. "I hate to see somebody go through that kind of breakdown. My first thought is still, 'What a horrible waste.' As angry as I am, and as betrayed as I feel, my primary response is still one of great sympathy. That such a talented guy is going to fall by the wayside."

Not everyone responds with such compassion. For Bissinger, the more he dug into the story, the angrier he became.

"Whatever the reason, it suggests the complete absence of any moral center whatsoever," he says with palpable disdain. "In the end, Stephen screwed everybody—his closest friends, people who helped him, people who liked him. He dishonored Penn; he dishonored *The Daily Pennsylvanian*; he dishonored *The New Republic*. He did a tremendous amount of damage to journalism. But maybe in a way that's good, because I think he tore the lid off a lot of the problems that are in the journalism profession. This whole blurring of what's real and what's imagined."

> *On the fourth floor of Washington's Omni Shoreham Hotel, eight young men sit facing each other on the edge of a pair of beds. They are all 20 or 21 and are enrolled in Midwestern colleges . . . The minibar is open and empty little bottles of booze are scattered on the carpet. On the bed, a Gideon Bible, used earlier in the night to resolve an argument, is open to Exodus . . . The young men pass around a joint, counterclockwise.*
>
> *"I'm telling you, I'm telling you, we don't know what we're doing," says Jason, a brown-haired freckled boy from Iowa, between puffs. "We've got no mission. We've got no direction. Conservatives—we're like a guy who has to pee lost in the desert, searching for a tree." The other seven young men nod and mumble in agreement . . .*
>
> *This is the face of young conservativism in 1997: pissed off and pissed: dejected, depressed, drunk and dumb . . .*

—From "Spring Breakdown,"
by Stephen Glass, in the March 31, 1997, *New Republic*.

D r. Alan Charles Kors, professor of history, recalls reading that piece with some misgivings. A conservative libertarian himself, he had been sufficiently impressed by Glass during his days as editor of the *DP* to recommend him for his first job at the Heritage Foundation's *Policy Review*, even though the Heritage Foundation is a conservative institution and Glass was, on many issues, a liberal. But Kors put his doubts aside. "I said to myself, 'Yeah, but it's Stephen who wrote it, so it must have happened that way.'"

It didn't.

After the article appeared, an old *DP* colleague, Gabriele Marcotti, called Glass in Washington to talk about it. "One of the things that struck me at the time," says Marcotti, "was how he got very excited about it. He regaled me with all these anecdotes, some of which were in the story, some of which hadn't appeared in the piece. Looking back, if you're going to make something up and write it and get away with it—at that point, unless you believed your own bullshit, you'd probably let it lie. You wouldn't go and try to impress somebody again with more anecdotes about it. I think that was an obvious sign that he was under a lot of stress. He needed help at that point, because it wasn't just a case of 'I can't cut it, so I'll stretch the truth.' It was a case of alternate reality."

> *Johnnie is the leader of his "posse," a club of several dozen homeless people that has its own intricate rules and traditions. All members of the club identify their allegiance by donning an American Heart Association button and a Zenith Data Systems painters' cap . . . Club members enjoy citing their hero, Kenny Rogers, as best expressing the philosophy of surviving on the streets. Twice that day June and Johnnie sang "The Gambler" in chorus . . .*

—From "A Day on the Streets,"
by Stephen Glass, in the June 6, 1991, *Summer Pennsylvanian*.

Since no one has proven otherwise, it's always possible that this story is completely accurate, right down to the first-person descriptions of homeless people smoking crack and picking up prostitutes and talking about murders they committed. There's no question that there really was a West Philadelphia homeless man named Johnnie who used to hassle Glass for money—"like Steve owed him," recalls Matt Selman—and whose photo accompanied the story. And Glass's roommate that year, Joon Chong, remembers him being away from the room for a day or two while he was working on the article. But the notion of a homeless "club" with matching buttons and caps seems *prima facie* absurd. Kenny Rogers seems a rather unlikely hero for African-American homeless men. And the very idea of the neurotic, khaki-clad Glass hanging out in a West Philly crack-house struck some of his colleagues as preposterous—though at the time, they kept their mouths shut. After all, says one, he was a person that "strange things happened to."

Later, Gabe Marcotti, who had done some work in outreach programs and once scored some crack for a story himself, talked with Glass about his "day on the streets." A number of things about it simply did not ring true. "It struck me as really, really unlikely," he says. "He was the most white-bread, preppy person you can imagine." (A prominent urban sociologist did later confirm that one of the points that Marcotti disputed, the price of a sex act, was in fact accurate.)

But while Marcotti didn't really believe Glass's story, he admits that he wanted to. "You sort of got the sense when you spoke to him that everything he told you, you wanted to believe him. When I heard the news about what happened to him, just talking to friends, a lot of us came to the conclusion that he had so many other things going for him, and so many people looked up to him, that you always wanted to believe him—and were willing to give him the benefit of the doubt."

The *DP* can be a very demanding master: reporters regularly log 30 to 40 hours a week there, while top editors often put in 50 to 60—a grueling load for a full-time student. In the words of Matt Klein, who preceded Glass as executive editor, it "weeds out weak-minded people." For all its self-importance, it has long been regarded as one of the best college newspapers in the country, with the awards to back it up.

It also inspires fierce loyalty—you have to be deeply devoted, and maybe a little nuts, to work that hard for free. Staffers talk about the "*DP* culture" that separates the truly devoted, fast-track insiders from those on staff whose entire lives do not revolve around the paper. Insiders tend to come from similar, affluent backgrounds; anyone in a work-study program, for example, is unlikely to have the time to get deeply involved.

"The *DP*, like any newspaper, doesn't reflect the student body; it reflects the people who make it up," says Marcotti. Glass, by all accounts, was an insider from the get-go who loved the paper and was one of its most enthusiastic cheerleaders.

Though not known as a great writer, he was considered a very good reporter: quick on his feet, energetic and resourceful, able to cover complex issues, ask the right questions, find the right people to talk to—and chat them up. Some of the subjects of his stories and editorial coverage remember him as fair and pleasant to work with; others still seethe about what they saw as deeply biased coverage.

Matt Klein says that while Glass was a "solid" writer and reporter, his rise through the ranks was based to some extent on a "cult of personality." Glass, he says, "had worked the hardest, put in the most hours, and was a good leader. He was someone people respected, trusted, and liked."

Sabrina Rubin, who says she and the rest of the editorial board "adored" him, puts it another way: "There are reporters who get ahead because they're great schmoozers, and I think Steve was definitely one of them." When he became the paper's executive editor, the editorial board hailed him as a "man of principle," and in her *Philadelphia* magazine piece, Rubin describes how Glass threw a righteous fit when she and a colleague concocted a funny and obviously made-up travel story for *34th Street*—going so far as to call an emergency session of the *DP*'s Alumni Association board to apprise them of the transgression.

"The *DP* at times has been a confluence of very talented people and very interesting events," says former editorial-page editor Ken Baer, now a speechwriter for U.S. Senator Robert Torricelli of New Jersey. "And Steve was an editor at one of those moments: 1993 was a big year for Penn. [Former President] Sheldon Hackney was leaving; the provost was leaving; there was the Water Buffalo case, the theft of the newspapers—and all of that came together at this one massive year. I feel fortunate that we had a very able staff working on it, and I feel fortunate that Steve Glass was the editor and was leading us at that time. I don't feel that anything that happens [now] should reflect on what happened then. No one should ever look back and say, 'What was going on there?'"

D r. Sheldon Hackney, who returned to Penn last year as a professor of history after four years at the helm of the National Endowment for the Humanities, is not particularly eager to revisit that confluence of events and people. But he has obviously thought about it a good deal, and when he finally agrees to talk, he does so thoughtfully and at some length. (At the end of the interview he also tells me, quite cordially, that he hopes this article never runs.)

"Journalists are basically telling a story," he says, sitting in his sunny office in the history department's temporary warren at 3401 Walnut St. "They're not just telling you what happened. They're arranging those facts and trying to fit them into a story that is recognizable by the public, and it's a story that has conflict and good guys and bad guys—a narrative, if you will. And if the narrative doesn't exist, then you have to sort of suggest one, and you rearrange things so that there are narrative elements to it. Otherwise it really isn't very interesting.

"What Glass was good at, of course, was finding those quotations and human beings who somehow embodied the meaning of the story, who carried the narrative impact of the story. And he was rewarded for that—quite handsomely. Since the rewards are so great, and people pat you on the back and say, 'That's a great piece,' the temptations for making sure the next piece is just as good or better must be tremendous." He smiles; a smile of many meanings. "This is an understanding of the press that I achieved through hard knocks," he adds.

"Now, he didn't invent the Water Buffalo incident. He didn't invent the theft of the newspapers. But his coverage I remember as being really over the top. That clearly was shaped by him, and in inventive ways, to portray the story that he wanted to portray. Which was the story, I think, of the *DP* as the defender of moral virtue and free speech being oppressed by the storm troopers of thought-control, epitomized by the president of the University. So every time there is a chance to shape the coloration of the story in that direction by inventing quotations or changing them a bit, and in the way the story was played—I wouldn't be surprised if he was doing that."

Just recently, he mentions, he and Linda Hyatt, a former senior member of his staff, had been reminiscing about Glass and his coverage of those incidents. "She remembers his quoting me on occasion, and she would ask me why I said what I did, and I didn't have any remembrance of even talking to Stephen Glass. So it sounds as if he was embroidering."

This is strong stuff, but it hardly constitutes a smoking gun. I call Hyatt, now president of the Landmark Foundation in Norfolk, Virginia.

"I can't remember specific quotes," she acknowledges, "but I can certainly remember saying to Sheldon, 'Did you say that?' And he said to me, 'No, I didn't say that.' Well, no one in the office said it. Where is this stuff coming from? We were quite puzzled by it. And there were a lot of incidents when I called Steve and asked about these stories when quotes appeared attributed to Sheldon, and he didn't return my phone calls." She promises to check her files and call me back if she finds anything solid. I never hear from her.

No one denies that both free speech and diversity are fundamental values to the University's academic mission. But in his so-called effort to "balance" the two ideals, Hackney has betrayed both.

When it comes to values, Dr. Hackney, there can be no compromise . . .

I have had less than 17 hours of sleep in the past four days. In the same half-week, I have logged over 50 hours of phone time with the media, attorneys, civil rights groups, and our readers. And I have spent almost that amount of time arguing with University administrators who perpetuate Hackney's unjust compromise of values.

In the past four days, I have been betrayed—and so have you.

—From *Hackney's betrayal*, op-ed piece by Stephen Glass in the April 20, 1993, *Daily Pennsylvanian*.

This one is not a fabrication. Depending on your viewpoint, it is either an impassioned and eloquent defense of free speech under assault by would-be censors or a biased, self-righteous attack on a free-speech defender who was trying to keep an already tense campus calm. Glass wrote it several days after a group of students who called themselves "The Black Community" and later "The Working Committee of Concerned Black and Latino Students" seized virtually the entire press run of the *DP* and deposited it into dumpsters. They were, they said, protesting the "blatant and covert racism" at Penn and, especially, in the *DP*. Not surprisingly, Glass was furious. In his opinion, which arguably helped shape the national debate, Hackney had not condemned the protesters strongly enough.

"One thing if I could do it over again is to write the statement that I released a bit stronger and more clearly," says Hackney. "But it does say, the famous sentence, 'Here we have two University values in conflict, open expression and tolerance,' something to that effect. That's what *The Wall Street Journal* picks up, and says, 'Here's this namby-pamby president who says, "We have two values in conflict."' Well, the very next sentence in that statement says, 'At a university, it's clear which value must take precedence. It's open expression.' Well, they never mentioned that. So there—I've always wondered why—I think Stephen Glass and the *DP* had a role in reinforcing that version of the story."

Actually, what the statement said was: "There can be no compromise regarding the First Amendment right of an independent publication to express whatever views it chooses," followed by: "At the same time, there can be no ignoring the pain that expression may cause." And in the same April 20 *Almanac* in which that statement appeared, Hackney added: "Though I understand that those involved in last week's protest against the *DP* may have thought they were exercising their own rights of free expression, I want to make it clear that neither I nor the University of Pennsylvania condone the confiscation of issues of *The Daily Pennsylvanian*." Right below that, Hackney had pointed out that the University policy he had promulgated in 1989 specifically banned such actions and warned that "members of the University community who are responsible for confiscating publications should expect to be held accountable." Glass and the *DP* were not assuaged.

"I've always wondered why they did not take the other option open to them," says Hackney, "which was to say, 'We won! The president is for it, free speech is upheld, we're victorious, let's get on with it.' But they didn't. They chose instead to go with, to reinforce what I think is an erroneous right-wing picture of the University of being totally under the control of left-wing radicals who have no respect for truth, who don't even believe it exists, who think that their job is to indoctrinate students rather than teach the truth and to enable students to learn."

Most members of the *DP* felt that Glass not only reacted appropriately to what they saw as a blatant attempt at censorship but that he handled the high-pressure situation with poise. "Steve really distinguished himself as a true leader," says Rubin. "The rest of us were basically in a panic—when we found out that the entire press run had been stolen and thrown away, we felt like we were under attack, and we didn't understand the reasons why. Steve originally thought the people who had done it should be prosecuted and all the other stuff, but then he cooled down and he calmed everybody else down. And he had a little talk with [editorial-page editor] Kenny Baer, and he said, 'Everything's got to come through me; we can't have everybody else talking; I'll be the spokesman.' Whenever he was quoted in all these different magazines, whatever he'd say, he could talk in sound bites. He knew exactly how to handle the situation—he knew people really well."

Well, most of the time. On Alumni Day that year, he did make the mistake of trying to hand a copy of the *DP's* annual graduation issue to Alvin Shoemaker, then chairman of Penn's board of trustees. The issue recapped the year's leading stories—including the Water Buffalo incident, the theft of the *DP*s and a number of other not-so-rosy incidents, none of which reflected particularly well on the University. Shoemaker, who found the paper's coverage infuriatingly one-sided, told Glass in very blunt language just where he could stick his newspaper. No need to ask "Are you mad at me?" this time.

Marcotti was one member of the *DP* staff who thought Glass had blown the *DP*-theft story out of proportion. "I disagreed with him deeply on that issue, on the confrontational tone," he says. "I still believed that the [trashing of the papers] was a form of free expression, not censorship. This did not endear me to the *DP* mainstream."

But some months later, he had dinner with Glass, whose term was soon to expire. They ended up talking about free speech and the trashing of the newspapers until the small hours of the morning. "This is one of the reasons why I genuinely liked the guy—and still do, in spite of everything—because he took all this time to try to persuade me to his point of view, and he had no reason to. Even situations where I disagreed with him, I would come out of talking with him, while maintaining my viewpoint, recharged. He was so charismatic and energetic. And I would go and I'd work my ass off for the *DP.* He really was a natural leader, and he had this power to really inspire people to go above and beyond what they would normally do. Even people who shared nothing with him in terms of goals and ideas."

Buzz Bissinger wonders how deeply Glass really believed in his free-speech rhetoric. "It seems to me that those are values that, if you believe in them, you believe in them your whole life. You don't turn them on; you don't turn them off. Certainly, later in his life, Stephen had no problem turning off the values of truth. So you have to wonder how much did he really, really believe in it when he was in college—or to what degree did he think, 'Hey, this is a way to get some fame for myself'? You know, a lot of people around the country had heard of him. George Will was writing about him, and Nat Hentoff was writing about him. I mean, a lot of big names were writing about him. And I'm sure it made him feel good.

"I don't want to insult anyone who writes for a college newspaper," Bissinger adds, "but a college newspaper is not a reflection of *anything.* And I'm saying that as someone who worked at *The Daily Pennsylvanian,* and it was a wonderful sort of seminal experience—but it's not the same."

Which leads to the inevitable question of how Glass, with such limited real-world experience as a journalist under his belt, got to such a lofty position by the age of 24.

"I've spent 20 years as a journalist," says Bissinger, "and I've spent those years in places that were not very sexy, like Norfolk, Virginia or St. Paul, Minnesota. But they taught me a hell of a lot about journalism. Regardless of how good or how bad a reporter or journalist Stephen was, how did he get to this level so quickly? When I was 24 or 25 years old, I was covering cops. And I'm glad that I did it, because Stephen never knew what it was like for someone to get in his face and say, 'You know what, that story was wrong, that story was inaccurate.' When you work at a relatively small newspaper, if you print one fact wrong, they are all over you, and they are all over your editor. It's an incredibly unpleasant experience, and for no other reason, you never want to go through it again."

It was "Hack Heaven"—a story about a bratty teenage computer hacker who was blackmailing software companies that appeared in the May 18, 1998, *New Republic*—that led to Glass's unmasking as a writer of fiction posing as a journalist. (And not a very good fiction-writer, either; the dialogue in that piece is ludicrous.) The former fact-checker was exposed by an online journalist from *Forbes Digital Tool* named Adam Penenberg, who couldn't figure out why he had never heard of "Jukt Micronics" and why Jukt's Web site (which featured a "rebuttal" of "Hack Heaven") was so blatantly amateurish.

"I am sure Glass would have been caught eventually," says Penenberg. "Usually when Glass faked a piece, he would use first names, or rely on anonymous sources and fabricated notes to fool editors and fact-checkers. But with 'Hack Heaven,' perhaps we were seeing the beginning of the end. He actually provided first and last names, a government agency and a law, a convention he wrote had occurred in Bethesda, Md. He was becoming careless. Perhaps he wanted to get caught."

*P*ostscript: Five years after Glass was unmasked, he broke his self-imposed silence. Simon & Schuster was publishing his novel, *The Fabulist*. (Full disclosure: I couldn't bring myself to buy the book, and have only read passages and reviews that appeared online.) Its hero also went by the name *Stephen Glass*. In the author's note, he explained that the book, "while inspired by actual events in my life . . . is a work of fiction—a fabrication and, this time, an admitted one." In the novel, he also took some shots at the thinly disguised stand-ins for people who he believed had wronged him. And yet, the character named *Glass* informed the reader, "What I truly wanted was to be well regarded by the people around me—actually, to be loved by them."

When the real Glass went on *60 Minutes* to flog his fiction, he was contrite, remorseful, as he described the slippery slope that led him to deceive his editors and his readers.

"I remember thinking, 'If I just had the exact quote that I wanted to make it work, it would be perfect,'" he told *60 Minutes* interviewer Steve Kroft. "And I wrote something on my computer, and then I looked at it, and I let it stand. And then it ran in the magazine and I saw it. And I said to myself what I said every time these stories ran, 'You must stop. You must stop.' But I didn't.

"I loved the electricity of people liking my stories," he added. "I loved going to conference meetings and telling people what my story was going to be, and seeing the room excited. I wanted every story to be a home run."

At one point Kroft asked him whether the Stephen Glass in the *60 Minutes* interview was really Stephen Glass "or just another character that he has invented."

"I know people are going to think that," Glass replied. "And while I know I am not inventing the person I'm sharing with you now, I can't make you believe that. All I can do is continue to behave in a way that earns your trust."

"I read the novel hoping for some insight into why Steve did what he did," wrote Hanna Rosin, a former *New Republic* colleague, in a review for *Slate*. "I learned some weird things—for instance, when Steve invented someone for one of his stories he dressed up to get into character, putting on rouge and lipstick the color of 'cherry Tootsie Pop.' But otherwise the insights were shallow."

Glass made it clear throughout the book that he anticipated reviews like hers, she pointed out: "His fellow journalists will never believe he's sorry or been punished enough, will just wish him to remain forever ashamed, he writes. But this too is just another form of narcissistic fantasy. Most of us don't think about him all that much unless he publishes a novel and goes on *60 Minutes* to hawk it."

She was sure that Glass was sorry for what he had done, she said. "He was always sorry for even minor infractions; how much more so for this extravagant, ongoing lie. I'm sure too he's been punished enough, having lost his career and all his old friends. I don't wish him ill. But I'm not convinced he's changed all that much."

Later that year, *Shattered Glass*, a movie based on Bissinger's *Vanity Fair* article and starring Hayden Christensen as Glass, was released. Glass's old *DP* colleague Sabrina Rubin Erdeley reviewed it for the *Gazette* in the January/February 2004 issue. Ever since the news of his deceptions broke, she had struggled to make sense of his actions, she wrote. "I resisted the explanation I've come to believe since then: that the adorable little weenie I knew from our days at *The Daily Pennsylvanian* was nothing but a con artist." She found the film "riveting," she admitted, but as she watched it, she was ultimately dissatisfied.

"What was Glass after?" she asked. "What was he running from? The movie ultimately doesn't shed much light, and Stephen Glass himself isn't telling. If, that is, he even knows."

For my purposes, the story could have ended there. Then, as I was poking around on the Internet, I came across a story titled "The Liar's Club" in *The Stranger*, a Seattle-based weekly, published in March 2004. An enterprising writer named Christopher Frizzelle had asked Glass and Jayson Blair, the *New York Times* reporter who was also forced to resign in disgrace for crimes of fabrication (and who also published a book about it), to sit down for a joint interview in a Brooklyn bar. Amazingly, both showed up. "I like giving interviews," Glass said.

At one point, as they exchanged war stories of humiliation and disgrace over beer, Glass remarked quietly: "I was called the greatest con man of my generation. Or the Western world? The biggest lying con artist in the Western world? Something like that. In *The Pennsylvania Gazette*. And old college friends wrote stuff in *The Daily Pennsylvanian*, where I was editor way back."

As I read those words, I admit to feeling a slight stab. (The precise phrasing from the *Gazette* article is slightly different than what Glass recollects, but it's not too far off, and I don't think he was intentionally distorting it.) Of all the ink-tipped arrows shot in his direction, apparently the ones that stuck under his skin and festered were not the denunciations by *The Washington Post* or the *Columbia Journalism Review* or *60 Minutes*. They were the ones in his alumni magazine and his old college newspaper.

Yes, he deserved most of them, if not all. He knows it, and I know it. I also know that Glass has a large talent for getting people to feel sorry for him, and for using that to his advantage. But still. This is a sad, sad story of a very talented young man whose world fell apart because he was trying, too desperately, to make his stories dazzle.

SEEKERS,
SCHOLARS, SEERS

SUMMING UP LEON HIGGINBOTHAM

LEON HIGGINBOTHAM JR.

(First published in February 1993.)

I f you stand on the upper floors of the United States Courthouse at Sixth and Market Streets in Philadelphia and look east, you can easily take in some history: Over there is the stretch of Delaware River where William Penn first landed in 1682; over here, the spire of Christ Church, where a number of Founding Fathers kneeled to pray; right down in front is the Liberty Bell, housed in a glass-sided pavilion that was built in the mid-1970s (and looks it). But unless you know your way around this part of town, you might not even see, way down and to the right, the handsome Georgian brick building that, two centuries ago, was known as the Pennsylvania State House. It was there, in 1776, that a group of patriots with names like Jefferson and Adams and Franklin signed a document declaring that "all men are created equal," and where, a decade or so later, during the steamy summer of 1787, they hammered out a constitution for the new United States.

From his comfortably cluttered chambers on the 22nd floor of the courthouse, the Honorable A. Leon Higginbotham Jr.—a senior circuit judge of the United States Court of Appeals for the Third Circuit, professor of law, adjunct professor of sociology, emeritus trustee, and, in the words of a colleague, "citizen of the world"—likes to point out that building to visitors. It is now better known as Independence Hall.

"I always tell people that the most important thing is to look to the far right and you'll see where the Declaration of Independence and the Constitution were drafted," Higginbotham says in his relaxed, deliberate bass, gesturing toward the window. "That was, in many ways, the beginning of the dream. It was not a fulfilled dream then—and it's not now—though there have been profound changes during the interim."

He leans his long frame back in his chair, pressing the ends of his fingers together. "I stay in touch with the historical roots," he continues, "because, at various times, I worked on drafting up constitutions for other countries, and it causes you to try to reflect on what the forefathers were thinking about when they initiated this extraordinary process. You think in terms of not merely what significant things they did but of the omissions."

There were, of course, some rather glaring omissions. You don't need to be a legal scholar to know that a constitution that permitted slavery, neglected to enfranchise more than half the inhabitants of the new nation (including all women), and gave slaveholding states the right to count slaves as three-fifths of a person for apportionment purposes was, for all its undeniable grandeur and genius, an imperfect blueprint for democracy. And few thoughtful people would contest Higginbotham's observation that there is a "nexus between the brutal centuries of colonial slavery and the racial polarization and anxieties of today."

Higginbotham has devoted much of his life to dismantling that nexus: as a judge, as a scholar and author, as a teacher, as a human being. And while it is never entirely easy for white Americans to be confronted with the nation's racial past and the shortcomings of the Founding Fathers, the tour of duty is somehow much more tolerable when Leon Higginbotham is the guide. A commanding presence at six feet, six inches, he is also an immensely likable man, possessing vast reserves of dignity and warmth and an easy laugh that reaches falsettos of delight.

Even on the delicate and sometimes seemingly hopeless matter of race, he does not smolder with anger or despair—though he does have a fine, if well controlled, sense of outrage. To get a notion of that, read his "Open Letter to Justice Clarence Thomas from a Federal Judicial Colleague" or get him going on the subject of *The Daily Pennsylvanian*'s front-page photo last term of a Thunderbird-toting black man that was captioned "West Philadelphian." Higginbotham lives in West Philadelphia, and he deeply resents it when privileged kids take cheap shots at it. "The person who authorized that caption," he says gravely, "is incompetent to build a better world."

As he approaches his retirement from the bench, the biggest challenge to writing an article about him (apart from trying to pack his extraordinary life and work into some sort of manageable form) is keeping it from turning into cloying hagiography. As Colin Diver, the Bernard G. Segal Professor of Law who serves as dean of the Law School, puts it: "You're not going to find many people who are going to say anything negative about Leon Higginbotham."

That is not just a matter of personal charm. We have here a judge who, when nominated by President Jimmy Carter in 1977 for the United States Court of Appeals, was unanimously rated "exceptionally well qualified" by the American Bar Association and who, according to *The American Lawyer* magazine (which surveyed a wide range of litigators who have argued before him), is "popular and highly respected by Republican and Democratic, conservative and liberal lawyers alike." And the respect goes pretty far up the line.

"I thought he was a better-than-outstanding member of the Court of Appeals," says retired Supreme Court Justice William J. Brennan Jr., who, between 1956 and 1990, served as Circuit Justice for the Third Circuit Court of Appeals, on which Higginbotham has been sitting. "He was just a crackerjack judge, no matter what your measurement was of what's a good one or a bad one," Brennan adds. "He was a crackerjack judge and a crackerjack administrator, and he contributed an awful lot. I had the highest regard for his ability and integrity and whatever it is that goes to make up a good chief judge. He had it all."

Higginbotham likes to talk about life's "probability curves," and he has spent most of his life pole-vaulting over them. The 8-year-old who was told to forget the little boy's dream of becoming a fireman because the Ewing Township (New Jersey) Fire Company would never hire a black man has gone on to preside over numerous cases involving racial discrimination, and he has helped douse racial fires and otherwise shape public policy by serving on a long list of commissions and other influential boards. Last month, *The Washington Post* reported that he was one of five candidates under consideration by President Bill Clinton for the post of United States Attorney General. On January 24, the *Post* noted that "an informed source said Higginbotham had been approached by the White House about the position but discouraged the possibility, in large part because he becomes eligible for his judicial pension when he turns 65 on February 25." ("That is a *very* accurate quote," says Higginbotham with a hilariously arch laugh, adding that at his age, he is no longer interested in taking on the pressures of that office.)

The 16-year-old who arrived at Purdue University in 1944 and found that he had to live in an unheated attic because the dormitories were off-limits to black students has gone on to receive more than 70 honorary degrees (including one from Purdue), not to mention the B.A. he earned from Antioch College and the law degree from Yale University. He has taught or lectured at Harvard, Yale, Stanford, New York University, the University of

Michigan, the University of Hawaii, and Penn—all while working full-time on the Federal bench. He was the first black trustee of two Ivy League schools—Penn, beginning in 1968, and Yale, from 1970 until 1976—as well as Thomas Jefferson University, from 1966 to 1978. During his quarter-century affiliation with Penn, he has served as head of the trustees' committee on University responsibility, as well as of the Graduate School of Education's board of overseers and the Law School's board of overseers. (He was also reportedly sounded out about the presidency of the University in 1980.)

The 24-year-old who was treated as a prime prospect by a prominent Philadelphia law firm until he showed up at the interview wearing black skin ("Marvelous record," said his potential employer, a fellow alumnus of Yale Law School. "Of course, you know there's nothing I can do for you, but I can give you the telephone number of two colored lawyers, and maybe they can help you.") has left a lasting imprint on American law.

His career on the Federal bench began in 1964, when he was sworn in as a Federal district judge for the Eastern District of Pennsylvania at the age of 35. In 1989, after 13 years as a circuit judge on the United States Court of Appeals for the Third Circuit, he became the chief judge for that circuit. More than a few legal observers believe that if the White House not been occupied by conservative Republicans during the 1980s, he would have ended up on the U.S. Supreme Court.

Higginbotham's 1978 book, *In the Matter of Color (Race and the American Legal Process: The Colonial Period)*, which plumbs the unsettling story of racial law in Colonial America, is considered the definitive work in its field. The *Harvard Law Review* put it this way: "No attempt to summarize the Colonial experience could convey the rich and comprehensive detail which is the major strength of Judge Higginbotham's work." It earned him a slew of awards, including the American Bar Association's Silver Gavel Award and the National Bar Association's Literary Award.

It is, for all its case law and voluminous footnotes, compelling reading, as it traces the evolution of racial laws in six of the Colonies through the time of the Revolution and compares those laws with contemporary English racial laws. Although its tone is measured, the book can spark a surge of anger, even a prickle of shame. That is, presumably, one of the points; the trick is to see that the anger doesn't just explode and the shame doesn't degenerate into hand-wringing. Constructive channeling is something in which Higginbotham has some experience.

"You have to look at life through a bifocal lens, or maybe a trifocal lens," he says. "You have to look through one lens which understands the historical roots of those who are in power denying—sometimes intentionally and sometimes unconsciously—full equity to others. But after laying all of that out, a minority has to never throw in the sponge. And, therefore, you have to look through the second lens. And you look at the subculture and you say, 'What is it that we can do, even when no one else is going to help us to make things work?' And I think that, as long as minorities have this dual vision, this dual philosophy, we're going to be able to make the maximum progress.

"Theodore Roosevelt once said—and I'll be misquoting him—'The test of life is whether one enters into the arena, and, at his or her best, has a fleeting moment of success and, at his or her worst, fails while daring greatly,'" notes Higginbotham. "Now, that is where I come from. That you've got to make the effort, give it your best; and you hope you will succeed, but you don't worry about whether it's actually going to come through."

That does not mean that he backs away from a fight—or potential controversy. His "Open Letter to Justice Clarence Thomas from a Federal Judicial Colleague"—which alternately congratulated, advised, scolded, and exhorted the newly confirmed Justice, accusing him of failing to understand and appreciate the work of the civil-rights movement inside and outside the law—helped crystallize the disenchantment with Thomas' nomination, both inside and outside the black community. In 1985, he spoke at the *Harvard Law Review*'s 100th anniversary banquet, and while he spoke respectfully of the contributions of its members over the years, he made it clear that he was not exactly impressed with their overall record, especially with regard to racial matters.

"He had researched how Harvard professors and graduates of the *Law Review* had dealt with the issue of racism in society," recalls Derrick Bell, the visiting professor of law at New York University who left his tenured position at Harvard to protest the absence of tenured black women on the law faculty there. "And he was able to cite chapter and verse about the number of *Law Review* members who had gone on from Harvard to be on the Supreme Court—what they had done and, in many instances, what they *hadn't* done. It was very intriguing and courageous for him to come to the home of the great institution and pretty much pin their ears back."

For a man who recently described himself as being "in the twilight of my life, perhaps the last inning," Higginbotham is still throwing a lot of pitches. In addition to his writing and his normal case load, he has kept a punishing schedule of teaching obligations and outside speaking engagements. (The amount of outside work Higginbotham takes on occasionally raises eyebrows among some of his fellow judges, but he has always kept his docket current.) No wonder that Higginbotham looks forward to "retiring," which will involve serving as a counsel, on a part-time basis, to the New York-based law firm of Paul, Weiss, Rifkind, Wharton, and Garrison; teaching at Harvard University; and working on the four books that he intends to publish by 1996. (The first two are continuations of his Race and the American Legal Process series, which began with *In the Matter of Color*; the third examines the racial similarities and differences between the United States and South Africa; and the fourth—which he hopes to have out by 1996, the 100th anniversary of *Plessy v. Ferguson*—will focus on race and the U. S. Supreme Court.)

"I think one of the extraordinary characteristics of his personality is that he can handle so many different things at the same time and still have time to really extend himself to people," says Edward S. G. Dennis Jr., a former United States attorney who worked as a clerk for Higginbotham in the early '70s. "He always seems to have time for a law student who has a problem or needs a hand. He has a real good sense of balancing his responsibilities."

Working for Higginbotham, say his former law clerks, can be an exhilarating experience, not to mention an instructive one. "He would often critique what was going on in the courtroom or in the settlement conference, and he would give us a sense of the dynamics of the adversary process," recalls Dennis, now with the Philadelphia law firm of Morgan, Lewis, and Bockius. "And there were always a lot of very well-known people going in and out of his chambers—like [former Secretary of Transportation] Bill Coleman and people going back to his civil-rights days when he was president of the NAACP in Philadelphia. He was really doing the work of three or four people, almost, on a full-time basis. He has a lot of energy, and he worked very hard—seven days a week, 12-14 hour days. It was just a professional whirlwind."

The long and impressive string of law clerks he has hired has included a lot of women and African Americans (some of whom are, of course, women too).

"He's probably in the forefront of black judges who are willing to hire blacks regularly as clerks," says Bell. "There are a lot of blacks on the bench who have never hired any blacks as clerks—if you can believe that—or have hired only one or two. Because they go strictly on the basis of who graduated highest in the class. I don't think they discriminate, but they're busy, and they feel that they have to have the best. And Leon has always been one who felt that you could be the best even though you didn't have the top grades. And I don't think his work has suffered because he has reached out in hiring blacks."

"From the enormous loyalty and affection that the people who have worked with him and for him feel, they were obviously treated with respect and regard," says Ralph R. Smith, associate professor of law. "He has had an enormous influence on the lives and careers of people who will be the leaders of the bar for years to come. It is his molding of the next generation—directly, through the extraordinary string of law clerks he has hired and, secondarily, through his teaching and his example—that I would perhaps put at the top of the list as his greatest contribution.

"As he recounts the story of his life," Smith adds, "as he reaches out to talk with young people and students, his story really is an inspirational one. And his telling and sharing it is always well received by the people in the audience. It's a real motivator—how to essentially beat the odds and succeed, despite what seem to be formidable obstacles."

"If everyone had a mother like mine, there would be no limits to what we could do," Higginbotham is saying. "She was a woman who disregarded the probability curve. She never, ever accepted defeat."

Having fled the tobacco fields and Jim Crow miasma of rural Virginia for the cooler racial climate of Trenton, New Jersey, where she found work as a domestic, Emma Lee Douglass Higginbotham determined that her bright young son would not spend his life as a manual laborer—regardless of the daunting lack of white-collar options for blacks. Example: When young Leon finished the eighth grade at a segregated grammar school, he and all the other black students went on to high school, where one of the requirements to enroll in the academic program was a year of Latin. The grammar school didn't offer Latin; ergo, none of its students had ever enrolled in the high school's academic program. Higginbotham's mother promptly persuaded the principal to allow her son to take second-year Latin—despite the fact that he had never taken first-year Latin. With the help of a teacher who tutored him—one Bernice Munce—he was able to compete; and he did well enough in high school to be admitted to Purdue.

"My mother was absolutely confident that, through hard work and education, anyone could make it," he says. "And I think that I'm a workaholic today largely because of her. It was very, very clear to me that we have to work harder than anyone else, and if we do that, we've got a chance."

Higginbotham talks less about his father, a deacon in the local church and a factory laborer—who, he says, was late to work only once in 45 years (and that was during a blizzard). "My father was a good human being," says Higginbotham. "I think he accepted the probability curve. He had a membership in the NAACP, but he was not at all confident that the system could be defeated. He had the work ethic, but I don't think he had the societal expectations."

If it hadn't been for a man named Edward Charles Elliott, Higginbotham might have become an engineer. Elliott was the president of Purdue in 1944, the year Higginbotham entered as a freshman. The story of their brief encounter is one that Higginbotham has told many times—once during a speech he gave at Yale Law School (later reprinted in the *Yale Law Report* under the title: "The Dream with Its Back Against the Wall")—but it is a powerful one, and one that bears telling again.

When he entered Purdue as a 16-year-old freshman in 1944, he told his Eli audience: "There were about 6,000 white students, 12 black students. The 12 black students lived at a house that [Purdue] had the temerity to call International House. We slept in an attic with no heat. And after December and January, going to bed every night with earmuffs on, sometimes wearing shoes, other times three or four pairs of socks, jackets, I decided that I should go and talk to the university president."

He did not go so far as to request real integration; he just asked if the black students could have a section in any dormitory on campus that was warm. Elliott, he recalls, looked him in the eye and said: "Higginbotham, the law doesn't require us to let colored students in the dorm, and you either accept things as they are or leave the university immediately."

That incident would change his life.

"I am a lawyer today because of Dr. Elliott's negative motivation," he told the Yale audience. "Because, as I walked back from his office, I had a thousand thoughts. How could it be that the law would not permit 12 good black kids to sleep in a warm dormitory? The law had been very effective in the draft. Some of my best friends had gone and died for our country . . . . And yet, the legal system that proclaimed equal justice for all would not give any semblance of dignity to a 16-year-old boy who had committed no wrong. I felt that I could not go into engineering—that I had to try to challenge the system."

Not long after that, his mind now focused on the law, he had another telling experience at Purdue. He had joined the university's debate team, and on the night before it was to debate Northwestern University, the team arrived in Evanston, Illinois, and checked into a hotel—whereupon the hotel manager informed Higginbotham that he couldn't stay there. (His debate coach's feckless response: "Is there a colored YMCA?") And so he went to a "mice-infested colored YMCA," arriving at 1:30 a.m., and didn't sleep a wink, since the debate was at 9:00 a.m. and he didn't have an alarm clock. That he still won second place says something about his mental and physical stamina.

Soon after that, he transferred from Purdue to Antioch College—thanks to one Jessie Treichler, a special assistant to the president of Antioch who had created a fund-raising committee to attract black students to the college. Higginbotham was one of two black students at Antioch that year; the other was Coretta Scott, who later married Dr. Martin Luther King Jr. Years later, when Higginbotham was sworn in as a member of the Federal Trade

Commission, he sent Treichler a first-class ticket and reserved her a suite at the Mayflower Hotel in Washington.

"I shall always remember the Jessie Treichlers of this world, who gave so much," he says quietly. And he has not forgotten the Edward Charles Elliotts.

"The Elliott incident convinced me that, in the final analysis, victims of oppression have to be willing to fight their own battles," he says. "And while maybe, along the way, you will get some wonderful allies, the major burden is yours. And if you don't articulate the unfairness and injustice of the system, it's not going to change."

But the incident symbolizes something else to Higginbotham, too: "You know, lots of people like to think of barriers and oppression in terms of individuals who wear hoods—the Ku Klux Klan, vigilante groups. But most of the massive, devastating oppression that has occurred in this society was perpetrated by individuals who did not have the facade of hate and hostility but who had the opportunity to have the doors closed or opened—and refused to open them. What the Elliott experience demonstrated to me is that it is the individual who is civil, who is polite, and says *No* who may be more of a barrier to equal access than the individual who calls you a *nigger*. I mean, as civilized as Thomas Jefferson was, as much of a philosopher as he was, as eloquent as Patrick Henry was—each of them owned slaves."

Higginbotham's disdain for the more genteel forms of racism extends to the Ivy League as well, despite his own training and service in its hallowed halls. He is fond of pointing out that in 1896, four of the seven Supreme Court Justices whose decision in *Plessy v. Ferguson* upheld the separate-but-equal doctrine of Jim Crow laws were graduates of Harvard and Yale law schools. *Plessy v. Ferguson*, says Higginbotham, was "the most wretched decision ever rendered against black people in the past century," and he argues that "If those four Ivy League alumni on the Supreme Court in 1896 had been as faithful in their interpretation of the Constitution as Justice John Harlan, a graduate of Transylvania, a small law school in Kentucky, then the venal precedent of *Plessy v. Ferguson*, which . . . legitimized the worst forms of race discrimination, would not have been the law of our nation for 60 years." (Harlan, a former slave-owner, wrote a remarkable dissenting opinion, which stated, among other things, that "Our Constitution is color-blind, and neither knows nor tolerates classes among citizens . . . . The destinies of the two races, in this country, are indissolubly linked together, and the interests of both require that the common government of all shall not permit the seeds of race hate to be planted under the sanction of law.")

The tragedy of *Plessy v. Ferguson*, Higginbotham wrote in his letter to Clarence Thomas, "is not that the Justices had the 'wrong' education, or that they attended the 'wrong' law schools. The tragedy is that the Justices had the wrong values, and that these values poisoned this society for decades."

Few people would deny that the seeds of race hate to which Harlan referred are still bearing their bitter fruit today, though equally few are likely to agree on the best way to rip out the root system. There is, after all, only so much the law can do to change a way of thinking. But as Higginbotham points out, the law can be "very, very effective in constraining conduct," and he cites the 1964 Civil Rights Act as an example.

"Prior to 1964, when I took my children on a trip throughout the South, there was no hotel, no restaurant, any major chain where we could stay," he recalls. "When I was president of the [Philadelphia Chapter of the] NAACP and we had our convention in 1961, or 1960, in Atlanta, all of us stayed at the all-black colleges—Clark or Morehouse or Spelman. Now, if you went back three years later, blacks would have had access to the best hotels in town without any serious problem with public accommodation. It would be foolish to say that, within three years, the poison of racism had been eradicated, but the conduct had changed. It can make a big difference.

"That cuts across not merely the question of race," he adds quickly. "If you look at the number of women who were attending or who were faculty members of the University of Pennsylvania in 1964—it was minuscule. If you look at it now, it has increased many-fold. It's not because women have suddenly become brighter. A whole series of laws which prohibit discrimination on the basis of gender, all of which are spinoffs of the legislation prohibiting discrimination on the basis of race, have caused many extraordinary changes in this country."

Furthermore, he says: "The law also gives a legitimization of prejudice. When it is the law, it has a certain aspect of moral approval in the eyes of many people, and, therefore, you are almost immoral when you challenge the law, which has been enacted by the people."

It is partly because of his appreciation of the legal ramifications of the 1964 Civil Rights Act that Higginbotham places himself somewhat to the left of center on social issues. Roy L. Brooks, a professor of law at the University of Minnesota Law School, has described Higginbotham as a "reform liberal," a branch of liberalism that "holds that other forms of liberalism, as well as liberalism in its most basic sense, presuppose equality of opportunity in economic, political, and social affairs. State intervention into private affairs may be necessary to make this presupposition a reality. The state may have to intervene to make certain that the playing field is, in fact, level—and, indeed, more level than it has been in the past."

Asked about such labels, Higginbotham hints at a smile. "Well, I've been called all kinds of things," he says. "I guess any thoughtful black has not been a status-quo advocate. I guess, as a judge for 28 years—others have identified me as part of a more liberal tradition. Sometimes, I'm considered more liberal than I once was, and I don't think it's because my positions have changed as much as it is that people in power have become increasingly conservative."

In his open letter to Clarence Thomas, Higginbotham wrote: "I must confess that, other than their own self-advancement, I am at a loss to understand what it is that the so-called black conservatives are so eager to conserve . . . . It was the white 'conservatives' who screamed 'segregation now, segregation forever!' It was primarily the conservatives who attacked the Warren Court relentlessly because of *Brown v. Board of Education* and who stood in the way of almost every measure to ensure gender and racial advancement . . . . Where were the conservatives of the 1950s when the cause of equal rights needed every fair-minded voice it could find?"

Now that the more blatant expressions of racism have been stricken from and by the law, the task of ferreting out—and correcting—racial discrimination moves into murkier waters. While many of those who dislike Affirmative Action programs are white and some may be racist, even some of those who agree with the aspirations of the programs are uncertain about the way they have been achieved.

"I think that Affirmative Action is an issue which reasonable people could disagree on," says Higginbotham. "However, it seems to me that these people who are so much against Affirmative Action on race—I would be perfectly willing to be tolerant of that attitude if they weren't for Affirmative Action in other areas.

"Let me give you a classic example," he says. "You ever heard of a person by the name of Dan Quayle? You know how he got into the University of Indiana Law School? He got in on a special-admissions program. It was designed for people who purportedly had not scored well on the LSATs and had not done well on grades. But they wanted to have this experiment, and they accepted 20 students, about 16 of whom were white. So Dan Quayle goes in—and nobody's arguing that he shouldn't be a lawyer now. So I just think there's an awful lot of hypocrisy going on. Some of the people who are arguing most hostilely against Affirmative Action programs are the individuals who have benefited from them in other ways.

"When I entered [Yale's] law school in 1949, if you took the entire academic enrollment in Ivy League law schools, in terms of minorities, you would have had five," he notes. "And the reason why you had only five was not because black people in '49 were so stupid and whites were so smart. It goes back to a whole level of advantages and opportunities and access.

"Now," he says, "let's turn the clock up 40 years. If, in 1990, a university announces that, all other things being equal, it will give the benefit of the doubt to children of alumni, that is Affirmative Action in its most positive fashion. And I have yet to hear any college president announce from any podium that they do not have a special interest in recruiting children from alumni. Now, if you start putting this in greater context, the implications are overwhelming. Up until the 1950s, there was not one black in any major college in the South, by statutory exclusion. So if you're going to talk in terms of children of alumni, all you're saying is those individuals who have been the beneficiaries of past oppression should be able to continue their relative advantage."

Some people—mostly white—argue that Affirmative Action programs should be more or less limited to education. In *Reflections of an Affirmative Action Baby*, Stephen L. Carter, a black professor of law at Yale, argues that some Affirmative Action programs have "run their course." Carter, who acknowledges his own debt to Affirmative Action programs in higher education and to the civil-rights movement in general, wrote that "perhaps, if the programs are to be preserved, they should move closer to their roots: the provision of opportunities for people of color who might not otherwise have the advanced training that will allow them to prove what they can do."

Higginbotham doesn't think the education-only argument tells the whole truth, and he uses the example of gender to dispute it: "I think education is the main area, but I just can't believe that all the men who've gotten into the American corporate complex have gotten there because men are so superior to women. I think a lot of them have gotten there because of the old-boy network, and the only way you can deal effectively with old-boy networks is to be concerned about getting pluralism. In our United States District Court for the Eastern District of Pennsylvania—for its first 180 years, they never had a woman! And no woman got on that court until President Carter nominated Judge [Norma] Shapiro. Now: Is a court better off if it has diversity, with women and people from a variety of different backgrounds? I submit to you that it is."

In November, after Clarence Thomas was confirmed as Supreme Court Justice by the Senate, Higginbotham wrote his now-famous letter. When, after two weeks, Higginbotham did not receive an answer, he decided to make the letter public. First published in Penn's Law Review last January, it was also picked up, in edited form, by newspapers across the country.

The response was staggering. The article sold nearly 20,000 copies—more than any other article in the history of the Law Review—causing some work-study students there to quit because of the heavy work load. More than 800 readers wrote letters to the author, and while Higginbotham says that "98 percent" of them "vigorously supported" the article, a few were sharply critical. The criticism fell into several categories. The first, he says, was exemplified by a black Federal public official who said: "Who appointed you as a judge of the qualifications and character of black judges?"

At a meeting of the National Bar Association, an organization of black attorneys, he responded: "I can only say that I have never suffered from any grand delusion of being the universal spokesperson for all black Americans, nor have I ever entertained any chimerical belief of being the anointed prophet for the entire black race . . . . I wrote to Justice Thomas not as the universal prophet for all black Americans but as an individual witness to the frustration and hopelessness that we feel when we see rights won at the cost of so many lives slowly eroded by the courts."

Another category of critical letters argued: "Why are you holding Justice Thomas to a higher standard than the other, white Justices? The other Justices can choose to be liberal or conservative, average or great, pro-business or pro-people. So what if Justice Thomas chooses to be conservative, average, and pro-business?"

"My response," said Higginbotham, "is what W.E.B. DuBois wrote almost 90 years ago, in a book called *The Souls of Black Folk*. He talks about double-consciousness and how what we always have to have in this country, as blacks, is this double consciousness, [being] an American and a Negro. And . . . when a black person joins in an opinion which is particularly harsh and unfair to black people, the damage is worse. Because it leaves the impression, 'Why are these colored folks complaining? A colored man was on the majority, and he said they didn't have any rights.' And that is why the debate was going on. We can't let Justice Thomas be, because the stakes are too high."

The reaction to Higginbotham's letter in legal circles was slightly more mixed.

"I heard from quite a number of lawyers and alumni of this school and other lawyers that I run into in my daily life," says Colin Diver. "Most of them were quite complimentary—but by no means all of them were. There were two lines of criticism. One was that it was just utterly inappropriate for a sitting judge to openly and publicly criticize a member of the Supreme Court—that it's OK for him to send the letter privately, if he wants, and it's OK for him to publicly take a position on the policy issues, the interpretive issues on which he disagrees with Thomas, but he should keep it on an impersonal basis.

"The other line of criticism went more to the substance of what Leon was saying in the letter. The theme or the tone of the letter was that Clarence Thomas has betrayed or turned his back on the struggle and the efforts of those who preceded him, and a line of criticism was that that does not necessarily follow, that that is not necessarily a logically correct basis for criticizing Thomas—that what Thomas would say if he chose to publicly respond to this was, 'I appreciate what people in your generation and earlier generations have done for me; those policies were correct at the time, but they are no longer correct. Circumstances have changed, times have changed, and my approach—Clarence Thomas' approach—is the right way to achieve justice for people of our race.' I think both of those are sort of legitimate points of view, but you can understand that people are somewhat reluctant to state them publicly."

For Higginbotham, one of the great ironies of Thomas' confirmation hearings was his repeated emphasis on his own struggles against the odds, as well as those of his grandfather.

"I think it's wonderful to note the fortitude, whether it's Clarence Thomas or Leon Higginbotham or anyone else who has persevered and overcome the obstacles," he says. "The tragedy is, when one does that, and there is the assumption that everyone else could have done it. And that's the tragedy of Clarence Thomas. His sister was a hard-working person; for a couple of years, she was on welfare. And why he would go and speak in public in condemnation of his sister, who never got his benefits—the truth of the matter is, she stayed in Pin Point, Georgia, and he had the good fortune of moving on to Savannah. It has all of the gender implications of lots of backgrounds where the men get the education, the women clean the dishes. So I think the tragedy of Clarence Thomas is not that he made it—I'm delighted that he made it—but that he speaks with besmirchment of his own sister. I think that is a profound character revelation."

Higginbotham has been championing women's causes for some time—not only in contemporary society but from the perspective of his scholarship. "In my view, Missouri's most venal racist case was not the well-publicized *Dred Scott v. Sanford*—Dred Scott was ultimately freed and died a natural death from tuberculosis," he wrote in an examination of Missouri's racial laws published in the *Washington University Law Quarterly* in 1989. "The most venal case was *State v. Celia*, in which the Missouri courts in effect held that a slave woman had no virtue that the law would protect against a slave master's lust . . . . Celia died at the gallows because she had on one occasion the temerity to defend herself against further sexual molestation."

For Higginbotham, the tensions that sometimes accompany the unraveling of gender and race can reflect the essential "duality within all persons—and maybe the duality within all movements." And as our second interview in the U.S. courthouse comes to an end, he sums up: "There has been an extraordinary gap between the egalitarian concepts uttered and the practices of Jefferson and George Washington, which are, from a racial standpoint, symbolic of that duality. I think that the task of each generation is: How do you extract the best performance they had and use that to build on, and how do you eliminate the contradictions of their particular era—and try not to duplicate them in ours?"

Twenty-two stories below and a block or so south, the afternoon sun splashes the west side of the old Pennsylvania State House, where respectful tourists wait in line to tour the shrine to freedom and liberty. In its shadow, just a few yard to the east, is another venerable brick building: Old City Hall. There, in the earliest days of the Republic, the Justices of the new nation's Supreme Court first met to set their agenda.

"The irony of the unfulfilled American Dream of equality is that of all those in the long line of dreamers who have sought the ultimately just society, none had to seek out alien sources for moral authority," wrote Higginbotham in *In the Matter of Color*. "They had only to say to the American people: Fulfill the largest promise in your first statement as a nation."

DECIPHERING PAUL KORSHIN

PAUL KORSHIN

(First published as "The Unforgettable Dr. Korshin" in October 1991.)

D r. Paul Korshin, professor of English, is sitting in the drawing room of his West Philadelphia house, surrounded by books and flanked by cats and talking animatedly about literature and mentors and codes. He is dressed casually, in powder-blue slacks and a white sport shirt—which may come as a shock to those who assumed that he sprang from the womb in a custom-tailored suit and bow tie. Every now and then, he jumps up with a haunted look on his face and straightens a picture on the wall.

The two cats—one yellow and willful, the other an overstuffed calico that looks like something out of a George Booth cartoon—are named Oscar and Sherwin, which happen to be the first and last names of the professor who introduced Korshin, as an undergraduate, to the world of Jonathan Swift and Alexander Pope and Samuel Johnson. It is a world of mannered styles and abstruse symbolism, one that Korshin has found congenial—and one in which he has been residing ever since.

"That's what I like: decipherment," says Korshin, his voice fusing the precise diction of a British scholar with the frenetic pace of a New York City cabdriver. "So that's what I look for in literature. The first book I read as a 19-year-old in that course in 18th-century British literature was Swift's *A Tale of a Tub*—one of the hardest books ever written. You can only understand it if you decipher it. So that's where I must have gotten started, puzzling out the meaning of things. What always interested me about works of literature was: Were they hard? Did they require decipherment?"

Deciphering Korshin himself is a task that may well rank up there with *A Tale of a Tub*. His code is not going to be cracked by a single intercepted message; he is too complicated for that, too many-sided—an Enigma Machine, if you will. One colleague marvels at the "almost incongruous combination of simultaneous and, presumably, mutually exclusive qualities," only to conclude that he's "the genuine article, but extremely strange." Another describes him as a "strange puzzle, with big chunks out."

He is known as, among other things: a polymath, an epicure, a dandy, a fop, a wit, a scholar, a mentor, a friend, a character, a snoop, and a pain in the ass. ("He is not simply a pain in the ass," says one colleague; "he is *also* that, but he is not *just* that.") He is a dynamic lecturer, a magnificent cook, and a generous host who gives legendary parties to which people yearn to be invited. He is a straight arrow who refuses to jaywalk lest he set a bad example, and he has a reputation for driving like a berserker. (He was once taken in by the Philadelphia police for allegedly trying to run over a striker, though he claims the accusation was mischievous, and no charges were filed.) He can be highly sensitive and perceptive, and he can be remarkably obtuse to the effect he has on others. ("He has a silver ear that is beautifully tuned," says a colleague, "but he has a lead ear also—he can't hear a thing out of that one.")

Some background: He is 52 years old and, for those who follow such things, a Leo. He was born in Manhattan, grew up in Queens, spent six years in Cambridge, Mass., and the last 25 in Philadelphia. (Education: Bayside High School, Queens; City College of New York; Harvard University.) He has two brothers, both younger than he, both medical doctors. His mother was a schoolteacher, his father a fundraiser for various universities before swapping the Academy for Wall Street; both are now retired. (Asked which member of the family he was closest to, he responds: "Oh goodness gracious me. My father was not around much, so it must have been my mother.") He is a stew of ethnicities, and requests that the individual ingredients not be divulged. As a youth, he spent his summers at his mother's family's farm in upstate New York; now, he spends them in England, always stopping at the British Library, where he has a regular desk and code names for some of the other scholars, e.g., the Scumbag Boy and the Lad of the Crimson Visage.

He is an opera-lover who has a very expensive subscription to the Metropolitan Opera and an Anglophile who claims to have had more letters published in *The Times* of London than any other North American. Though he is deeply immersed in the world of 17th—and 18th-century British literature, he is considered a bottomless well of knowledge about taxes and lawyers and moving companies and the other practicalities of 20th-century American life. A self-professed, outspoken liberal and a white-collar elitist, he wishes there were more blue-collar African-Americans in his West Philadelphia neighborhood, where he moved in order to live by his principles.

His name evokes powerful reactions: from worshipful adoration to amused fascination to grudging respect to a sort of appalled disdain. Many of his students and former students are devoted friends and disciples who talk and meet with him regularly, but there have been others who have violently disliked and distrusted him. He likes to say that it's almost unfair that he should get paid for doing what he enjoys so much—"playing school"—yet he is said to be a vigorous advocate for raising his own salary. He claims to be uninterested in the student-guide ratings of professors, yet he rattles off his own numbers—which tend to be quite high—like a baseball announcer. He professes great relief at having avoided the tedious administrative chores of his department, yet he is rumored to have coveted the chairman's post. Fascinated by spies, he is regarded by some of his colleagues as a shameless snoop. (The more English departments change, the more they remain the same.)

Within the department, he is an anomaly: a professor of literature who doesn't much care for novels, dislikes the current rash of literary theories, and suspects that his real aptitude may be in the sciences, not the humanities. (He often takes the Graduate Record Exam and the Mensa tests to amuse himself, regularly registering perfect scores in the quantitative sections, better than he scores on the verbal parts.) He is extraordinarily well-read in all manner of subjects, yet he has argued that there should be no course requirements at all in the humanities. (He once gave a speech to the Faculty Senate in which he proclaimed that "Erasmus and Isidore of Seville did not become Renaissance men by having to take required courses," though that was nothing compared to the speech 18 years ago in which he predicted that the proposed office of provost for University life, with its inevitable growth in personnel, might "significantly lengthen the alimentary canal but will never be able to disguise the final product.")

No one questions his abilities. "One of the most intelligent men I've ever met," says a colleague. "Able in many ways. He could run the United States easily. He could also wreck the United States," the colleague adds, referring to Korshin's sometimes imperious way of dealing with people.

Nor does anyone question his reputation as a serious scholar with a high-voltage intellect and insatiable, omnivorous curiosity.

"I've never heard his most serious detractors claim that he was anything but a responsible scholar," says Dr. Robert Lucid, professor of English. "He's *good*. He's a living computer-bank of information with respect to his field—and not just literary studies but 18th-century cultural studies, a very broad mix."

"Paul has always been a rigorous student of the context and times that defined the work," says Dr. Alan C. Kors, professor of history, whose shared interests led him to edit a book with Korshin called *Anticipations of the Enlightenment in England, France, and Germany.*

"If one branch of a literary history is to add empirical historical context," Kors explains, "so that one might read a text with historical understanding, it is essential to know and decipher the symbolic language and meaning of the times. And Paul has done outstanding work in that period."

Korshin has been vigorously involved in the University of Pennsylvania Press—having sat on its faculty editorial board for six years, including three as chairman—and, by all accounts, he has been an invaluable force in helping it to attract authors from within and without the University. Since the press publishes a good deal of material related to 18th-century British literature, there is a natural connection between it and him.

"He's up to his ass in it," says one colleague, in an amused way. "It's a genuine passion with him. It's almost as if he takes publishing to its logical conclusion, as if it's a religious experience. After all, universities do treat it like that; he's just carried it all the way."

Korshin has published some 50 essays and more than a dozen books (many of them collections of essays by various authors) since coming to Penn in 1966, and his *Typologies in England: 1650-1820*, which examines symbolism in religious and secular writings, is considered the definitive work in its field. He has several new books in progress and on the drawing board—two on his longtime literary hero, Samuel Johnson; one on the concept of credibility; and another on code (tentatively titled "Private Language, Private Parts").

The leitmotif of code and decipherment surfaces often in Korshin opera, and wants explaining. One might start with the premise that it is his way—a highly logical and scientific way—of understanding the hidden meanings of life, literature, and the people who inhabit and create them.

"The art of referring to the things that we have hidden is often very complex," he writes in the introduction to "Private Language, Private Parts," "involving special signs, languages, and messages known only to ourselves and to certain select others to whom we desire to transmit intelligence of what we have hidden . . . . So the methods of concealment that men and women contrive to keep knowledge secret may be especially difficult for outsiders—people not in on the secret and the methods of its conveyance—to grasp."

Ergo, unraveling secret knowledge requires a great deal of knowledge about a great many things.

"In order to know how to decipher a code," he says, "you must know the language the person's writing in, and you have to know his culture as well.

143

To do what I do, you can't just know a few books. You have to know a vast amount of stuff and have a great deal of material at hand.

"How did the British manage to decipher some of the messages that the Nazis were sending to their U-boats in World War II?" he asks. "Well, one of the decipherers was English but had lived much of his life in Germany. And, knowing that the Germans were very formal, he was able to surmise that every message would begin with the same two words: '*Heil Hitler.*' They all did. They were never the same, because they changed the code daily, using their famous Enigma Machine. But knowing that, or surmising that, was the beginning of the key that unlocked the code."

He is somewhat more perfunctory on questions regarding the role of code in his own life, which might or might not support one colleague's contention that a key to Paul Korshin is a lack of self-knowledge. Then again, he might be just concealing his thoughts from the hoi polloi.

"I think that, for the longest time, he believed that historical research was totally disinterested," says Dr. James Cruise, a friend and former graduate student who now teaches literature at Purdue University, "but he betrayed to me, I guess a year ago, that his interest in codes also has some bearing on his own life. I found that shocking, because with that revelation, there was evidence of a personal point of view. I don't know that he's thought seriously about it, but he did see some bearing on the work he did and the way he lived his own life."

Whatever the personal implications have been for Korshin, his fascination with decipherment has yielded a rich vein of publishing material. It started with his dissertation at Harvard, which evolved into his first book, *From Concord to Dissent* (published in 1973), then branched out to his *Typologies in England: 1650-1820* (published in 1982) and the upcoming "Private Language, Private Parts." He also teaches a course on decipherment at Penn.

"I had one very good idea in the mid-1960s," he says, "and that's led to three books. Some people only have one idea in their whole life. But this one happens to have been very good. The dissertation was based on the argument that there'll be passages in certain poems where the author is talking surreptitiously, subconsciously, secretly, about what it's like to write about composition—theories of composition or 'vocational passages,' as I call them. Most people said, 'We don't believe that in a poem by Alexander Pope, say, or John Milton, that there are certain passages of verse in which the poet is talking indirectly, figuratively, allegorically, about his theories of art.' In the late 1980s, this became quite accepted, and now it's quite widely understood that there are all sorts of key passages of this sort in all sorts of works. And, in fact, the so-called deconstructionist movement has more or less insisted that was the case. But there I was writing about it about 20 years before any of this happened."

His first book, *From Concord to Dissent: Major Themes in English Poetic Theory 1640-1700*, continues his examination of "vocational passages"; it also traces the evolution of the era's poetry from one of harmony—reflecting the intellectual community's quest for social and political stability—to one of discord. It's an ambitious work, and it played to mixed reviews. In a peevish write-up in *Criticism*, John Fleischauer of Columbus (Georgia) College acknowledged that "Professor Korshin shows exceptionally broad reading experience, so his notes are very helpful; and when he is not after a point, his readings of Dryden, Denham, and Oldham are really very sound," but added: "I just wish that Korshin had used the history, theories, and poetry of the 17th century to develop a thesis, rather than starting with a thesis and concocting the poetry."

Far more successful was his 1982 *Typologies in England: 1650-1820*, which explores the densely coded symbolism in that era's literature—thereby providing a broad stage for Korshin's erudition. In a *Church History* review, Dr. Horton Davies, professor of English at Princeton University, called it "indispensable in its field" and added that it "is the work of many years of wide and reflective reading."

Few would argue with the latter assessment, least of all Korshin (whose accomplishments include creating a catalogue of every book published in the English language from 1701 to 1800). "I spend a lot of time reading old books and curious things that have nothing to do with literature—pamphlets, calendars, almanacs, auction catalogues—in order to get a taste of what was happening in the culture," he says. "I have tremendous curiosity. Never stopping, but always reaching out in new directions. It gets so broad that sometimes I wonder whether I should just give up, because I seem to be interested in everything. That's what polymaths do—though, of course, most polymaths never get anything done because they're so badly directed. They just fiddle around. That's not my way, of course. I've luckily been better directed.

"I could become master of one very narrow specialty," he adds, "but that never has been my idea. Spread out as much as possible—that might have been part of the Harvard experience. They go in for a lot of breadth. Huge humanistic constructs covering many disciplines—interdisciplinarity, if you will. That hasn't been Penn's way. It's not a popular notion here. But I can't change myself. So I must try to impose my own view in my own little way."

Some say that his curiosity extends beyond the bounds of scholarship.

"He is said to be able to read upside down," says one colleague dryly. "That is to say, if he's standing in front of your desk and you're sitting there with some messages, he can read them. Certainly, no one questions the fact that he would if he *could*. He is absolutely shameless about trying to find out everything that he can find out about everybody."

There is yet another side to that curiosity, though, and that is the genuine interest he has shown in his students—their opinions, their backgrounds, their careers—and one that has often translated into generous help and advice.

"Paul was very unusual in that he had an extraordinary sense of initiative with his students," says Barbara Kirschten, whom Korshin encouraged to apply for a Thouron Scholarship (to Cambridge University, of course) and, eventually, to Harvard for her Ph.D. She is now a lawyer in Washington.

"He was extremely interested in students he thought were talented," she adds. "He gave people a sense of initiative and ambition that a lot of people who are a little bit shy about these things might not have taken. He would take them in hand and say, 'Of course you can do that!' And especially for someone like me, who was a transfer student at Penn and who didn't have any friends and was just starting out, that was very important. And he continues to be interested in what his former students are doing."

"He's excellent about keeping up with his graduate students after they've left, and advising them on manuscript placement, grant proposals, and professional advancement," says the Rev. Dr. Girard Reedy, a Roman Catholic priest who teaches English literature at Fordham University. Reedy, who is dedicating his second book to Korshin, points out that "there are people out there who he's not only helped get their first job, but their second job as well. He's always out there promoting them."

Although some of his colleagues in the English department view him as an egocentric irritant, there is no question that he has also been helpful to some colleagues, especially younger ones. Dr. Nina J. Auerbach, the Morton Kornreich Professor of English, remembers coming to Penn in 1972 and being overwhelmed by the size and impersonal nature of the English department.

"I didn't know anybody," she recalls, "and nobody was very forthcoming except Paul. He was wonderful. He sat down a little group of us one day and told us how to do our taxes now that we were members of the University.

"He also put together his Humanist Luncheons, which brought together people from different disciplines. They were always at some upscale restaurant like La Terrasse or at the Faculty Club. They were sort of precious in a way, but they were a good initiation to Penn, and we met people whom we never would have met. It was very generous of him to do them. I always liked him a lot. He was a very crusty, strange person, who comes on very waspish and nasty, and he's really very kind—and very much of a mentor."

Korshin's penchant for mentoring seems a close relative of his generosity as a host. "The old hospitality has not passed away in Paul Korshin's household," says Cruise, whose wedding reception was held at Korshin's house.

The Korshin house is often aswarm with guests, and the parties there are legendary. Mention Korshin's Christmas party to anyone who knows him, and a certain reverential delight spills out.

"His Christmas party has the best food in Philadelphia," says Kors. "It's also one of the few events at Penn where radical academics, feminists, and benighted conservatives such as myself can meet in good cheer. Black tie is optional, so that those who wish to put on the ritz can do so, and those of us who wish to remain rumpled academics can do so, too."

"Everyone's fear is that they'll be cut off the Korshin list," adds Auerbach, "and he's very capricious about the list—suddenly you're blacklisted, and you never know why. You can be reinstated, but you never know why he's doing that, either."

His talent for entertaining guests apparently accompanies Korshin wherever he goes. "The best thing in the world is to meet him in London," says Lucid, "because then he's host on a grand scale. What he's giving you is London—the restaurants, the galleries, and so forth. He's fabulous."

Lucid recalls a London evening with Korshin at an Indian restaurant: "Of course he knew the owner, and so forth. At some point, Paul says to the guy, 'How are the chilies? So the guy says, 'Bring the chilies.' And the waiter brings some green chilies. And they each pick up one of these chilies and chew it meditatively, and finally, Paul says, 'They're not what they used to be, are they?' So I reach in and take a bite of one, and they're absolutely blazing hot chilies! You couldn't eat them! And here these two guys are, going through this macho, *mano a mano* thing: 'How are the chilies . . . .'"

Certain symbols have come to be identified with Paul Korshin. For some, it is the bow ties and Savile Row suits. His own sartorial code is a dapper one that lends itself to any number of decipherments.

"I guess he believes that there is ultimately a precision to the kind of codes he perceives operating in the 17th and 18th centuries," says Cruise. "Those codes are important in his own life as well. He's an impeccable dresser and an epicure."

"He's properly in 18th-century studies," says one colleague, "because he's a fop—an actual fop! It may well be that's why he went into 18th-century studies—so he could emulate Beau Brummel."

"He's a manufactured man, in Dickens's phrase, if I've ever seen one," says another, "but I think that's very 18th century, also. So in a certain sense, the persona and the professional identity are not so different."

"My view is different from that of most people," says Korshin. "When I went to college, I dressed every day as if I were working in an office. Because, my argument was, if I didn't go to college, I'd be working in an office. This is my work; therefore, I should dress as if I were dressing for work—not in play clothes or simulated stevedore outfits, as some of my colleagues or as many students wear. I'm not a stevedore. There's no need for me to dress like one. I must distinguish myself. And, in fact, your clothes do distinguish you by occupation.

"Of course," he adds with what might be described as a smug snicker, "being the best dressed man at the University of Pennsylvania is not something that is hard to accomplish. Once, a colleague of mine wanted to be introduced to my tailor. So I sent him along. He heard what the prices were and never went back."

O scar the cat jumps into Korshin's lap, prompting a grimace. Though he may not be as literary as his master or his namesake, Oscar has sharp claws and a critic's sensibility. He once emptied his bladder all over Korshin's copy of *Poems on Affairs of State*—seven volumes of satirical, antigovernment works by anonymous 17th- and 18th-century British authors—which may or may not confirm Korshin's contention that "gesture is a private language which, if we can decipher it, may serve as a key to a person's character."

"Somehow, Paul feels it rather appropriate," says Cruise. "It doesn't bother him that there's this lingering cat-pee smell. They're all rather ironical poems and satires and that sort of thing—'pissing poems,' as it were."

There is no question that the man after whom the two cats are named changed Korshin's life. Until he took that course in 18th-century British literature at City College of New York, he was planning to major in economics.

"What happened to me happens, I suppose, to everybody," he says now. "You get intellectually engaged because of a certain teacher's enthusiasm. In this case, it was Oscar Sherwin. He was a specialist in the 18th century, also in American literature, and a famous collector of antiques. One day, handing back a paper of mine—which he didn't give a particularly good grade to, maybe a B-plus—he said, 'You've got to learn to write better, Paul. You're going to be a professor, aren't you? You have to learn to write.' Well, I hadn't ever thought of that. I had no notion of being a professor. He naturally thought that someone taking an advanced elective in the 18th century would only be there because he planned to go into college teaching. That's when I got interested."

It was during that course that Korshin came across his first and most abiding literary love, Samuel Johnson. He was, he recalls, reading Johnson's series of essays, *The Rambler*. And what he remembers most is the challenge it provided:

"As I read the thing, I thought, 'God, these are hard.' I had no idea, as a boy of 19, how popular they were, and had been for two centuries. They were incredibly difficult. But at the same time, I thought, 'My goodness, for one person to have written these suggests great genius.' Because each of these pieces was so brilliantly reasoned. And so magisterial in its ability to teach. So—how shall I say?—didactic. You know, *didax* is the index finger, and it's the finger the teacher uses when admonishing or teaching. And *didactic* means so teaching-like.

"So I formed a lot of thought on Johnson, and spent a lot of time thinking about my own career in Johnson-like terms—even though, of course, it's very, very different when you're a scholar, a teacher, not a man of letters. Not the most popular and famous man of letters of a whole century, if not of all time."

On the surface, the disheveled, conservative Johnson seems an odd choice of heroes for the well-tailored, liberal Korshin. But surface appearances, he says, can be deceiving:

"Johnson's a rumpled character in some ways—although he did dress very well on occasion—but he's not as conservative as people think. His biographer, Boswell, makes him sound conservative, because Boswell himself was archconservative. Far more conservative socially than Johnson, with terribly reactionary views about the position of women in society, the transmission of property from one generation, and so on. He doctors the life of Dr. Johnson by asking him a perpetual, unending series of questions, all of which make Johnson sound far more conservative than he really is. Hence, you would never know from the *Life of Johnson* that Johnson was far more advanced in dealing with women—and in wanting them to have education, advancement, equality with men—than anybody else in his time. Johnson was very much opposed to slavery, and against the slave trade. Boswell barely hints at this. And you would never think from reading it that this was a man who was very much in favor of many of the advanced ideals of social welfare of the 18th century.

"So maybe I'm not that much different from Johnson," he concludes. "I might not be as smart as Johnson—he was, of course, one of the smartest and most widely read people of the century—but that's one reason I put off writing about him for 25 years, until I could get a little bit smarter."

In fact, Korshin has averaged roughly one essay on Johnson a year since he came to Penn, so the two forthcoming books—the research for which was aided by a Guggenheim Fellowship—are not entirely new material for him. One is on the concept of the literary relationship: those authors whose work influenced Johnson's development as a writer. The other focuses on *The Rambler*—which, he argues, is not only much more of a unified work than most people think but also the high point of Johnson's literary career, though it's seldom given the attention it deserves.

"Even though it's Johnson's most famous and biggest work, nobody's ever written a book about it,' he says. "It's as if there were to be no book about *Middlemarch*, or no book about *Ulysses*. People have always thought, 'Well, it's a miscellany, it's a collection, it's not really a single work. It's an unconnected series of essays.' But I had a theory that it wasn't. Which I think I proved.

"But careers are allegorical, in a way," he says thoughtfully. "Johnson saw that. Everyone's career has had a series of turning points. In my case, it was a teacher who directed me, and then my first patron. Everyone needs a patron. Johnson had a patron. He would never admit it, but, of course, he did. People who directed him, who helped him and got him his first work, as it were. His first promotion. That's what it was for me: my first patron."

Korshin's patron was Dr. Robert Lumiansky: chairman of the Department of English at Penn, former provost at Tulane University, chairman of the board of directors (and, later, president) of the American Council of Learned Societies, a moving force behind the creation of the National Endowment for the Humanities, and even a chief lobbyist for the creation of the College Retirement Equities Fund. He died in 1987.

"If we can decipher who Robert Lumiansky was in Paul's psychic cast of characters," says James Cruise, "we might be on to something. I think he was a kind of spiritual father to him."

Korshin calls him a "great man—the greatest of great men." And he means it.

"He was a kind of kingmaker," he says emphatically; "the sort of person you always consulted on anything. No one started a major program in the humanities without first meeting with him. An ideal person to have as your patron, if you could have one. Certainly he shaped me in every way—and, in fact, it transformed my life, having someone like that behind me."

It certainly transformed his life at Penn. Lumiansky hired Korshin at Penn after one interview, shortly after Korshin had completed his graduate work at Harvard. But the real test of his influence came a couple of years later, when the English department voted, by an overwhelming margin, not to renew Korshin's contract as assistant professor.

"The vote was decisive—19-3," recalls Korshin. "One of the younger professors told me to leave at once. I went to see Lumiansky, because Lumiansky had told me he had recommended me for a three-year renewal. I said, 'But the vote was decisive!' He said, 'Forget about it.'"

Korshin was rehired. But the question that has to be asked is: Why—considering his academic credentials—was the vote against him so strong?

"It's been a mystery to everybody for many years," he says, shrugging sharply, "but I came here, and in one year, I had four articles published—which had never happened at Penn. And the older people in my field took offense, because I'd not asked their advice at all. And they declared that I was not very good. And, of course, everyone else believed them; people believe your colleagues.

"But as it was, it didn't matter. You see, Lumiansky was a person of such tremendous power that, even with a decisive, almost unanimous vote against the candidate, the dean listened to him and not the department. We could never do that now. Because we have no one so great."

Although no one challenges the gist of the story, some remember the details differently: that it was essentially a personality clash between Korshin and a senior member of the department (who has since retired). Korshin may have rubbed some others the wrong way, too.

"When they battled, they were openly moving their troops into place," recalls one observer. "It was a David-and-Goliath situation, in a sense, since Korshin was an assistant professor without many troops to move. But ironically, [the other side] made it so much a matter of temperament and personality that Lumiansky, a very judicious guy, disapproved. He looked at Korshin's work, and I dare say that he was correct in deciding that, on the basis of his work, Korshin was a deserving candidate for promotion. I don't remember a 19-3 vote, but there's no question about the fact that if Lumiansky hadn't brought pressure to bear on people to support Paul, then [the other side] presumably would have prevailed. And eventually, Paul must have received a majority of positive votes, or the thing could not have gone forward. There may have been two rounds of votes. The first round may have gone down heavily against him, and then, almost comically, when they counted [the votes] they said, 'Let's count these again—let's poll the jury.'"

To say that Korshin has never forgotten the episode is putting it mildly.

"When you write this article, I would appreciate it if you would call him '*Mr.* Lumiansky,'" he says at the end of our last interview. "I wouldn't want to trifle him by calling him 'Bob,' or 'Lumiansky.'"

"Paul was really shaken by the death of Robert Lumiansky," says James Cruise. "He called him a great man, and adjectives of that order are not something that Paul is inclined to use. He's very careful about the way he frames things."

"The thing that was great about Paul," says Barbara Kirschten, "is that I think he recognized how much his mentors had done for him, and he, in turn, wanted to do that for people who were coming up through the ranks."

Korshin himself quotes Dido: "'Not ignorant of misfortune, I have learned to assist the unfortunate.'

"If you've had some problems yourself," he adds, "you're better equipped to help your students."

Even students who haven't been helped by Korshin, and those who don't care for the Korshin style, concede that he is a dynamic speaker and lecturer. Words like *gripping, witty, brilliant,* and *creative* almost inevitably surface, and he has a reputation for being a fair grader and a constructive critic. Furthermore, he not only listens to his students; he admits to learning from them.

"I always felt in class that whatever we were exploring was a common endeavor," says Ira Robbins, who took a freshman English class with Korshin back in 1967 and is now a professor of law at American University.

"Almost in a Socratic way, he would help students explore their own prejudices and assumptions," Robbins explains. "Paul also helped students be creative. He didn't thwart creativity as so many professors do. He helped build up my confidence. I remember that when there was an argument, or a discussion, he called on me as the 'universal arbiter.' I was fresh out of high school, a freshman in college, and here I was in his class, and he thought my ideas were good. My sense was that he did that with everyone in the class."

"It sometimes happens that a student changes my whole way of thinking about something," Korshin acknowledges. "It goes without saying that, in every class, there's always one student who's superior to you in some way—usually a lot superior. The brightest students you teach at Penn are so fantastic that everything they say is worthy of note. And the brightest I've taught are unforgettable."

In recent years, Korshin has become famous for his "Madness and Literature" class, which has the largest enrollment of any course in the humanities, regularly attracting 150 to 200 students for each of its two parts. One semester usually begins with Rabelais and Erasmus's *In Praise of Folly* and goes as far as *A Tale of a Tub* and *Tristram Shandy*; in the second semester, students unravel the works of the Brontes, Poe, Mary Shelley, Kafka, Virginia Woolf, and more recent writing.

Korshin, who has been teaching "Madness and Literature" for some 15 years, says it evolved out of a course on Surrealism that he was teaching in the late Sixties: "I discovered that much of Surrealism was basically about different levels of bizarre behavior. Deliberately so, of course; the Surrealists meant to shock and offend. And I thought about the idea for a while, and then in the mid-Seventies, we decided to restructure the teaching of courses in the 18th century. We decided to offer courses based on genres—the novel, for example—or histories of ideas. And I thought, 'Well, here's one.' So I began offering a course on madness. It began, oh, perhaps with the late 17th century and went as far as Blake. But I kept enlarging it, and as I enlarged it, the course got larger. More students took it. And then I divided it into two courses, so it covers the whole year, and moved it back to about 1500 and forward to the 1950s. You could carry it much further, of course. Students always want me to."

Madness has an undeniable allure in our society, though the realities are usually a lot less glamorous than the literary depictions. I ask Korshin what he thinks is the course's appeal to students.

"Well," he says archly, "I have to put aside my own skill. It might be that. There hasn't been much of a tradition at Penn of great lecturers. And it may be that there has always been an attraction of the person who pleases a large crowd. But I think the attraction is that students are ever more aware of the derangement of the 20th-century world."

Some years ago, one class got a firsthand taste of that derangement when a student began making loud and inappropriate pronouncements from the floor. It turned out that he was schizophrenic.

"I was the last person to discover it," says Korshin. "Yes—all the students knew this already. He kept interrupting me and making remarks from the floor of a large lecture hall. His interruptions were much disliked and quite offensive. But, of course, I didn't show any sign of this. I finally learned that he was in the psychiatric wing of the hospital, but they thought it would do him good if he went to a few classes. So he was dosed up on lithium, or one of the other anti-schizophrenic drugs, and let free on purpose to go to my class."

Perhaps he was merely inspired by the course material—say, the "Digression on Madness" section of *A Tale of a Tub*:

> IS any Student tearing his Straw in piecemeal, Swearing and Blaspheming, biting his Grate, foaming at the Mouth, and emptying his Pispot in the Spectator's Faces? . . . Is another eternally talking, sputtering, gaping, bawling, in a Sound without Period or Article? What wonderful Talents are here mislaid! Let him be furnished immediately with a green Bag and Papers, and *three Pence* in his Pocket, and away with Him to *Westminster-Hall*.

There have been other oddities in Korshin's classes. Many years ago, a student claimed to have discovered a witch in the class—and proceeded to point her out to his fellow students. In another, Fellini-like incident, a student came to class dressed in opera clothes, then climbed a tree outside College Hall and eventually had to be removed by a maintenance crew in a cherry picker. One wonders if his performance might have been a commentary on Korshin's teaching style.

"It is interesting, isn't it, that his undergraduate reputation to a large extent rests on this 'Madness and Literature' thing," says a colleague, "because it is such an emotional literature, and you don't feel that he is himself very closely in touch with those subterranean fires."

Certain images of Paul Korshin linger in the memory. This last one comes from Bob Lucid and is set in the department chairman's office. A search committee was meeting during lunch hour, and the members had all brought their own lunches, which, in most cases, consisted of a paper bag with a cheese sandwich in it, and maybe a piece of fruit.

Korshin, resplendent as usual in his custom-tailored suit, arrived with a wicker hamper, which he placed on the table before him. He opened it up and pulled out a linen napkin, then a half-bottle of claret, then a long-stemmed wine glass, then a fork and knife, and finally a serving dish filled with duck *á l'orange*, which he began serving to himself, ever-so-carefully, onto a china plate.

"By this time, everybody had completely stopped eating and was just sitting there looking at him, completely overwhelmed," recalls Lucid. "It was like watching some wonderful mime, like Victor Borge or something."

He laughs for a long time at the memory. "But you know," he adds, "Paul carries his world with him. That little hamper: It's a perfect symbol, in a way."

Smoke and Steel

Robert Strausz-Hupé

(First published as "Robert Strausz-Hupé's Long Walk
on the Right Side," October 1995.)

The smoke curls toward the ceiling, fading into the muggy Pennsylvania air. Dr. Robert Strausz-Hupé, emeritus professor of political science, finishes his demitasse and offers his visitor a thin Sumatran cigar.

"My father caught me smoking at the age of 12," he says in a dry, faint voice tinged with the accents of Austria-Hungary. "He said he was delighted. He said, 'Promise me that you will only use French rice paper and good Macedonian tobacco, and you can smoke as much as you like.'"

There is a glimmer in his pale blue eyes as he recounts the advice, given eight decades earlier, when the borders of the Austro-Hungarian empire were about to go up in smoke. Now, in the study of the Chester County farmhouse that he has called home for more than half a century, he sits back in his rocking chair and listens while his visitor reads him a passage from his 1965 autobiography, *In My Time*: "Since my barque will never float again, I need not concern myself unduly with voyages ahead and cock my ear anxiously to the distant rumble of the tide." An uncharacteristically inaccurate prediction, I suggest, since just a few years after writing those words, he would embark on a 20-year career as a diplomat.

"I didn't expect it," he responds. "I thought I would settle here, teach my classes at the University, and enjoy the countryside. I didn't know that some of my facilities were relevant in politics."

Some people are at their most charming when they are being modestly disingenuous. And Strausz-Hupé probably did not expect, as a retirement-age Republican during a Democratic administration, that he would be called upon to serve his adopted country in such an active capacity. By then he had already made his mark: as a highly popular professor who had introduced the study of international relations to Penn; as a writer who had already written some seminal books, one of which served as a blueprint for United States foreign policy during the Cold War; as founder of the Foreign Policy Research Institute, then still part of the University; and as editor of FPRI's influential journal, *Orbis*.

But as he wrote in *In My Time*, "Life has taught me to expect the unexpected and not to try to outwit it." And so he found himself putting his geopolitical insights and his subtle charm to use as the U.S. Ambassador to Sri Lanka, Belgium, Sweden, NATO, and Turkey, stepping down in 1989 at the age of 86. He was, by all accounts, one of the most astute and effective American diplomats of his day.

"He was one of the very best," says a protégé, John F. Lehman Jr., the former Secretary of the Navy during the Reagan Administration who had also served in the National Security Council under Henry Kissinger. "That is why he was used so consistently and so long in some of the more sensitive positions, because even the most hard-core foreign-service officers admired him and respected him in the State Department. His cables were perhaps the most read cables that came back from any embassy. And the reason was that every event, he viewed in the larger geopolitical context."

Today, Strausz-Hupé is 92 years old, and his diplomatic barque is unlikely to sail again. But his mind is still astonishingly keen, and his battery is still charged up. This year, Transaction Press published his latest book, *Democracy and American Foreign Policy: Reflections on the Legacy of Alexis de Tocqueville*; he has completed a book of aphorisms; and he has another autobiography in the works, which will take up where *In My Time* left off, shortly after World War II—"*Deo Volente*," he says with a small, engaging smile.

There is an intriguing duality to Strausz-Hupé's old face. In conversation, a cordial sort of inner twinkle holds sway; at other times—when he gets to his feet to hunt for a book or journal article that will illustrate his point—a tough, bulldog-like determination shades his features. Over the years, both the twinkle and the determination have served him well.

"He's pixie-like, but he's a very worldly fellow," says former NATO Commander Alexander M. Haig, who served as Secretary of State during the Reagan Administration and as White House Chief of Staff toward the end of the Nixon Administration. "His background just drips with both European elegance and plain old American good sense. He's a happy blend of the two."

Strausz-Hupé is a man of many layers, personally and intellectually. The tough realist who conceived and vigorously advocated a hard-line policy of "containment" toward the Soviet Union also has a strong current of idealism and little patience for repression anywhere. ("A foreign policy inconsistent with the principles of democracy," he notes, "is both a philosophical lapse and a strategic blunder.") His bookshelves hold almost as many books on art and archaeology as they do biographies of statesmen and journals of foreign policy; ask him about a wintry landscape hanging on the wall and he'll describe it as a "modernized Brueghel the Elder," then tell a brief story about the artist. Though he once expressed doubts that America's "great cultural wherry-mixer will blend all races, classes, and castes into a stable compound," he himself is happily married to a woman from Sri Lanka. As Martin Meyerson, emeritus president of the University, puts it: "At a time when we talk of multiculturalism and so on, he was about as multicultural as a diplomat could be." ("I tolerate almost everybody," Strausz-Hupé once wrote, "except men who smoke cigars between courses.")

A few years ago, when Dr. Walter McDougall, the Alloy-Ansin Professor of International Relations, was asked to write a piece about Strausz-Hupé for the 35th anniversary of *Orbis* (which McDougall now edits), all he knew about his subject "was that he was this old Penn professor who was known to be conservative and had founded the Foreign Policy Research Institute." Then he went back and read Strausz-Hupé's writings.

"I had this image of him as simply being a kind of generic hawk," says McDougall, "and that he had founded this institute and this journal because he thought that the sort of Eisenhower, middle-of-the-road moderation and so forth was wimpy—and that he was a real, roll-back Cold Warrior. And then I discovered in his writings that, whereas you could interpret that to be his position in a long-range sense—that communism will collapse some day, and we have to be tough in standing up to it—nevertheless, his intellectual vision was remarkably liberal, in the sense of human rights, democracy, a new-world-order idea."

"I have not been the identical man to those whom I knew well enough to bid the time of day, to address with levity or pondered thought, and to like and to dislike," Strausz-Hupé wrote in *In My Time*. "Nor have I been on any day the same man to myself." Yet he has left an indelible imprint on American foreign policy.

"My crystal ball about myself was obviously cloudy," he says, "but I think if you read my writings, I take pride to say that I've been fairly consistently on the right side. Because I do have one truth, and it has, in a way, guided me through all the labyrinths of life and politics. I can say that I've seen the world fairly clearly."

"One of my friends has suggested that my next autobiography should be entitled 'Memoirs of a World Federalist,'" Strausz-Hupé is saying, not without amusement. "I believe it's in the nature of events that the nation-state will come to an end. The nation-state has outlived its usefulness—its *raison d'etre*. All the tendencies of our age are toward a universal state, and one question, of course, is: What kind of universal state? Will it be a state of freedom or will it be a state of tyranny?

"Americans are the first real federal state in history," he adds. "We have the remedy that's elixir, suitable for every nation in the world. And I'm immovable in my conviction that this is so."

Unlike Nazi Germany and the Soviet Union, which also attempted to realize a "universal state" in this century, the United States is "uniquely fitted for leadership in global unification," Strausz-Hupé suggested in 1957.

As he wrote in the premier issue of *Orbis*: "The economic benefits that flow from the American association to all peoples and the sheer decency of the American scheme for universal partnership will inexorably persuade the Soviet masses (who, too, aspire to a middle-class status) across the heads of the communist bosses to defect into freedom."

The name *Orbis*, incidentally, comes from *novus orbis terrarium* ("new world order"). And in that first article, titled "The Balance of Tomorrow," he asserted:

"The coming world order will mark the last phase in a historical transition and cap the revolutionary epoch of this century. The mission of the American people is to bury the nation-states, lead their bereaved peoples into larger unions, and overawe with its might the would-be saboteurs of the new order who have nothing to offer mankind but a putrefying ideology and brute force."

That internment, he suggested, would take about 50 years, and might well "exhaust the energies of America." But by the end of that time, he predicted, "The American empire and mankind will not be opposites but merely two names for the universal order under peace and happiness."

This was the essence of the vision that drove Strausz-Hupé in the decades that followed. His prescience regarding Soviet communism (among other things) was remarkable, though the demise of nationalism still seems a long way off.

"Today," he notes in *Democracy and American Foreign Policy*, "nationalism is reasserting itself and gaining ground with ever increasing speed, reawakening atavistic and disruptive passions wherever it appears . . . . But if the contagion is to be stopped, prophylactic measures will have to be taken at once . . . . And this means that the American people will have to join in a foreign policy aimed at stopping nationalism." To do so, he added, "the American people will first have to be asked to silence their immediate needs with a view of the future, something that does not come naturally to a democratic people."

It is not entirely clear just what sort of prophylactic measures Strausz-Hupé envisions, since even he concedes that he would "not like to see our resources squandered on a war in the Balkans," the latest example of atavistic nationalism.

I ask Dr. Harvey Sicherman, the current president of the Foreign Policy Research Institute, whether he thinks Strausz-Hupé's statement that "the task before American diplomacy is to create a new world order in which the United States reduces conflict by asserting its position as the leading world power" could be interpreted as meaning that the U.S. should be the world's policeman. Sicherman gives a long, measured response that concludes: "He doesn't think we ought to be the policeman, but he probably thinks we ought to be the chief of police."

B ack at the farmhouse, a flame is being put to another cigarillo. "My mother had a very simple method of imposing sanctions," says Strausz-Hupé, exhaling a wispy cloud. "When she said, 'Now we are going to speak English,' and I said, 'Mother, I don't want to speak English,' she would say, 'Then you'll have nothing for lunch.' And when French lessons came around, she taught me exactly the same way. My mother realized that she had nothing to leave me—not a penny. So the next best thing was to leave me a facility, a talent."

Her precocious son did more than just learn English; he also became a compelling prose stylist, capable of trenchant lyricism. ("Americans, more open-faced than other peoples, decry secret diplomacy," he once wrote. "Yet, the enticing scent of the flowers which grow in darkness stirs strange desires, especially in puritan breasts.") *In My Time* sketches his youthful wanderings in Europe after the destruction of his homeland and his impulsive coming to America in 1923. Arriving almost penniless, he worked as a picture-framer in Chicago; as a real-estate broker in Manhattan; in the "engine room" of Wall Street; and finally in banking. ("Like all introverts," he noted, "Wall Street is terribly sensitive to itself.")

"There is only one trespass that our civilization does not forgive," he says now, "and that is being poor. So I did everything I could not to be poor. But I was not interested in business per se, and I was not very good at it."

What he was good at was international relations. His first book—which predicted that France would be defeated in the coming war with Germany— failed to interest a publisher. After marrying his first wife, Eleanor Cuyler, whose family owned the farmhouse where he still lives, Strausz-Hupé turned to lecturing. In 1938, the circuit brought him to Philadelphia. "Since I had only one song to sing," he wrote, "I talked about the coming war." A Penn dean—"the first member of this formidable species to enter my life"—invited him to speak at the University. A few months later, he signed on as a part-time instructor.

That "most unexpected" turn of events proved to be a happy one, both for him and for Penn. In America, he wrote, "the decent and lively relationship between teacher and student comes closer to the Greek ideal than in any other country." For him, the relationship has been one of mutual respect—and affection.

"Whenever I've talked to alumni groups," says McDougall, "he is the college lecturer that a lot of these old guys remember fondly—whether or not they agreed with his politics."

Strausz-Hupé found academe "congenial," as well as something of a life-saver professionally. "It took me until my early thirties to get my footing there," he says. "I gained it in academe, thank God. I wonder if I would have gained it anywhere else.

"But this was a time when my goods were salable," he adds. "I mean, people wanted to know why Hitler raped Austria. They wanted to know why Hitler expelled the Jews—and worse: killed them. And having lived abroad, speaking foreign languages, I could give answers to some of their questions."

His next book, *Geopolitics: The Struggle for Space and Power*, published in 1942, was a probing examination of the German school of *Geopolitik* (roughly, the relationship between politics and geography), and it is said to have introduced the word *geopolitics* to an American audience. For the leaders of Nazi Germany, he wrote, "geopolitics is the blueprint for world conquest . . . . As the nation grows it requires more space, and it must anticipate future growth by acquiring still more space to satisfy the needs of yet unborn generations."

"I believe that books sell for one reason only," Strausz-Hupé says now, "and that's by chance they strike a note which reverberates to the public. So people were ready for a book on geopolitics. And it brought me a sudden fame."

B y the 1950s, America's enemy had become the Soviet Union. Strausz-Hupé was at the forefront of those warning against its evils—though the notion that there was a communist under every bed still strikes him as ludicrous.

"The wing in American politics to which I belonged put everything in the basket of ideology," he says. "To them, it was what was horrible about communism. To me, the most significant thing was, you have an ideology to be sure, but the ideology happened to be armed with the most powerful weaponry and military in the world, next to ours. If Marxism-Leninism would have been a sectarian undertaking, like those crazy people [in Waco, Texas] who got killed—the Branch Davidians—that was very regrettable and awful, but it's of no consequence at all."

It was *Protracted Conflict*—published in 1959 in collaboration with several other members of the FPRI, which Strausz-Hupé founded at Penn in 1955—that would influence a generation of foreign-policy-makers.

"You know, *Protracted Conflict* was perhaps one of the most important contributions of his life," says Haig, "because it shaped American strategic thinking for generations. It was really a benchmark document or treatise on the current state of the world—and East-West relations in particular. It was hard-headed, and we needed a degree of that—as we do today, and which we're lacking so badly. You need people like Bob Strausz-Hupé to keep sobering people up."

I ask Haig if Strausz-Hupé's worldview as set forth in *Protracted Conflict* has been vindicated. "Nobody writes something 40 years ago that would withstand every scrutiny of time," he says, "but I think that to an unusual degree, *Protracted Conflict* has withstood those tests."

As Harvey Sicherman sums up the message of *Protracted Conflict*, the Soviets, and later the Chinese, "understood that in any immediate, straightforward contest with the West, they were likely to be outgunned and out-produced, so their idea was to nibble way here, push a bit there, till they could turn the balance, which ultimately turned on the European theater."

Western democracies are ill-equipped for this kind of struggle, he adds, "because, short of a mortal threat, we tended to dissipate our assets, our discipline, and to compromise where we didn't need to—and where it was cumulatively dangerous for us to do so." The logical consequence of all that, Sicherman notes, was "that we ought to bring this test to a head—sooner rather than later.

"Now, Strausz-Hupé himself shrank from that," Sicherman adds quickly. "He was always careful to say that logic and policy were not necessarily the same thing, and that what ill-suited us for protracted conflict ill-suited us for the kind of Machiavellian derring-do where we created a crisis in order to press a point. But a lot of people were very critical of him because of that logic train—and considered him to be dangerous."

"I think *Protracted Conflict* was a mind-set and an outlook which led to Vietnam," says Dr. Alvin Z. Rubinstein, professor of political science.

"The failure to differentiate between the Soviet threat and the threat from 'international communism' was what brought the kind of confusion that led to Vietnam. It ignored the Sino-Soviet dispute, which, by the mid-1960s, was pretty serious. And therefore, you could no longer say that there was such a thing as a united world-communist movement manipulated by the Soviet Union. I think it was, by the mid-Sixties, clear that *Protracted Conflict* had big cracks in the theory."

"Strausz-Hupé's writings were a part of the intellectual foundation that led the generation of the Sixties to pursue an active containment policy in Vietnam, as in Eastern Europe and Latin America," says Lehman. "As to the specifics of how it was done and the whole idea of turning it over to a kind of Army bureaucracy to fight a land war in Asia, he never supported that. But he still believes that the commitment to support the South Vietnamese against the North was a correct one, geopolitically and morally. And he remains unreconstructed."

Well, yes and no. Strausz-Hupé—who is quick to say that he "never became an expert on Southeast Asia, thank God"—decries the fact that "tremendous resources, both spiritual and material, went into this wretched war, which, in my view, should have gone into NATO.

"I was a critic of that war," he says, "chiefly because I thought it was a diversion of the resources of the free world from where it mattered—namely Europe—to where it mattered not the damned least bit: a wretched country on the other side of Asia. I thought it was ridiculous that one of the great Western nations could be stuck in an unhealthy jungle war for stakes which I never understood. 'Domino theory'—no one believed that anymore. My God, what were they, these dominoes?" (Be that as it may, it's worth noting that the editorial column in *Orbis* was cautiously advocating ever-stronger military measures in Vietnam as early as the winter of 1964.)

The problem, Strausz-Hupé says, is: "Once you start that kind of war, can you afford to lose it? I believe you couldn't. Wrongly or rightly, I thought that if we had become involved as deeply as we had, we really had no choice but to fight it through. Mr. Kissinger's peace—it really was not peace at all. By any other name, it was surrender, by a man who had a wonderful ability to make green look blue, or blue look orange. We finally got kicked out, and in the most humiliating circumstances—and we're still paying the bill. Asia has not forgotten the circumstances. Nor have the Serbs. Nor have the Croats."

During the Vietnam controversy, Strausz-Hupé acquired a reputation "as a man with both the rapier and the broadsword," in Sicherman's words. "He had a particular gift for writing and for speaking. He was not afraid of controversy—and he probably enjoyed it more than his critics thought he should have. He was not a man to leave unsaid the witty expression, simply on the grounds that it skewered someone else. He was strongly critical of the Johnson Administration—of [former Secretary of Defense Robert S.] McNamara, of people of that sort."

Some of Strausz-Hupé's criticism of McNamara went beyond disputes over the political wisdom of being involved in Vietnam.

"Strausz-Hupé was never a fan of the philosophy and the methodology that McNamara brought into the Pentagon—to make decisions through computer analysis and body counts," says Lehman. "And that spilled over into the running battle that Strausz-Hupé had with the political-science department at the time, which was so enamored of the empirical methods. Computers were just coming in, and the classical approach of Kissinger and Strausz-Hupé was very much out of favor—'Why bother to read Sun Tzu when you can do statistical analyses of the body counts or the bicycle flow down the Ho Chi Minh Trail?' That was the McNamara approach, and it had swept academia as well. Nobody could get tenure in the political-science department at Penn unless their dissertation had been on regression analysis and statistics and use of the computer in political theory—all of which Strausz-Hupé thought was hocus-pocus and charlatanry."

Yet for all the controversy, the courteous, urbane Strausz-Hupé never lost the affection of his students.

"He was never a Dr. Strangelove figure," says Rubinstein. "His courses were too popular among undergraduates, and he had never made any kind of statements that aroused the ire of campus. He was someone who, at least in private discussion, would be prepared to listen, debate, disagree, and discuss it in a very urbane and civil fashion."

"Strausz-Hupé's courses were always among *the* most popular at the University," says Lehman. "I mean, the students loved him—even though many of them hated his political views. They had to put his P.S. 50, I think it was, in the biggest lecture hall available."

"He was a superb lecturer," recalls Rubinstein. "I never saw him lecture from a note. He would come into class, and he would ask his teaching assistant what the subject was, and he would then proceed to talk for an hour and a half—without so much as dropping a sentence."

Strausz-Hupé himself has a more modest explanation for his popularity. "Students were, on the whole, more gentle on foreigners than on Midwesterners," he says, "and I was even more of a foreigner then than I am now. I had more trouble with members of the faculty. There were some who I thought were inordinately critical of the foreign policy of the United States, and I didn't like what they said about the military or about myself."

By the end of that turbulent decade, the FPRI had become something of a lightning rod for the antiwar movement on campus. In 1969, an ideological struggle erupted in the Faculty Senate over who would appoint the institute's successor to Strausz-Hupé, who had been named Ambassador to Sri Lanka and had nominated William Kintner, a retired Army colonel, to succeed him. After a not-so-protracted conflict, the FPRI severed its ties with the University. It was, says Rubinstein, "divorce by mutual agreement."

I ask Strausz-Hupé if he is sorry that the FPRI and the University parted ways.

"Personally, yes," he responds. "You know, I'm a very conservative person, and this arrangement had proven itself. We had done all kinds of things together which I thought were very valuable—to the nation and to the University. And it would have been nice if we had stayed the way we were. But I don't think that the divorce was unpleasant—or not in the best interests of either the University or the institute itself."

When Strausz-Hupé was confirmed as Ambassador to what was then known as Ceylon—after his nomination as Ambassador to Morocco had been derailed by Senator J. William Fulbright—it seemed an idyllic assignment. As it turned out, the incoming socialist regime of Sirimavo Bandaranaike was openly hostile to the United States.

"We had to fight for our diplomatic life," he recalls. "At one point, Mrs. Bandaranaike seemed to want to throw us out altogether—and most certainly throw out the [Central Intelligence] Agency. So it became my task to prevent that."

Through hard work and diplomacy—both personal and professional—he succeeded, and by the end of his tenure he and Bandaranaike had become good friends. (He also emerged from Sri Lanka with an even better friend—his second wife, Mayrose. He describes the marriage as "the best thing I ever did—an undeserved benefit.")

Strausz-Hupé also struck up a friendship with another left-leaning critic of U.S. policy: Olaf Palme, the Prime Minister of Sweden, where Strausz-Hupé became Ambassador in 1974.

"There were, in a way, two Palmes," says Strausz-Hupé. "There was Palme the firebrand and leader of the Socialists, and Palme who came from an aristocratic background and married a very aristocratic wife—who was more radical than he. He was a very charming man when he wanted to be. We discovered a common interest in tennis doubles, and he sent me books on how to play doubles. I came to like him very much."

Al Rubinstein, who visited Strausz-Hupé in Sweden as well as Sri Lanka, says that he came away with an "extraordinary" impression of the man's diplomatic skills. "When I talked to journalists about their view of the American Ambassador," he recalls, "they all said, 'Well, your Ambassador has been quite a surprise in terms of how well he's gotten along with our Prime Minister'—in each case, clearly one who was critical of American policy."

Respect for Strausz-Hupé's diplomacy eventually crossed party lines. "Strausz-Hupé metamorphosed into a kind of bipartisan figure," says Sicherman. "I attended his confirmation hearings for his post in NATO in 1975, and a resolution was moved by Hubert Humphrey that Strausz-Hupé was the right man in the right place at the right time."

"He was an absolutely indefatigable advocate of his views—persistent, reasonable, rational, and yet unyielding," says Alexander Haig. "And that was always in the best interests of the United States with his various host countries—but in a way in which those countries could relate. So many times, American representatives abroad are familiar with our objectives, goals, and policies, but they just don't know how to market them. Bob was a superb marketer of the American point of view. I mean that in the best sense."

Donald Rumsfeld, White House Chief of Staff and later Secretary of Defense under President Gerald R. Ford, came to know and admire Strausz-Hupé when they were both stationed in Brussels—Rumsfeld as Ambassador to NATO and Strausz-Hupé as Ambassador to Belgium.

"This was a man who had a worldview, a world perspective, who'd served in a variety of ambassadorial positions," says Rumsfeld, who later recommended Strausz-Hupé for the NATO post. "Having a person who has that background—and can speak knowledgeably and thoughtfully and insightfully in a multi-dimensional way—is a great advantage."

Asked about his contributions to NATO, Strausz-Hupé singles out his recommendation to assign top priority to "remedying one of the most obvious shortcomings of the NATO military setup: intermediate-range weapons," since the Soviets then had "an overwhelming superiority" in medium-range missiles. The recommendation was approved.

"The Soviets were very indignant," he acknowledges. "They recommended dire consequences for us—a soupçon of war—if we risked. Well, we decided to risk. It is my conviction that the defeat of that Russian bluff had a lot to do with the collapse of the Soviet Union. Because the more I saw of it, the more I was convinced that it was the loss of the armaments race that upset the Soviet applecart."

He comes back to this point several times, worried that it might be misinterpreted. "It's not as simple as that," he concedes. "There are many other factors, too. But in my view, it probably was the conclusive one."

Strausz-Hupé's experience with NATO was undoubtedly part of the reason he was nominated by President Ronald Reagan to be Ambassador to

Turkey in 1981. "Reagan made it clear to me that there was one concern he had" vis-à-vis Turkey, says Strausz-Hupé. "He was a very curt man when he chose to be, and when I asked him what he wanted me to do in Ankara, he said, 'Keep them in NATO.'"

And so he did, despite a contretemps that developed when the Administration's proposal for an aid package to Turkey—supported by all the NATO allies—was watered down by a Congress heavily influenced by the Greek lobby in America. That American foreign policy is often driven by domestic interest groups—there are many more Greeks in America than Turks, and they have proportionately more influence in Congress—disturbs Strausz-Hupé, though he recognizes it as a political phenomenon that has plagued American democracy since de Tocqueville's day. And according to Haig, Strausz-Hupé displayed a "very significant degree of moral courage" in conveying the realities of Turkey's strategic importance to the State Department.

"Robert was immensely admired by the Turks," says Martin Meyerson, who notes that Suleyman Demirel (then Prime Minister and later President of Turkey) "regarded Robert as not only the best American Ambassador but among the very best of all the Ambassadors to Turkey." When he visited Ankara, Meyerson was fascinated to see how many leading cultural figures—"from the universities, from the arts, and so on"—kept company with Strausz-Hupé. He recounts a lengthy conversation the two had about Islam, and concludes: "Here was somebody who took the trouble to understand the culture."

H e could have retired to the Italian Riviera, Strausz-Hupé is saying, or to an island somewhere. But in the end, he could not see himself living anywhere but in the United States. He loves the gentle beauty of his farm, and on the whole, he likes Americans—"the most orderly, the most kindly people in the world."

"I've lived here in comfort in high office, and I've also lived here in great poverty," he says. "I can safely say that I had no other support than $15 when I arrived in Hoboken [in 1923]. Instead of perishing in the tremendous current of energy, in the tremendous rushing forth, I made good—not necessarily by my own standards, but by the standards of most people. Even people who used to be my enemies."

He does voice one surprising regret: that he never attended an American high school, which he views as a rite of passage that separates insiders from outsiders. Had he done so, I suggest, the idea might have lost some of its allure. He smiles gently, conceding the possibility.

After our last interview, Strausz-Hupé insists on walking me out to my car, despite heat rivaling Sri Lanka's. At the driveway, he looks out toward the sturdy stone-and-wood barn and the grass fields sprinkled with Queen Anne's Lace. Over it all, the humid summer air hangs like a faint blue cloud of smoke.

"I love my acres here," he says with feeling, the inner twinkle surfacing again. "I often wonder, when I go away, why I would ever want to be anywhere else."

*P*ostscript: A few years after that interview (one of several I conducted for that article), I drove out to Strausz-Hupé's farm for some tea and wisdom. In the wake of my *Gazette* article, he had proposed that I assist him with the second volume of his autobiography, and though that fell through for financial reasons, I stayed in touch with him—partly to keep open the possibility of some sort of collaboration; mostly because I enjoyed his company. It took a couple of years before he stopped calling me *Mr. Hughes* and switched to *Sam*, at which point I felt sufficiently comfortable to call him *Robert*. Despite his faint voice and flagging energies, he was still a most engaging conversationalist, and I was always aware that I was hearing a brilliant and singular voice on world events.

The madness and circularity of history fascinated him in his last years— and at times frustrated him deeply. Once, when the Kosovo crisis was in full sway, I found him incensed at the inept American response. ("It's an *embarrassment*," he fumed, disgusted by the military's inability to get Apache helicopters into the combat zone, and appalled that those "schoolboys in Pristina" could cause so much trouble.) But what really galled him was the fact that the Balkans were still a killing ground at the end of the 20th century, just as they had been when Bismarck famously dismissed them as "not worth the bones of a single Prussian grenadier."

"You must forgive me," he said finally, "but I am so *god*-damn sick and tired of the Balkans. I am probably as fed up with the Balkans as my father was, nearly a hundred years ago." It occurred to him that he had not been to Bosnia-Herzegovina for 80 years.

Even as his strength was fading, his will showed its steel. One windy November morning in 1997 he announced that he wanted to dictate an essay. I was surprised, as the plan had been for me to go into his basement and bring up some old files for him to look over, but I had my laptop with me, so I set it up in his study and began to type as he spoke. His voice was so faint that I could barely make out the words, and he often paused for 15,

30, 45 seconds between phrases. Yet he eventually delivered, off the top of his head, a subtle, insightful essay—about 750 words if memory serves—on the geopolitical relationship between Russia and China, the U.S. interest in that relationship, and its potential flashpoints.

At one point, he abruptly stopped talking and shuffled off to the bathroom, leaning heavily on his walker. Just before he reached the hallway, he turned and, in a wryly mournful voice, quoted De Gaulle: "Old age is a shipwreck." Five minutes went by; then 10. When he finally shuffled back into the room, his first words were: "Dash-dash." It took me a moment to realize that he was simply picking up where he had left off, in mid-sentence. And so it went, for well over an hour. When he finished, he listened as I read back what he had dictated. I believe he changed two words.

I visited a few times after that, and attended the FPRI's celebration of his 95th birthday, but my time was consumed with my young family and my job, and to my regret I did not see him for the last year and a half of his life.

One of my last memories came during the Monica Lewinsky furor. We were not on the same side of that issue, and while that may have dampened my wit it didn't affect his. "The cow has fallen into the well," he shrugged, adding that Clinton had brought the whole mess onto himself. "Clinton is a great tactical perjurer," he added dryly. "Perhaps the greatest we have ever had."

When he suggested that the entire political process was "rotten to the core," I agreed; when I suggested that the rot included Newt Gingrich, then Speaker of the House, he did not. "I don't mind Gingrich," he said, though he conceded that the Congressman had a "serious flaw." I leaned closer, not wanting to miss the trenchant character analysis that would inevitably follow. "A *bad* haircut," he said finally, and settled back in his chair, enjoying my hilarity. It was the mark of a great diplomat: able to disarm a potential opponent with a quip without giving an inch on his fundamental beliefs.

A few months after the planes of Al-Qaeda slammed into the World Trade Centers, Strausz-Hupé wrote a brief essay for the FPRI. It was titled "The New Protracted Conflict."

The new conflict, like the last one, "will end only when one side vanquishes the other," he wrote. "Either the United States, at the head of the international order—such as it is—will forfeit its leadership, or international terrorists and the states who use them will find violence against innocent civilians a tactic too dangerous to be used.

"I have lived long enough to see good repeatedly win over evil, although at a much higher cost than need have been paid," he concluded. "This time we have already paid the price of victory. It remains for us to win it."

When he wrote that essay, the deep divisions between the U.S. and "old Europe" (in the words of his old colleague Donald Rumsfeld) had not yet been exposed by the U.S. decision to invade Iraq. I've often wondered what he would have thought of the invasion, which was being planned when he died in late February 2002, shortly before his 99th birthday. I like to think he would have been wiser than some of his protégés at the FPRI, who were practically salivating at the prospect of going to war with a small Middle Eastern country headed by a genuine bad guy. At least, he might have counseled giving diplomacy more of a chance than the Bush administration did.

But I'm probably fooling myself. He would have wanted the U.S. to take the battle to the enemy, and since the enemy was and still is an elusive beast, there's a very good chance that he would have bought into the neoconservative delusion that by toppling one bad regime in the Middle East and replacing it with a representative democracy, the U.S. could knock some sense into the rest of the region. I'll never know for certain. And ultimately, it doesn't matter.

"In history—real history—there stands at every turning point one man with an idea." Strausz-Hupé wrote those words in *In My Time* more than 40 years ago. They apply to him as well.

Mother Superior
Makes Her Case

Kathleen Hall Jamieson

(First published in February 1995 as
"The Story on Kathleen Hall Jamieson.")

M any years later, as she was writing a book on Presidential debates,
Dr. Kathleen Hall Jamieson would remember the afternoon when
the nuns took her Catholic-school class to watch the Nixon-Kennedy debate.
In her memory, she was a high-school freshman again, trying to keep track
of the candidates' thrusts and ripostes on a grainy black-and-white set that
she could barely see.

Jamieson, now dean of the Annenberg School for Communication, is one
of the nation's leading scholars of political discourse, and she has come to
view those contests as a high-water mark in American Presidential politics.
After all, the two men did actually debate the issues. But the experience of
watching them was less rosy-hued in her memory.

"I had a very high level of evocation of this poor little freshman who was
trying desperately to make sense of it but couldn't really write very well,
because she was crouching in a corner," says Jamieson, now sitting in an
empty conference room in the Annenberg School and talking at roughly the
speed of light. "And here I was, sitting at my desk—a big, expensive desk.
I had all the space in the world. I had a videotape—I was shutting the tape
off, I was turning it on—and I said, 'Ah, *heaven*—I've made it.'"

Hard to argue with that. Nowadays, students take notes on *her* television performances; she's a star on some of the very forums she critiques, providing razor-sharp analyses of Presidential campaigns and public-policy debates for all manner of media. She has been the media analyst on Bill Moyers' *Listening to America*, the political commentator on National Public Radio's *Morning Edition*, a regular guest on the *MacNeil/Lehrer News Hour*, and an irregular guest on *The Tonight Show*, to name just a few. Open any major newspaper during the final weeks of a Presidential campaign or in the course of certain public-policy debates and, chances are, you will be greeted by one of her punchy, meaty, diagrammatically correct quotes.

Jamieson is in high demand not *just* because she is extremely smart, lucid, and insightful but because she also has the scholarly brawn to back up her assertions.

"She has the remarkable ability to appeal to two communities and be well respected by both: the community of practitioners—the news writers, the political reporters—and the community of scholars," says Dr. Joseph Cappella, professor of communication, who has collaborated with Jamieson on a number of projects. "She's widely respected among scholars for her scholarship on Presidential campaigns and political rhetoric, and at the same time, her insights into the issues that are facing political actors, particularly in the media environment today, are sought constantly by national journalists in both the print and the broadcast news media. I think that's truly unique."

On the print side, syndicated columnist David Broder describes her as "the most influential voice from academia in reminding journalists of their responsibility in both the political arena and in this recent health-care debate." He mulls that over for a second. "I don't think anyone else even comes close."

Broder's remarks are often echoed on the broadcast side. Jamieson "is one of the most thoughtful—and original—interpreters of political news coverage in the country," says Andrea Mitchell, the alumni trustee and chief foreign-affairs correspondent for NBC News. "She certainly has affected the way we do things at NBC."

For someone who meets the press as much as Jamieson does—and toward election day, she is umbilically connected to reporters—she is surprisingly loath to be the subject of a story. When *The Philadelphia Inquirer's* Sunday magazine was attempting to do a feature on four powerful women at Penn, one of them Jamieson, she went so far as to send down a memo to the school's faculty and staff that strongly suggested they not talk to the reporter. Yet once she finally agreed to be interviewed by the *Gazette*, she was candid, thoughtful, funny—quite delightful, really, as long as I didn't start poking around in her family life. (For the record: she and her husband, Robert, an engineer, have two sons: Robert and Patrick; the latter is a junior at Penn, and the former works for an advertising agency in Manhattan. That's as far as we're going to poke.)

Having cut her scholarly teeth on papal pronouncements—her doctoral dissertation at the University of Wisconsin was titled "A Rhetorical-Critical Analysis of the Conflict over *Humanae Vitae*" (the 1968 papal encyclical on birth control)—she leaped headlong into the Presidency when her first job, at the University of Maryland, so demanded. Her well-received books include *Packaging the Presidency: A History and Criticism of Presidential Advertising*; *Eloquence in an Electronic Age*; *Presidential Debates: The Challenge of Creating an Informed Electorate*; and *Dirty Politics: Deception, Distraction, and Democracy*. She describes her most recent book, *Beyond the Double Bind: Women and Leadership*, as her "visceral" response to Susan Faludi's *Backlash*, which she calls a "prescription for perpetual victimage." Don't try to tell Jamieson that all women are doomed to be oppressed.

There is certainly nothing oppressed about her. Watch her stride across campus at full throttle, and she seems to push the air behind her with her arms as she walks. Listen to her introduce a speaker or analyze a political dilemma, and chances are you'll feel like a kid watching a magician produce showers of coins from thin air. She can be brusque, some colleagues say ("*very* brusque," says one); she can be thoughtful and kind; and she can be funny as hell. She is an administrative whirlwind, a green-thumbed fund-raiser, and a scholarly "idea machine," as one colleague puts it.

As a teacher, she is a supernova—and she knows it. "She referred to her course, in class, as 'the greatest experience of your nonsexual life,'" noted the 1993 *Undergraduate Course Guide*, "and many students agreed." "Dean Jamieson is hands-down the *best* instructor I have ever had," wrote one student who had taken her Introduction to Political Communication course. "Taking her class is one of the few ways to get your $20,000 worth at this school."

She did take some heat for inaccessibility, however. "Dean Jamieson is entertaining, as well as intelligent," wrote one student. "I hope to actually meet her someday." Another grumbled that it was "pretentious for her to miss class and leave a tape of her appearance on the Bill Moyers show instead."

David Broder tells of meeting a former student of Jamieson's at a television station out in Omaha: "I said, 'That must have been a treat, to have her as a teacher.' He said, 'It was a treat—and it was a terrible challenge, because she talks so fast and she wastes no words.' I told Kathleen, 'You'll either have to slow down or learn to waste words,' and she said, 'Well, I know I'm not going to slow down . . . .'"

"She talks faster than almost anyone you'd ever meet," says Dr. Larry Gross, the professor of communication who headed the search committee that chose her to be the school's dean. "You walk in and"—he snaps his fingers four times—"you can't quite tell how much of this is planned and how much of it is improvised off the top of her head. And I'm still not always sure. If anything, I've moved toward thinking more of it's planned, but then I've been in situations where I *know* some of it's improvised—arguments where she's making up rationales for something right and left . . . . She certainly operates at an extraordinary speed."

During the search process, Gross called a friend at the University of Texas (where Jamieson was head of the speech-communication department from 1986 until 1989, when she came to Penn) and asked for some feedback. Most of the comments were quite positive, as he had expected, but when he pressed the guy for negatives, the man said: "Well, I think people here think she's not laid back enough."

"And I thought, 'Well, that's Texas, she's from the North, they don't think she's laid back enough, big deal,'" Gross recalls. "Later, I found out that there probably isn't anyone in the *world* who thinks she's laid back enough. I told that story to another friend from Texas, and he hooted in laughter—like, 'Right, and who would?'"

After the search committee had interviewed her, one member told Gross: "I've met her before—as a type. She's a Mother Superior."

"If you think about it," says Gross, "in other times or places, she might well have been one. She came out of an environment in which that was often what smart, dynamic women would have done. And to some extent, she does have those character traits."

T he Voice of Responsibility is on the line. It's a caring, polite voice, ready to praise where praise is due; not quite ready to forget transgressions, even youthful ones. It belongs to Sister Romaine Theisen, who taught young Kathleen Hall at St. Benedict's, an all-girls, college-preparatory Catholic school in Minnesota that closed in 1973. Sister Romaine was the adviser to the school newspaper, which Hall edited for two years, and also taught her Latin III.

More than 30 years later, Sister Romaine still remembers her well. A "wonderful" student, Kathleen was. Oh, yes. Very excellent. Graduated at the top of her class. First out of 34. Very high percentile in the National Merit Scholarship exams, too.

"She was very good in communication skills," Sister Romaine says, "and she was very active in extracurricular activities—in dramatics and music and, of course, debate—and the school paper. She was just in everything, you know. She was an excellent writer. Oh, she was so good. When she was a sophomore, she just wrote articles, but she had such a vivid imagination, and her choice of words, for a sophomore—she was just very good. That's why I chose her to be the editor."

Here, Sister Romaine pauses for a moment. "But you know," she adds, "Kathleen was in so many things, and she wasn't always able to give her best potential to the projects, because her energies were so scattered. She sometimes did not take her responsibilities as seriously as she should have. So I really got on top of her many times. She really should have had an award, at an awards program, and I never gave it to her, because I was just so irked at her because of her lack of responsibility when she was an editor."

She laughs, a shy, rueful little laugh. "Did she ever mention that?" she asks. "Oh—well, you wouldn't want to mention that in your profile, either." Well, actually, I confess, I might . . . . Sister Romaine softens—for a moment: "She was so active, you know, and it was really not her fault that she wasn't able to do it. She just let me do most of the work."

One still senses the imprint of those years on Jamieson. "They told us that college was going to be more difficult than high school," she says now, "and they *lied*. The most difficult part of my academic life was high school. I struggled. I worked all the time. I was always behind. Never thought I was going to make it.

"But as a result," she adds, "I don't have any trouble saying, 'I've got to get these eight things done, and I'm going to get them done in a fairly compressed period.' I don't procrastinate. I do take on more than I should; that's the down side with that kind of a background. You get an unrealistic sense of your ability to always meet deadlines when you've got an awful lot to do. But it was a Catholic school, and they really were running it as if they were running a monastery. They believed they had 24 hours of your day and you were going to use it."

And yet, says Larry Gross: "She doesn't play the Catholic-school-veteran victim-routine that a lot of them do. I mean, I know lots of Catholics who tell you these stories, but I've never heard *her* tell any."

Which is not to say that young Kathleen was always the picture of obedience.

"They tried to throw me out a number of times," she says, looking decidedly unrepentant. "I wrote an editorial for the paper that said one shouldn't give uncritical respect to nuns simply because they were nuns. It didn't go over well at all. Fortunately, there was a very strong nun [Sister

Annerose Wokurka] who headed the history area, who was also the woman who got me into debate. And when I would take an anti-authority position and get too far out of line, she would come and defend me—saying, 'This is good; we do not want to crush her.'"

There were no boys at St. Benedict's, though it was near an all-boys' school. Jamieson—like many women who have gone to girls' schools—now considers that a blessing.

"It never occurred to me that there were things that women were not supposed to do," she says. "Somebody was going to be a leader, and it was going to be a woman, because you were all women. Social life was weekends, in which case you weren't worrying about competing academically; now, you were in a completely different domain. And the boys were all in their own highly competitive environment; if anything, they thought the notion that you were, too, was attractive."

With the help of Sister Annerose, she won a full scholarship to Marquette University, where, in three years, she earned her bachelor's degree in rhetoric and public address (and co-authored a book titled *Debating Crime Control*). Then it was on to the University of Wisconsin to pursue her master's degree and her Ph.D.

I ask Dr. Edwin Black, the emeritus professor of communication arts at the University of Wisconsin who served as Jamieson's dissertation director, how her Catholic-school background might have affected her.

"I expect it accounted for her academic conscience," he says. "The industry, the stubbornness with which she insisted on pursuing questions until she had exhausted them, the dedication that she had then and has demonstrated in her career to inquiry and scholarship. Those are manifestations of a kind of professional conscience, and though I'm not certain what the origin of such a thing is, I suspect that her background had a lot to do with it."

Yet as someone with strong feelings about women's rights and a skeptical eye for authority, she was unconvinced by Pope Paul VI's 1968 encyclical on birth control, which essentially forbade all forms of contraception but the rhythm method.

"I think she was very skeptical of it," says Black, "and on occasion, I found myself, in the course of directing her dissertation, having to construct arguments in favor of it—though I am not even remotely Catholic. In a sense, it was routine, a normal part of the interaction between a dissertation director and a dissertation writer, but she certainly wasn't strongly disposed to write favorably of the encyclical."

Jamieson's arguments were scholarly, subtle, and persuasive enough to earn her the Speech Communication Association's Outstanding Dissertation Award.

"The question I was trying to ask," Jamieson says now, "was: how does rhetoric function to create and sustain institutions? And I used *Humanae Vitae* as a moment to analyze that, because it throws the Catholic Church into crisis over a single rhetorical document—and lets you, as a result, look at how the rhetoric came to be, what it does when it faces challenges, and how it ultimately adapts."

Noting the "striking similarities between the papal encyclicals and the Roman Imperial Decrees" (including the Ciceronian Latin, the complex sentence structures, the authoritarian tone, and the fact that both were issued by men "claiming the title 'Supreme Pontiff'"), she argued that "not only was *Humanae Vitae* inevitable but so also was the dissent from the document. The Pope and the dissenters are separated by a rhetorical as well as a philosophical chasm . . . . Because they are communicating in languages derived from antagonistic strains of early Latin, the Pope and the dissenters may have been affected by subtle tensions produced not by the content or form of the messages but by the languages themselves."

A year after issuing *Humanae Vitae*, the Pope would have some sharp words—which Jamieson would quote—for the Fourth Estate.

"Modern communications media today," he wrote, "invade public opinion with a noisy facility and give disproportionate importance to minimal facts."

Going from the papacy to the Presidency was an accident of circumstance for Jamieson, but it was a "fairly natural move" as a scholar. Her husband was working for the United States Navy in Washington, and the only job-opening in the area was a rhetoric job in political communications at the University of Maryland—which, she says, "did not want a papal-rhetoric theorist; it wanted a political-communications scholar." Both look at institutions, and since she was an institutional theorist, she figured she could handle Presidencies. "So I became a political-communications person. It seems like a big jump to people, but it doesn't seem like a big jump to me.

"My interest as a scholar is how institutions come to be and survive, and how they adapt to publics and how publics are changed—and change [the institutions]," she adds. "Besides, you have intrigue in the Presidency, you have intrigue in the papacy, and you have corruption in both."

Jamieson's talent for argumentation also stood her in good stead. She had got her first taste of debating life as a freshman at St. Benedict's, when she openly questioned the existence of God in a class. After listening to her argue her case, Sister Annerose took her aside and told her she was joining the debate team—which later won the state championship.

She kept debating through her undergraduate years at Marquette, and even now, as director of the Annenberg Public Policy Center, she sponsors a National Debate Tournament team at Penn. She considers much of her recent work—including her analysis of the recent debate over health-care reform—to be "essentially an extension of varsity debate."

"If I were in charge of the world for a day, I would ask all college students to take a course in argumentation," she says. "Because I think it's a life-skill. It's very helpful, regardless of the discipline. And I think it's also extremely valuable for somebody who's going to be an administrator. When they first talked to me about this job and said, 'What do you think your strengths are to do the job?' I said, 'I know how to argue. Give me a case that is worthy of argument, and I think I can make the strongest possible argument for it.'"

Debating, she adds, "creates a disposition toward fairness, because the first thing you do is weigh the other side. You don't take an argument forward unless you believe that it is the better argument that will withstand the scrutiny of someone who is arguing as well as you can argue when arguing from the other side. And there's an absolute equality in debate. It doesn't matter what your class is; it doesn't matter what your gender is. It's an extremely pure form of intellectual engagement."

No surprise, then, that Jamieson has adopted what she calls the "rational-citizen model" for an electorate.

"My model of how the public-policy process should work is really based on the notion that, given enough argument, given enough evidence, given enough good clash, reasonable people will be able to come to a considered judgment," she explains. "The critique of my position is that I presuppose a rational public-policymaking. And it's true—I do. Because I think that's the fairest way to take the other factors out. If you can get into that domain, you can take money out of the equation—because, ultimately, you can't buy the one person who's standing up there. In my model, the argument is going to be the strongest argument that can be made for a position.

"Now, in fact, the real world doesn't work that way. But I'm an academic. There's a plausible alternative which says that low-level rationality's fine; let people work on the basis of heuristics and intuition. And they'll vote more often against the incumbent than they probably should, but they'll still come to judgments that aren't going to be grossly different. It will ultimately be a self-interested decision—and it's less time-consuming. I don't buy into that, but it's probably the way most people make political judgments."

Don't expect to find out where Jamieson herself stands on the issues. "She is very careful to maintain a neutrality which gives her credibility as an expert," says Gross, "as opposed to being identified with any position."

Jamieson agrees. "People usually guess that I'm whatever the party is that's not in power, because I'm always critiquing what's in power," she says. "So people who read *Dirty Politics* said, 'Oh, she's got to be a liberal Democrat who wanted Dukakis to be elected.' During the health-care debate, they said, 'Oh, she's got to be a Dole supporter.'

"I usually ask the students at the end of the semester how many of them think I'm a Republican, how many of them think I'm a Democrat, and how many of them think that I'm a vegetarian anarchist," she adds. "And most of them vote that I'm a vegetarian anarchist."

She hasn't entirely abandoned her first scholarly love, however. In the works is a new book about "three moments in the history of the Catholic papacy"—which, she says, asks "what those moments tell us about changing roles of women, about philosophies about birth regulation, and about the institutional papacy."

Jamieson does know a thing or two about the changing roles of women. When she first applied for a Woodrow Wilson Fellowship, she showed up at the interview wearing an engagement ring.

"I came in and the guy, in essence, said, 'Why would you think we ought to fund your graduate education if you're going to get married?'" she recalls. "And I said, 'Why would you assume that if I'm going to get married, I'm not going to make use of the graduate degree?'—which was not the right answer."

She did not get the fellowship—not that year, anyway. And when she first applied for a position at the University of Maryland, she happened to mention that she was planning to take "a couple of days out in November" to give birth to her first child. "We do not hire pregnant women," she was told. End of interview.

The second time around, the University of Maryland was feeling the heat from Affirmative Action. Hired in 1971 as an assistant professor, she stayed there until 1986, by which time she was a full professor.

"I'm in the generation that came into the academy with Affirmative Action behind me," she says. "I got my first job because of Affirmative Action and the women's movement. I know it was easier for me to be promoted because people had fought very hard to insure that there'd be fair tenure standards. And I don't want to lose those gains by believing either that that was accidental or I was lucky. Competence with opportunity makes those kinds of things possible."

Which is why she had such a "visceral" reaction to Susan Faludi's *Backlash*—a reaction that led to her writing *Beyond the Double Bind*, which examines the myriad "Catch 22" situations faced by women, especially those who wield power.

"I read *Backlash* on a plane, going on vacation, and I was just outraged by it," she recalls. "All my friends were reading it, and they were thinking it was wonderful. I read it, and I said, 'This is the prescription for perpetual victimage.' That's the first problem with it; the second is that it is bad history. And so I decided on a plane that I was going to write a response."

The main thrust of *Backlash*, she says, "is that, historically, women have moved forward and then been driven back by a backlash, then they move forward again, and then are driven back by another backlash. The question then is, 'Why should we then try to move forward?' There's an inevitability of another backlash. A rational position would be collective suicide. So I said, 'What are the underlying claims about where this has occurred?' And then went back to the evidence to say, 'How legitimate are these claims?' and concluded that the book just simply does not acknowledge history as it occurred—at least, as I see it occurring.

"I also think that there is a very strong tendency on the part of women who have made it to pretend they haven't made it," she adds. "And it seems very odd to me to have tenured, full professors at prestigious universities who are women talking about how oppressed they are."

The pause that follows is pregnant, though it could be measured in microseconds.

"As the dean of the number-one school of communication in the country," says Jamieson with a look that is two parts triumph and one part scorn, "I do not feel oppressed."

Stand By Me

Alan Kors

(First published in March 1994 as "Alan Kors As Others See Him.")

Dr. Alan Charles Kors, professor of history and scourge of orthodoxies, is defending the followers of Christ as if his very soul depended upon it. He is standing before two dozen members of the Newman Center, speaking as though his thoughts are being fired by an inner blast-furnace, cast into words by some keen precision instrument of the mind, then forced through tortuous nasal passages into the autumn air. The object of his wrath is—once again—the administration of his employer, the University.

His point of departure is a crucifix dunked in urine—the "Piss Christ" of sculptor Andres Serrano. It seems that, several years before, students at the Graduate School of Fine Arts invited Serrano to deliver a lecture—an invitation, Kors explains, that sparked an angry letter from the Newman Center's executive board, which argued that no other group on campus would have to suffer such an insult to its most sacred symbol. The school argued that universities should be open to all points of view, artistic and otherwise—a defense, says Kors almost parenthetically, with which, as a libertarian, he agrees. But that, for him, is not the issue. Listen as he asks his audience to reflect on the following scenarios:

"Supposing we had an artist at Penn who had immersed a Star of David or a picture of the survivors of Auschwitz in urine and represented that as a major work of art. Do any of you have *any* doubts whatsoever whether or not that artist would have been the recipient of that invitation and that defense from the University? *Imagine* if an artist had immersed the writings of the

---

180

Honorable Elijah Mohammed in urine, or a portrait of Martin Luther King Jr. in urine, and exposed that for an exhibit? Not only is it unthinkable that that person would have received an honor in the form of such an invitation, but should such an honor have been given, we would have had an administration leading candlelight vigils on sensitivity, mandatory sensitivity-education for all people at the School of Fine Arts associated with the exhibit, and lecture after lecture from the administration—as they said this past June—about the terrible tensions that exist in their mind between the full freedom of expression on the one hand and a welcoming community on the other.

"You live in a university," he continues, with swelling fervor, "that, under the guise of commitment to diversity, wants to say to certain groups—among them, believing Catholics, evangelical Christians, believing Muslims, Orthodox Jews, but above all, believing Christians—that *your* sensitivities, *your* being welcomed, *your* not being offended, does not count equally with the claims of others. And *your* outraged sensibilities—to the point of the honoring of the artist who put your most sacred symbols in urine—are the price we must pay at the University for freedom. That is not diversity. That is a double standard. And double standards are the enemy of everything sacred, in a secular sense, that has to do with freedom—above all, equality before the law."

There is more—a great deal more—all of it dramatic, all of it intensely provocative, whether one agrees with him or not. But for now, let us cut to the moment of elocutionary Armageddon, when he challenges the faithful to toss the swarms of secular social workers out of the temple of the University's soul:

"We are all rendering unto Caesar that which is God's: the inner conscience of the human soul. And to participate in something evil is to *be* evil. It is time you stood up for your rights, for your vision of an authentic human dignity and equality—and it's time that all of us stop collaborating in their project of evil."

Right now, Kors is in my living room, discussing the Mind of the Enlightenment. He's a captive, of sorts: When I want him to talk, he talks; when I want him to stop, he freezes in mid-syllable while I attend to my young son's latest Brio-train crisis, then resumes his monologue. His presence is owing to a series of videotaped lectures—the "Superstar Teachers"—put out by an outfit called The Teaching Company. Since he declined to be interviewed for this article, this is the closest I can come to having a real one-on-one with him, so I start and stop him with giddy abandon. He still won't say, for example, what led him, personally, to atheism, but he does speak with staggering erudition and insight on the challenges to received wisdom in the 17th and 18th centuries and on their effects on the European intellectual landscape. It is a landscape in which he is obviously very much at home.

"In many ways, an intellectual historian chooses the era and the problems which most closely match his or her own view of the world," says Dr. Alfred Rieber, the professor and former chairman of history who hired Kors as an assistant professor back in 1968. "Alan resonates the Enlightenment and varieties of Enlightenment thought. He loves the keenness, the excitement of the intellectual debate about fundamental issues. And, of course, he is a very secular person and admires the secularists for attacking the overweening role of religion in the late 17th and the 18th century."

On the surface, this might seem odd, in light of his defense of the Newman Center. But then, Kors does not lend himself to simple deconstructions. Consider: He was born a Jew, has long been a devoted atheist, and spent many years "sounding like a broken record," in the words of a friend, about the dangers of the Moral Majority and the religious right. Yet there he was, passionately defending evangelical Christians and the Catholic Church. He has served as head of the academic-freedom committee of the American Civil Liberties Union of Greater Philadelphia—and as a member of the Republican Party caucus that works for women's rights, gay and lesbian rights, and rights of privacy. Dr. Martin E. P. Seligman, professor of psychology and a friend of Kors' since their undergraduate days at Princeton University, suggests that "Alan's loyalties have always been to the side that needed hearing"—though those on the other side of the fray might not always agree.

"You're dealing with a human being who's complicated in many ways," says Dr. Bruce Kuklick, professor of history, "and yet there's a kind of core which leads him to do his work in a certain way; it leads him to present himself to people academically in a way; and it leads him to his politics. They're all connected in Alan."

Kors has a withering contempt for the "pinched, parsimonious" efforts to diversify college campuses and for the "Orwellian" efforts to sensitize their residents. Yet when he served as master of Van Pelt College House, he worked hard to bring in African Americans and other minorities, and he still takes great pride in the fact that Van Pelt was then one of the most successfully integrated campus residences. ("Never in my life," says one former resident, "have I lived among such diverse people as I did there.")

No one questions his commitment to undergraduate teaching, for which he has twice won major University awards. ("He is passionately committed to high-quality undergraduate education," says Dr. Richard Beeman, professor of history and associate dean of the School of Arts and Sciences, "and he has

---

put his own career and efforts where his words are, in ways that few have.")
His student evaluations border on the worshipful—"I've never been so
transfixed by anyone in my life," recalls one former student—and no one who
has heard him lecture would deny his formidable intelligence or rhetorical
skills. Those who follow such things closely speak in superlatives about his
scholarship and his books: especially *D'Holbach's Coterie: An Enlightenment in
Paris* (1976) and *Atheism in France: 1650-1729, Volume 1* (1990).

Just what led Kors to atheism is surely a personal matter, but the over-
throwing of God by the intellect is a subject he has plumbed deeply in his
scholarship—and even, one could argue, in his politics.

"These issues of belief and disbelief are of great personal importance
to him," says Dr. Marc Trachtenberg, professor of history. "It's not like
someone like me, who's like, 'Well, I don't know whether God exists or
not; how does that affect my daily life?' For him, this stuff really matters, in
personal terms."

Adds Beeman: "I think he is—*obsessed* may be too strong a word, but I
can't think of a better one at the moment, with the whole question of religious
belief in the early modern and modern world. Basically, his whole approach
to the history of the ideas of the early modern world is the investigation of
the process by which men subject received beliefs to rational scrutiny. And
virtually all of his work—in his first book on this circle of thinkers, many of
whom were atheists and proto-atheistic thinkers, around the Baron d'Holbach,
to his massive history of the rise of atheistic thought in the early modern
world—is basically around that question of thinkers subjecting received belief
to critical, rational scrutiny. And what Alan does as an intellectual historian is to
proceed ever-so-logically to call these thinkers to task for inconsistencies—so,
I mean, he's just as critical of people in the past as he is in the present."

"If you think of the history of Western thought as an area," says Kuklick,
"he's unparalleled. He knows the languages, he knows the arguments,
he knows the philosophy well, he knows the theology well—he's just
outstanding."

But campuses can also be highly political worlds, and Kors, who has been
involved in some very politically charged campus episodes—he served as
the faculty adviser for Eden Jacobowitz during the infamous Water Buffalo
incident—has often infuriated his opponents with his blazing rhetoric, his
willingness to deal with the national media, and his apparent relish for the
fight. Yet his friends describe him as a warm, gentle man with an engaging
sense of humor, a "monkish scholar" at heart who would much rather spend
his time studying and writing about the Enlightenment. The problem, says
one, is that he "happens to be very good at doing something that he would
prefer not to do."

Which leads to another word that no one who has followed him closely would contest: *committed*. Kors has his principles—and woe to those who cross them.

Beeman, who has known Kors since they arrived at Penn as assistant professors together in the fall of 1968, shortly after Kors received his doctorate from Harvard University, describes him as a "master of the logically consistent argument" and acknowledges that there is an edge to that compliment: "Alan is committed, in his life's work—intellectually, professionally, and personally—to that kind of logical consistency. What I've noticed—and I've been not only his friend and history colleague but I've been department chair and now [associate] dean—is that the conflict of opposing ideas, and even of opposing logical systems, is a constant reality. I often have to compromise my commitment to logical consistency in order to produce a consensus among people of differing views—and, indeed, that has been the primary source of conflict between Alan and myself over the years. Occasionally, his commitment to that kind of logical consistency gets in the way of accommodating inevitable differences among human beings."

In that sense, he adds with a telling wince, "Alan is a very stern judge of friendships—of human relationships. There is a tendency to draw a line, and if you step over that line, then it's hard to maintain those relationships."

"That commitment of logical consistency," he says, "you know, it embarrasses us sometimes, but it's very, very good for us. And it's not just an ideological consistency: it really is his fundamental honesty. He is true to himself."

"Alan Kors," wrote an admiring student some years back, "should have been a prophet." The image—of Kors, dressed in flowing robes and preaching in the desert wilderness beneath a burning sun—somehow, for all its absurdity, resonates. There is a fire to his rhetoric that brings to mind the Old Testament prophets and the struggle between light and darkness, good and evil.

Kuklick agrees with that assessment, though only up to a point. "There is an Old Testament aspect, if you think of the prophets and the Jeremiahs, but it's more Enlightenment," he says. "You have the world of reason and responsible discourse. I think he romanticizes that, to some extent, and then he makes that romanticized version of intellectual debate the absolute norm for all peoples at all times. And that does become a debate between good and evil, between the reasonable people and the unreasonable ones, and between principles and expediency. And there's a lot of truth to what he says, which makes it all the more compelling."

"He takes the rhetoric to the extreme position," says Dr. Sheldon Hackney, former president of the University, "so that it's no longer of reasonable people disagreeing about how to accomplish a good end. It's good versus evil. You fall into the Manichean fallacy." Yet despite some deep and very public disagreements about issues of campus policy, Hackney also professes some admiration for Kors, whom he calls a "principled libertarian" and a "useful figure" on campus.

"The ironic thing," says Trachtenberg, "is that people like Alan, in the 1960's, were considered on the left. If you believed in treating everybody equally without regard to color; if you believed in freedom of speech without limit; if you believed in getting a university administration off the backs of the students and not taking on the role of *in loco parentis*—that was the position of the left at that time. He hasn't changed his views; it's the general standards of the university culture that have moved so far to the left that somebody like Alan appears to be on the far right. But because he's got this very strong anchoring in firmly held beliefs, because his mind works to sort out these intellectual questions in such a powerful way, he doesn't simply drift with the academic culture the way so many other people do."

"I really think that the long-term effects of what he has done for this university won't be felt for some time," says Dr. Richard Wernick, the Pulitzer Prize-winning composer and Magnin Professor of Music, "but they will be felt—and they will be very, very important. It's extremely important that someone like him was willing to speak out and act the way he did and defend students the way he did against what some of us consider to be kind of forces of oppression."

"Alan's central belief is still that people should be allowed to be themselves and be individuals with the freedom to live their lives according to their consciences, as long as they don't interfere with somebody else," says Harvey Silverglate, a partner in the Boston law firm of Silverglate and Good and a close friend of Kors' since their days at Princeton.

"I call him a paradigm university man," says Martin Seligman. "I see Alan as a courageous and staunch defender of the university as a place where free speech and the exchange of ideas thrive. And when I think of the University of Pennsylvania and what's valuable here, Alan's right up at the top of my list.

"He's certainly got a lot of enemies," Seligman acknowledges, "and that runs along political lines. It used to be that Alan could often defuse his enemies by getting to know them. He's such a delightful character. But over the last few years, I've noticed a hardening by his enemies, even though they know him and may even like him at some level."

One of those on the opposite side of the rostrum is Dr. Houston Baker, the Greenfield Professor of Human Relations and director of Penn's Center for the Study of Black Literature and Culture. Baker describes Kors as a "genuinely non-collegial, self-promotional person who has interests other than those of the University as a community at heart." Kors himself might not disagree with the second part of that comment, since he has always viewed group beliefs and group interests with a skeptical eye.

Although most people would use the word *conservative* or *libertarian* to describe Kors these days, there was a time when he was considered a counter-cultural liberal, and even today, he would probably be considered a southpaw on certain issues. One of his old mentors from Princeton, Dr. Lawrence Stone, now an emeritus professor of history, goes so far as to call him an "extreme liberal" who "pushes liberalism to its logical extreme—which makes him have some curious bedfellows."

Dr. Peggy Sanday, professor of anthropology, takes a dimmer view, arguing that people like Kors "project political correctness onto those who are trying to deal with hostile-environment types of issues, when, in fact, the political correctness is coming from their rather broad-based universalizing the notion of freedom—meaning that by *freedom*, you can say anything, whenever you want, wherever you want, and there can be no social restraints to speech. But there can be no society without some form of social mores and norms.

"I find his arguments always to restrain," she adds. "That's why I say *he* is politically correct, within a conservative framework."

On the other hand, Wernick, who describes himself as a liberal on most issues, says that, on the "whole subject of political correctness and speech codes and free speech," he and Kors see "absolutely eye to eye—as, I think, many liberals do."

Furthermore, says Silverglate: "He has gigantic differences between himself and the conservative movement. And the reason for that is, Alan is a libertarian conservative, and most conservatives are not. They believe in libertarianism in certain areas but not in others. Whereas Alan would take exactly the same position right down the line. What he says is subtle—so you really have to listen to him."

In a 1988 speech to the National Association of Scholars, Kors criticized "the heart of the feminist and black-liberationist paradigm, that radical-feminist theory is women's experience, that radical black analysis is *the* voice of a diversified American black community. Nothing, of course, could be more sexist or racist than the assumption that these congeries, 'female experience,' 'black experience,' can be reified into such programs."

Kors has also been a point man in the fight against attempts to mandate a more diverse, non-Western academic curriculum, a key issue for the

National Association of Scholars. Sanday recalls, with more than a trace of annoyance, Kors' "very, very strong and important voice raised against our attempts, a couple of years ago, to diversify the core curriculum," saying that Kors "essentially killed that effort through his lobbying and his speech in the Faculty Senate."

And yet, says Beeman: "Alan has no truck with Allan Bloom's *The Closing of the American Mind,* which is one of the principal texts criticizing the P.C. movement. Alan believes that the utopian world of 30 years ago, in which undergraduates studied the great texts and had a mastery of the Western political tradition, is nonsense—that, in fact, the traditional liberal-arts education was a pretty un-rigorous smorgasbord. And Alan believes that a lot of the aspects of non-Western tradition are a *very* important part of any first-rate curriculum—he just doesn't believe in mandating them."

And from all accounts, any attempts to force such changes will cause him to fight like a cornered wolverine.

"I don't know what leads someone to feel the intensity or the passion that he feels about these things," says Kuklick. "He is genuinely driven by these principles. You see the assault on the canon as an attack on these principles, so you react." Kuklick sighs: "I mean, I see it as an assault, too, but I guess I'm more secure about the future of the West, let's say, than he is."

W hen Eden Jacobowitz yelled the controversial—and still disputed—words *Shut up, you water buffalo! If you want to party, there's a zoo a mile from here,* he touched off a firestorm that still smolders. Jacobowitz says that he got in touch with Kors (whom he calls a "saint") after reading an article in *The Daily Pennsylvanian* that described how Kors had helped get racial-harassment charges dropped against Gregory P. Pavlik, a conservative columnist for the *DP* whose columns had struck some as racist. After checking out Jacobowitz's story, Kors agreed to help him.

At first, he tried to resolve the dispute internally. He asked two black scholars—Dr. Elijah Anderson, the Charles and William Day Professor of Social Science, and Dr. John Roberts, the associate professor of folklore and folklife who serves as director of Penn's Afro-American studies program—whether the phrase *water buffalo* had any racial connotations. He then asked top administration officials to intervene on Jacobowitz's behalf.

When they did not, Jacobowitz, with Kors' encouragement, began taking his case to the national media—at which point, a potentially explosive case went thermonuclear.

"Last spring," recalls Hackney, "Alan called me before he began to stir up national attention to tell me that that was what he was going to do if I did not intervene, and since I felt I could not intervene in the Penn system and the Penn rules, then he went ahead and stirred up a lot of national attention. But in that instance, he was doing what he thought he had to do to win for his client."

Sanday, who served as a faculty adviser to the five women, is still angry about the role Kors played. "I'm extremely concerned about how he allowed that case to get totally pressed out of shape by going to the media," she says. "And he seemed to enjoy it in the process." The whole discourse, she adds, "got completely bent out of shape by the media's discussion of it without ever hearing the side of the complainants."

Kors' friends say that he tried hard to avoid a public battle, but that he felt forced to do so by an administration that was unwilling to intervene in the judicial process.

"I genuinely believe that Alan was driven to go public," says Beeman, "that he believes that Eden Jacobowitz was victimized, [and] that his decision to go public had to do with the fact that here was a student-life bureaucracy—and, ultimately, a central administration—that was unresponsive to the real predicament that this innocent kid found himself in."

Baker sees it differently: "The way you go at advocacy for a libertarian policy on a campus that is presumed to be guilty of collegiality is not by generating a set of letters to the national media of a particular stamp—George Will and so forth. And Alan did that. It seemed to me that it hurt the University that he put it in the public arena and cast it in the light of persecution of a poor, pure student who had not used a racial epithet.

"He made telephone calls to people," Baker continues, "and sandbagged them, as far as I'm concerned—like Elijah Anderson and John Roberts. He asked them: 'Have you ever heard this word used in a negative or a racial context?' without explaining why he was doing it. And then he summoned them up as sort of expert witnesses, saying that this was not a racial epithet."

Baker was also disturbed by Kors' attempts to convince the administration to intervene. "I guess I interpreted that as a threat rather than an attempt not to go public," he adds. "That's part of what conditioned my feeling of complete self-promotion—Alan's profession of one set of in-the-marketplace-of-ideas and free exchange, and then this kind of Booker T. Washingtonian campaign of threats and power politics going on behind the scenes."

Yet Hackney, who was flagellated by commentators of all stripes for not intervening on Jacobowitz's behalf, believes that Kors behaved in an "honorable" way, and says he took Kors' warning as an "observation," not a threat. Although he acknowledges that the experience was "incredibly" painful for him personally, he says he is not bitter about the course of action Kors chose.

"He and I have a very curious relationship that goes back some way, in which I do have some respect for his positions, his point of view," says Hackney. "I understand that he pushes that point of view very hard and that he pushes it hard in a way that was not good for me—and not good for the University, I felt—but it's hard to fault him for that, because he was really representing a student, and was doing what he felt was necessary. So I don't come away feeling bitter about him.

"He doesn't always look at the context in which a policy exists," Hackney adds, "but that's what happens when you're something of a monomaniac about free speech and academic freedom."

To understand some of the intensity behind Kors' commitment to principles, go back to Princeton University in the fall of 1960. Kors—then a full-scholarship freshman from a close-knit family in Jersey City—is sitting in his dorm room, listening to a recording of Pete Seeger singing union songs. He's a little awed at finding himself at a prestigious Ivy League university, and he's quietly excited about the intellectual adventures awaiting him. All of a sudden . . . but let Beeman tell the story:

"Into the room comes a delegation of classic Princeton eating-club WASPs, led by Tommy Smathers, the son of Senator George Smathers. They go over to his record player, take the needle off the record, pick up the record, break it in half. Tommy Smathers takes his wallet out, puts the amount of the price of the record on his desk, and they walk out.

"That, in combination with the kind of enforced Christian religiosity, in the name of Christian values, was Alan's introduction to Princeton," says Beeman. "And I really and truly believe that some of his libertarianism—and his revulsion against a lot of what he sees as political correctness—comes from those kinds of experiences."

By "enforced Christian religiosity," Beeman means mandatory chapel, and in his talk to the Newman Center audience, Kors recalled going to the dean of the chapel and telling him: "My conscience is my own"—whereupon the dean of the chapel responded: "It's good for you."

"Alan didn't like mandatory chapel at Princeton any more than he likes mandatory sensitivity training today," says Silverglate. "He refused to go to chapel. He made a deal with Ernest Gordon, who was then the dean of the Princeton Chapel, that instead of going to chapel, he would sit and talk to

Ernest Gordon about the existence of God." Silverglate laughs: "Of course, the problem was that if that went on too long, it's quite possible that he would have turned Ernest Gordon into an atheist. But I don't think it went on long enough."

Martin Seligman tells another story about Kors that took place during those formative years:

"We had a friend—you should change his name—who was really quite a good friend of both of ours, and Alan somehow found out that 'John' had—I don't think raped, but forced himself sexually on a woman, whom Alan didn't really know. And after that, for Alan, it was as if 'John' didn't exist. He was sort of cut from Alan's list of human beings. He ignored 'John,' didn't talk to him—sort of like the father in *Fiddler on the Roof* whose daughter marries outside the faith. And that was a time when, I think, people were very tolerant of the sexual exploitation of women. But Alan just thought it put him into a different moral universe."

There was another bit of social stratification that Kors didn't care for at Princeton: the eating-club system. According to Silverglate, Kors was "very instrumental" in organizing the "first blow" to the system. "Alan didn't like the kind of selectivity that it was based upon in those days," he explains. "It was based upon race; it was based upon your family background; in some of the clubs, it was based upon money; in some of them, it was based upon how important your father was—never your mother, of course. And that grated Alan the wrong way. So Alan refused to participate, as did I, and he and I and a couple of others started the Woodrow Wilson [Society]. It was a facility for upperclassmen eating together without the selectivity of the clubs."

It may have been Kors' success with the Woodrow Wilson Society that led him and Dr. Mark Adams, professor of the history and sociology of science, to help found the college-house system at Penn in the early 1970s. Their first project was Van Pelt College House, where Kors was a resident for eight years, including three as master. (It was there that he met his future wife—Erika Wallace, then a student. After the Vietnam War—which Kors supported, reportedly on the grounds that the United States had made a commitment and should honor it—he and Erika became adoptive parents of a Vietnamese refugee. They have two biological children of their own, too.)

Harrison Tao has fond memories of Van Pelt College House, which he describes as "a way of bringing a small-college atmosphere to a very large and impersonal place." Kors and Adams, he says, "were truly intent on having the dynamics of an intellectual atmosphere and a very strong family atmosphere. They opened their doors and minds and hearts to the students. Alan was a real presence in the house—he truly lived the life that he had wanted for it, in the sense of participating with students and being available.

"One of the beauties of the place," he adds, "is that it really tried very hard to integrate. I don't mean just in the racial and ethnic sense—I'm Chinese, and there were many African-American students who lived there and were personal friends—but in terms of interests. For instance, I'm not a jock by any definition, but I got a chance to make friends with and play touch football with guys on the varsity football team. I wouldn't have even met them otherwise."

One of those football players (and African Americans) was Adolph Bellizeare Jr., who says that Kors recruited people to come and live in Van Pelt.

"He made an active effort to get a number of athletes in there and a number of blacks in there," recalls Bellizeare. "There were probably representatives from every nationality at Penn in that building. We talked about all kinds of customs of all kinds of people. There was diversity among *blacks* in the building. We talked about Long Island blacks versus South Carolina blacks or Louisiana blacks—I mean, there was all kinds of different stimulation there among students. It just helped us to get to know and learn about each other."

Bellizeare laughs. "Alan did have a knack for stimulating conversation and thought. Fortunately, he had a bunch of big-mouth people in the dorm who loved to talk. I mean, he could start a heck of an argument, but in a place like Penn, I guess that's what makes great things happen—arguments."

"We did no social work" at Van Pelt, Kors told his Newman Center audience. "We had no diversity education. We said, 'You come here as an individual: no violence, no theft, no destruction of property, no terroristic threats'—in the early Seventies, you had to add the latter. The speakers we brought in weren't to morally instruct little children; they were scientists, theologians, philosophers, historians, critics of religion, literary critics. We addressed their minds, as adults. I lived there eight years, and after the first year, there was never less than 20-25 percent blacks. We had the first wave of leaders of gay liberation—and of Campus Crusade for Christ, living in the same house. We had Marxist revolutionaries. We had people on the governing board of the Newman Center. You know what that's called? A *university!*"

"Alan was very committed," says Debra Wollens, another Van Pelt resident who also took two history courses from Kors. "He was certainly the most dynamic member of the house. He was always willing to help any student who was having problems of any sort—that's an important thing for a professor in a house situation to do for kids who are becoming adults in a transitional and volatile time of their lives. And he always tried to get the students to help each other."

"He's a real treasure, as somebody who connects with students," adds Tao. "Part of me thinks I should qualify that and say, it's been 20 years; he may be a different person. But I doubt it."

He pauses a moment, then adds, in a quiet but emotional voice: "I would stand by Alan through anything."

Born Under a Bold Sign

Martin Seligman

(First published in June 1994 as "On His (Mostly) Best Behavior.")

Chances are, if you were looking to understand why somebody responded in a certain way to a traumatic episode in his youth, you'd round up the usual suspects: heredity and environment. You'd probably lean toward one camp or the other, depending on what you'd read recently and on your own philosophical bent—and then, if you were seeking clues to the mystery of the grown man, you might even work the youthful episode itself into the equation.

Take the case of Dr. Martin E. P. Seligman, the enormously influential professor of psychology, whose father was paralyzed some 40 years ago by a series of strokes that left him, in Seligman's words, "physically and emotionally helpless." It was a foundation-shaking event for a 13-year-old boy, one that he describes in sobering detail in his 1990 book *Learned Optimism*. But while he acknowledges that it had an "immediately depressing effect" on him at the time, he also says that, on an intellectual level, it "lit a fire about doing something about helplessness and passivity, which has not been extinguished."

Given Seligman's long and much-decorated track record—which includes books like *Helplessness: On Depression, Death, and Development*; *Learned Helplessness*; and *Human Helplessness: Theory and Applications*, as well as innumerable articles on the subject of helplessness and its offshoots—it's hard to dispute that claim. But the real question is, *why* did it spark that kind of fire, and not render *him* helpless and passive, too—or, at the very least, cause him to lock the whole scary subject in some deeply buried vault of the soul until he was a good deal older and less likely to be spooked by it?

"I'd like to know the answer to that," he says simply.

"I've often wondered about my father's success versus my own," he adds. "While my father was a pretty successful man—and cut down at just the age I am now—I think I've done better than my father, and I've wondered why. I don't think it's something like intelligence: he was a very smart man. But it is something like doggedness and persistence and competitiveness. I don't lie down and die. But I don't know why that is."

Since Seligman doesn't have an identical twin from whom he was separated at birth, and since it might take years of analyzing childhood stories to come to any conclusions about his home life (which would probably be completely off-target anyway), I take a wild stab and ask him what time of day he was born. I know that he was born in Albany, New York, on August 12, 1942, but to my surprise, he answers with scientific precision: 11:58 a.m. He explains that, when he was in the eighth grade, a "very serious astrologer" cast his horoscope—and was "quite stunned" by what he found.

"He said I had the same configuration as Caesar and Stalin," recalls Seligman, not without amusement. "There were several great world leaders he named. He also prophesied my mode of death—which I think I'll keep quiet, lest someone try to bring it about."

So maybe we should just say that he was born under a swashbuckling sign and that his character, and thus his fate, was more or less predetermined by the stars. But while Seligman, again to my surprise, doesn't dismiss the stars' influence out of hand—"No one can explain the mechanism," he says of astrology, "but for some of the things there are good statistical predictions"— he does dismiss the notion that he is simply a born optimist.

"I think, in fact, I'm a pessimist," he says. "I don't know if it's genetic or not, but I think by the time I was out of adolescence, I was pretty much a pessimist. And I've had to invent techniques and use the techniques that people like [Dr. Aaron T.] Beck and [Dr. Albert] Ellis invented, most every day of my life, to work effectively."

Frankly, *I'm* a little bit skeptical about that. Seligman is undoubtedly a tough-minded scientist who casts a pitilessly realistic eye on his own work and others', and he may sometimes be, as he puts it, a gloomy sort of "nimbus cloud" around the house. And he's the expert on this stuff, not me. But too many people who knew him in the early days of his career describe him as *enthusiastic* and *brash* and *self-confident* for me to entirely buy the notion of him as a deep-rooted pessimist. ("I think one ought to accept someone's self-evaluation on that," says one old friend, "but he has always struck *me* as an optimist.") The jury may still be out on this one.

But there is a well-researched theory, to which Seligman subscribes, that pessimists, for all their depressions and failings, are the ones who see the world most clearly. "We must be able to use pessimism's keen sense of reality when we need it," he writes in *Learned Optimism*, "but without having to dwell in its dark shadows."

So let's try this: Seligman has within him powerful alternating currents of optimism and pessimism, and he has learned to harness both for his own ends. If you look long enough, you may sense those twin currents pulsing, in various guises, through his work. *Pessimism/optimism, heredity/environment*: The usual suspects are still the hardest to crack.

R ight now, Seligman is sitting at the end of the long wooden table in his office in the psychology building, wearing an olive green sweater and a tropical tan, explaining why he does what he does and what he tells his graduate students to expect. His speaking voice—deep and relaxed, yet vigorous—would be perfect for a radio call-in show, and his remarks are both thoughtful and concise. He looks robust, in a solid, stocky way, and the combination of his high forehead and retreating hairline gives the odd impression that his brain has blasted the follicles right out of the front end of his dome.

"Science, as I see it, is very much in the Jonas Salk image," he says, referring to the inventor of the polio vaccine. "Which is, you do things toward ends of alleviating human suffering. That's what you're after. There are a lot of people out there who want to lead rational lives, and it's your job to take hard information and try to translate that for the public.

"But in your twenties, you do that at your own risk," he adds. "If you're pursuing the academic route, which most of my students are, you can expect that those people who don't have the Jonas Salk view of science—which is 80 percent of scientists—are going to hold that against you."

Seligman speaks from some experience. Internationally famous before he was 30 for his work on learned helplessness, he says he was told "in no uncertain terms, by lots of the tough-minded people I respected, that this was really bad for me—to be known." It was a price he was willing to pay, and now, apart from minor snubs like not being in the National Academy of Sciences ("I long ago made peace with that," he says. "Some of my best friends are in the National Academy"), he is so well established, so enormously successful, that his critics are more or less resigned to his fame and influence. He's been doing his own bold brand of psychology for 30 years now—by which time, he says only half-jokingly, "your critics think you're long gone anyway."

He was recently voted (along with another Penn psychology professor, Dr. Robert Rescorla) one of the world's 10 most influential living psychologists in a survey of those who head psychology departments—a fairly tough-minded lot themselves.

"He is a huge figure in the world of psychology," says Dr. John Sabini, professor of psychology and chairman of the department. "He never proposes timid hypotheses; he proposes bold hypotheses. It's always fun to watch him defend the limbs he's crawled out on. He does it with great verve—and pithily, I might add."

Dr. Henry Gleitman, the white-haired, German born psychology professor who has known Seligman for 30 years now, describes him as a "swashbuckling kind of scientist."

"There are some people who carefully, diligently, patiently stalk nature, like the Red Army used to wage war," Gleitman explains in his rich and somewhat formidable accent. "And there are others who are like, oh, General Patton—daring. Marty is more the latter—the Patton. Is this good or bad? Well, which do you prefer: peonies or roses? It's my belief that science needs both.

"Then the question is, are you good as a swashbuckler? Are you good as a patient tracker? Marty's good. I mean, clearly he's good—look at his record. Swashbucklers, of course, are more likely to make mistakes. They're also more likely to bag big game."

Seligman himself says that while he doesn't mind being wrong, he greatly minds being boring. He divides the world of psychology into "simplophiles and complophiles," and he describes himself as an "unabashed simplophile" who seeks—and often finds—the "simple red threads" connecting complex phenomena. "I think most clinical psychologists are complophiles, who believe in how complicated people are and how important it is to have very rich and widespread clinical experience," he told an interviewer from *The Behavioral Therapist*. "I believe the richness of the clinical experience is something to be fought against."

But there is nothing simple about him. He is a political conservative who nonetheless worries that the "extreme individualism" of contemporary America is contributing to an epidemic of depression, and his suggested remedies include performing acts of service for the "commons" (his term for, roughly, the commonweal) and "immunizing" children psychologically to ward off depression. While he attributes his own "failings as a clinician" to a "limited capacity for love and an impatience and impulsiveness," and sees himself as that brooding nimbus cloud around the house, he appears to be quite devoted to his wife, Mandy McCarthy, and their three children. (He also has two children from an earlier marriage.)

One undergraduate student, who decided to major in psychology after taking Seligman's abnormal-psychology class, describes him as a riveting lecturer, though she also remembers one afternoon when he became so annoyed and distracted by a sing-along outside College Hall that he finally stormed out of class, saying: "I can't continue under these conditions!"

His darker side has been known to emerge when he is with his graduate students, too. While some of his former grad students say that he creates an atmosphere that encourages high standards and creativity, and that he can be helpful and supportive, others—who will not speak for the record—say that he can be extremely unpleasant to work under.

"Marty believes that a graduate student will succeed in large measure insofar as that graduate student is tough," acknowledges fellow psychology professor Dr. Robert DeRubeis, "so his treatment of them follows."

Seligman doesn't deny that he has stepped on some graduate toes over the years. "My mission as a graduate teacher is to turn out those psychologists who will make a difference in the 21st century," he says firmly, "so when I think someone's not living up to that for one reason or another, it gets to me. It engages all my negative emotions. I'm very hard on students who don't live up to it.

"Fortunately, this is a garbage-in, garbage-out situation," he adds with characteristic bluntness. "I've been able to get very good students, and by leaving them alone and sort of having the ones who didn't live up drop off, I've been a good graduate educator."

"The question is whether you primarily see yourself as a teacher," observes Gleitman. "If you do, you're going to have students who tend to love you. That's not how Marty sees himself. And not all his students love him.

"I don't believe that it is Marty's primary goal to 'make friends and influence people,'" Gleitman adds. "I'm not saying that he is a curmudgeon who hates people, but he's a pretty independent guy."

"He's a very complicated personality," says Dr. Paul Rozin, professor of psychology. "For someone who is as successful and focused as he is, he is amazingly un-driven, amazingly tolerant."

But, says a colleague, "there are a lot of people who don't like him. Part of it's because of his success and part of it's because one of the ways he's efficient is to not waste a lot of time being just sort of pleasant. He is both extraordinarily nice to people and extremely standoffish with them."

Even if he were an utter misanthrope in his personal relationships (which he is not), Seligman will undoubtedly be remembered as someone who has helped a lot of people.

"You know, psychologists have devoted so much energy to make sick people normal, and I've paid my dues in that area," he says. "I think I've contributed to that. But so much of what psychologists have discovered now bears directly on making normal people much better—not just relieving misery but getting normal people to live up to potential. *Learned Optimism* is an attempt to tell healthy, normal people the things they should know to make their lives much better."

That may strike the skeptical as suspiciously akin to pop psychology. But when Seligman talks about learned optimism and its flip-side, learned helplessness, there is some pretty rigorous science behind it. The research—some his own, some others'—has involved hundreds of doctoral dissertations and hundreds of thousands of experimental subjects, some four-legged, some two-. When he balked at putting his work on learned helplessness and its offshoots in a popular, mass-appeal format, a literary agent (Richard Pine) told him: "Religions are made out of books like this." And, in fact, *Learned Optimism* is one amazingly persuasive—even uplifting—book. His next mass-market book—*What You Can Change and What You Can't*—is considerably more sobering, even pessimistic. It's what publishers call a "Don't help yourself" book.

Seligman has spent much of his career building bridges between those two sometimes-hostile psychological camps, the clinical and the experimental. While he has sometimes been accused of being too clinical and unrigorous by the experimentalists and too experimental and rigorous by the clinical crowd, he may have done as much to create common ground as any psychologist on the planet.

He is also one of the few serious psychologists in his field to bridge the chasm separating the academy from the general public—something not always appreciated by his peers.

"He paints with a broad brush, though he's quite a rigorous thinker," says Rozin. "Anyone who's as successful as him is going to breed jealousy and a certain amount of resentment. You can't have one without the other. And he does play to the intelligent lay audience as well as to academics. It's hard to say what an academic's proper role is."

Having earned his Ph.D. in psychology at Penn three years after graduating summa cum laude from Princeton (where his major was philosophy and his thesis was on "mind-body identity"), Seligman is routinely described as "brilliant"; yet he cheerfully suggests that many of his colleagues in the psychology department could outscore him on an IQ test.

"Henry Gleitman once jokingly called me the single clearest case of overachievement he'd ever seen," he says. "I think my work does outstrip how bright I am, and I've wondered why. Because I think there are half a dozen people in my own psychology department whose psychometric intelligence is higher than mine. I still, whenever I look at a mathematical equation, have to sit there and think about it, and I get a headache. And yet I do sometimes see to the core of things, without understanding how I got there."

F lashes of insight have certainly illuminated his professional career. The first came shortly after he arrived at Penn as a graduate student in the fall of 1964—"their star student, with trumpets blaring," in the words of Dr. Steven F. Maier, now professor of psychology at the University of Colorado, then a fellow first-year graduate student. Maier, who came from a poor background and had some doubts about his own place in such an elite academic environment, remembers Seligman as "very self-confident, with a very clear vision as to what he wanted to do and what he wanted out of life."

One thing Seligman "desperately" wanted to do was study under Dr. Richard Solomon, then a professor of psychology at Penn. Solomon, notes Seligman in *Learned Optimism*, was "engaged in the very kind of work I wanted to do: He was trying to understand the fundamentals of mental illness by extrapolating from well-controlled experiments on animals."

The day Seligman arrived, a group of dogs in a Pavlovian "transfer experiment" were failing to respond as expected. The dogs had been exposed to two kinds of stimulation: high-pitched tones and "brief tingling electric shocks"; the idea was to get the dogs to associate the neutral tone and the noxious shock. The investigators assumed that the dogs would react to the tones the same way they had learned to react to shock—by jumping a barrier to get away. But these dogs, he recalls in *Learned Optimism*, "had just lain down whimpering. They hadn't even tried to get away from the shocks. And that, of course, meant that nobody could proceed with what they really wanted to do—test the dogs with the tones."

As Seligman looked at the whimpering dogs and listened to another graduate student (Dr. J. Bruce Overmeir) describe the problem, he realized that something of profound significance had already occurred: "Accidentally, during the early part of the experiment, the dogs must have been taught to be helpless. That's why they had given up. The tones had nothing to do with it. During Pavlovian conditioning, they felt the shocks go on and off regardless of whether they struggled or jumped or barked or did nothing at all. They had concluded, or 'learned,' that nothing they did mattered. So why try?

"I was stunned by the implications," he adds. "If dogs could learn something as complex as the futility of their actions, here was an analogy to human helplessness, one that could be studied in the laboratory. Helplessness was all around us—from the urban poor to the despondent patient with his face to the wall. My father had his life destroyed by it. But no scientific study of helplessness existed. My mind raced on: Was this a laboratory model of human helplessness, one that could be used to understand how it comes about, how to cure it, how to prevent it, what drugs worked on it, and who was particularly vulnerable to it? . . . It would take the next 10 years of my life to prove to the scientific community that what afflicted those dogs was helplessness—and that helplessness could be learned and, therefore, unlearned."

It was a pivotal moment, both for Seligman and for psychology. Thirty years later, in his office in the psychology building, he describes the impression it made on him.

"I know it sounds strange," he says, leaning forward slightly on his arms, "and this isn't the way people talk about it, but my whole life flashed in front of me then. In fact, about a month ago, I was talking about this question with someone who works on battered women. The helplessness stuff has been used in court very frequently as a defense for battered women. And she asked me, had I ever thought of that. And I said, 'When I first saw the helpless animals, all of these things flashed in front of my mind . . . .' Everything was there in the first moments."

To confirm the theory, he and Maier devised an experiment: Taking three groups of dogs, they gave one group "escapable" shock (the dog could learn how to stop the shocks by pushing a panel and thus have control over its fate); another would get the exact same shocks but would have no control over them; and a third group would get no shocks at all. The dogs in the first and third groups, Seligman and Maier hypothesized, would quickly learn to escape, while those in the second group, which had found that nothing they did mattered, would give up. They were right on both counts.

(Seligman, who has taken some heat from animal-rights groups for those experiments, describes at some length in *Learned Optimism* how he wrestled with the moral dilemma of subjecting the dogs to the electrical shocks, which he likens to the "sort of minor jolt you feel when you touch a doorknob on a dry, winter day." He says that before he began, he consulted one of his philosophy professors at Princeton—who, in a Socratic way, led him to the conclusion that there was a good chance that he could eliminate "much more pain in the long run" than he was inflicting in the short run. Seligman also promised his professor that once he had "found out the fundamentals" of what he needed to know, he would stop working with dogs. A few years later, he did.)

In *Learned Optimism*, he sums up the implications of those early experiments: "Clearly, animals can learn their actions are futile, and when they do, they no longer initiate action; they become passive. We had taken the central premises of learning theory—that learning occurs only when a response produces a reward or punishment—and proved it wrong."

This was something of a death-knell for behaviorism, though he says that the behaviorists "did not blithely surrender." One of them, the late Dr. Francis Irwin, wrote him a note saying that a draft of the article had made him "physically sick." ("He was a serious teacher of mine," says Seligman now, "someone I have enormous respect and affection for, so it was a shaking experience for me.") Since behaviorists believed that animals—and human beings—could only learn actions (technically, "motor responses"), never a thought or expectation, they argued that something must have happened to the dogs to *reward* them for lying there and staying still during the shock—and that the cessation of pain, as the shock ceased, was a "reinforcer." At that point, writes Seligman, Maier designed a "brilliant" test proving that once dogs learned that they really did have some control, they would not become helpless and would quickly learn how to escape the shocks. "Our findings," wrote Seligman, "along with those of thinkers like Noam Chomsky, Jean Piaget, and the information-processing psychologists, served to expand the field of inquiry to the mind and to drive the behaviorists into full retreat."

In addition, he and Maier found that they could "cure" learned helplessness—by dragging "those poor, reluctant animals back and forth across the shuttlebox, over the barrier and back again, until they began to move under their own steam and came to see that their own actions worked. Once they did, the cure was 100 percent reliable and permanent." They also discovered a phenomenon they called "immunization"—which he describes as "learning beforehand that responding matters actually prevents learned helplessness. We even found that dogs taught this mastery as puppies were immunized to learned helplessness all their lives. The implications of that, for human beings, were thrilling."

Not everyone was thrilled. Among the unconvinced was Solomon, whom Seligman describes in the book as "skeptical" but "supportive." He is still skeptical, though he speak fondly and admiringly of his former student.

"I was never terribly enamored of the theory, as you probably know," says Solomon, now retired and living in New Hampshire. "Marty thought that we were studying depression. I never thought we were. As a matter of fact, I thought we were studying habituation, or getting used to, tingling electric shocks, which were initially frightening for the dogs. But it looked to me as if, as they received more of them, the dogs were getting less frightened. And I don't think they were getting helpless; I think they were just habituating.

"Furthermore, the relationship with depression is just what I call a theoretical leap. Depression was never studied in the dogs. I begged several of the students working with me to study depression—because it's study-able. And the first clue to depression in man and animal is interruption of sleep patterns. The second is interruption of dietary habits. The third is suppression of sexual behavior. So you can go on listing all the features of human depression that could be studied in animals—but they never were. So I lost interest. As far as I'm concerned, the jury's still out."

When Seligman left Penn, Ph.D. in hand, in 1967 (by which time he had already published five articles with titles like "Effects of Inescapable Shock Upon Subsequent Escape and Avoidance Learning"), he headed to Cornell University, where he spent three years as an assistant professor. His work on learned helplessness was already making waves in psychology circles, and by 1969, it had caught the attention of Dr. Aaron T. Beck, the Emeritus University Professor of Psychiatry and director of the Center for Cognitive Therapy, which fosters a style of treating depression that he invented. Beck invited Seligman to join him back at Penn.

"I had already met him before he left Cornell, and I thought he was brilliant," says Beck. "I also thought that his learned-helplessness theory, which he was developing at the time, could be a real breakthrough. So I thought this would be a good thing for us to pursue together, working in some kind of collaborative style—which, indeed, we did do."

A s a theory, learned helplessness had much to commend it, and in 1976, Seligman's work on it earned him the American Psychological Association's Early Career Award for "distinguished scientific contributions" within the first 10 years of a career. It didn't hurt that learned helplessness had Seligman's imagination, flexibility, and talent for synthesis behind it, not to mention his salesmanship. As Gleitman puts it: "The trick is to somehow see the true significance and run with it. Swashbucklers do this."

"Unlike some scientists," adds Rozin, "Marty has come up with a rather strong theory and not defended it—that is to say, he's modified it consistently. He's been very receptive to concerns about what it was not accounting for, and he's changed it. He and his colleagues—particularly [Dr. Lyn] Abramson and [Dr. Christopher] Peterson—have done quite a bit of change. So what it looks like now is not what it looked like 15 years ago. It's a very flexible response to some of these concerns."

Open-mindedness is, apparently, an old habit for Seligman. History professor Alan Kors, a friend of Seligman's since they were both undergraduates at Princeton, says that what stood out most about Seligman then was a "categorical open-mindedness" and adds: "Two of the most common phrases heard in discussions with Seligman in those days were, *What if?* And *Have you ever considered the possibility that . . . ?* He taught me that it was an act of friendship to challenge someone in his particular or fundamental beliefs—not an act of hostility."

"Throughout my career," Seligman writes in *Learned Optimism*, "I've never had much use for the tendency among psychologists to shun criticism . . . . I've preferred the humanistic tradition. To the scientists of the Renaissance, your critic was your ally, helping you advance upon reality."

One such critic-turned-ally was Dr. John Teasdale, a British psychiatrist who gave a "piercing critique" of a 1975 speech on learned optimism that Seligman gave at Oxford University. It helped lead Seligman to the conclusion that the way in which people explain bad events to themselves can lead to helpless behavior and depression—and that changing their explanatory style could help alleviate their depression. Many other psychologists would make important contributions to the theory, and a few years later, Seligman and Peterson, a social psychologist, modified it still further, examining comments for their qualities of permanence, pervasiveness, and personalization. Someone who reacts to a head cold by saying, "Things like this always happen to me," for example, is explaining it in language that is permanent ("always"), pervasive ("things like this," instead of "a cold"), and personal (these things "happen to me," not everyone). That style of thinking, they argued, can be a major cause of depression, not just a symptom.

Other psychologists, including a young professor at Yale named Judith Rodin, performed experiments that provided dramatic evidence that learned helplessness could influence the immune system and even, in situations such as elderly patients in nursing homes, lead to death.

Soon, using a technique developed by Peterson called Content Analysis of Verbatim Explanation, or CAVE, Seligman began using "explanatory style" to predict the outcome of baseball pennant races and even Presidential elections. While these sorts of things are fascinating and fun, they are somewhat risky from a scientific point of view.

In *Learned Helplessness: A Theory for the Age of Personal Control*, he, Peterson, and Maier laid out the parameters for a phenomenon to be considered an example of learned helplessness. It has to have "the contingency (that nothing you do matters); the cognition (that you expect that nothing you're going to do will work out); and the behaviors of passivity, depression, and giving up," Seligman explains. "Insofar as something that's proposed has all three of those characteristics, then it's a good model, and if it's only got one, which is very often the case, it's a bad one."

Seligman's questionnaires to determine whether a person is prone to pessimism and depression (and thus failure) have been used by everyone from insurance-company personnel directors to the admissions office at Penn.

Given the accessible nature of the theory and its profound implications for individuals and society, it's not surprising that it made its way out of academic circles and into the public sphere. Pine, the literary agent, says that Seligman was the "best and quickest" student of writing he has ever met.

"This is a man who had never written anything beyond academic prose, and within three months of editorial coaching, he became one of the most proficient, accessible writers of psychology that I have ever read," marvels Pine. "Which I think is proven if you've read either of his books."

B ack in his office in the psychology building, Seligman has just uttered a four-letter word, one that would elicit icy glares in some psychology circles. The word is *soul*.

"I'm very much interested in questions of the soul—what some of my colleagues would call 'hot psychology,'" he is saying. "They're much more interested in the mind. And the mind seems to me a sort of accouterment."

It's an unusual statement for a self-proclaimed environmentalist with cognitive leanings to make, though don't get the wrong idea. Seligman is not using the word in any sort of religious or spiritual sense. He's referring to that which is "deep" in human personality, as opposed to the superficial; that which we are born with, as opposed to that we have learned—and that which is, as a result, deeply resistant to change, not malleable.

"Lest purists among you be put off by my using the word *soul*," he writes in *What You Can Change and What You Can't*, "let me remind you of Freud's terminology. Freud's word for his subject matter was not *psyche* (as it has been rendered in English by his medical translators) or *mind* (as the modern cognitivists prefer) but *die Seele*, 'the soul'—an entity connoting much more than cold cognition.

"I intend to revive an idea long neglected by scientists other than the Freudians: the idea of depth," he adds. "I believe it is the key to change. Changing that which is deep requires mighty effort—massive doses of drugs or interminable therapy—and the attempt is likely, in the end, to fail. That which is near the surface changes much more readily."

This is a far more somber portrait of the world and human perfectibility than the one he painted just a few years before in *Learned Optimism*, though in one sense it is optimistic. We are not prisoners of our past, he argues—just of our DNA. While such near-the-surface things as panic, sexual dysfunctions, moods, depression, and pessimism can be changed, dieting almost never works in the long run; children "do not become androgynous easily"; homosexuality does not become heterosexuality; and reliving childhood trauma "does not undo adult personality problems."

What You Can Change and What You Can't reflects a lot of work by others, but its origins for Seligman go back to a pair of insightful flashes that occurred some 30 years before—in, of all places, his bathroom.

The first came about when he was sitting on the toilet, reading an article by Dr. John Garcia about x-radiation in rats, he recalls. "Garcia noticed that when you gave x-rays to rats, who subsequently got stomach illness, they went off their chow, but they didn't mind him at all," he explains. "So he asked the question, *Why?* Why did they get an aversion to the taste but not to the external stimuli? And from an evolutionary point of view, it makes a great deal of sense—because in nature, [food is] what's going to do the poisoning, not external stimuli."

He would spend the next few years trying to explain the significance of the "Garcia flash," as he calls it, to the psychological community. Although Garcia was dealing with rats, Seligman had a corroborating "flash" of his own just weeks after reading the article. Late one night, after a delicious dinner of filet mignon served with Bearnaise sauce, he became violently ill, "retching until there was nothing left to throw up." For years after that, he could not abide the taste, smell, or even the thought of Bearnaise sauce.

It was not, as the behaviorists would have it, simply a Pavlovian response. As he points out, he didn't develop an aversion to filet mignon, or the plates it was served on, or his wife (who was with him at that dinner). Moreover, it was only one meal, not the half-dozen or so repetitions usually needed for a conditional response, and he didn't get sick until several hours after he had eaten. When he found out that he had not been poisoned but had simply been hit by a stomach flu then sweeping the psychology department, he *knew* that the Bearnaise sauce wasn't the culprit—but it still tasted terrible to him. In *What You Can Change and What You Can't*, he offers an explanation:

"For millions of years, our ancestors repeatedly encountered, among their other woes, stomach illness . . . . Those of our ancestors who, after stomach illness, learned rapidly and well to hate the most distinctive taste that accompanied sickness, passed on their genes. We are *prepared* by our evolutionary history to learn some things well."

The "Garcia flash" and the *sauce Bearnaise* theory, as it came to be called, led to his first book, *The Biological Boundaries of Learning*, published in 1972. The implications of those ideas, which he continues to pursue, were profound—and politically charged. American psychology as a whole is "militantly environmentalistic," he argues in *What You Can Change and What You Can't*, and the "underpinnings of American environmentalism are very deep, both intellectually and politically." It is no coincidence, he adds, "that

Locke fathered both the idea that all knowledge is associations and the idea that all men are created equal.

"The behaviorists, scientific Lockeans all, domininated academic psychology from the end of World War I to the Vietnam era. We may have been working on rats and pigeons, but in doing so, we were trying to show that human beings were the product of their upbringing and their culture, not of their race . . . . Garcia denied [behaviorism's] most basic premise: that we are wholly the creation of our environment, not of our genes." And Garcia's modest suggestion that "our genes limit what we can learn," Seligman notes, "opened—just a crack—the door that environmentalists wanted shut forever."

In a sense, the two strains of Seligman's work—the environmentalist strain and the inherited strain—have mirrored the optimistic and the pessimistic factions of his own soul.

"I think of myself as an environmentalist," he says, "and all my science has been about the environment. But for 25 years, I've worried about the problem of why certain things, like personality, don't change.

"It's the twin studies and the adoptive studies of the last 10 years that I think have been the most important work in personality in my lifetime," he continues. "They have argued—more than argued, documented—that more than half the variance for most personality traits is genetic in nature. Now I'm starting to think about what's called 'breaking the genetic-environment co-variation' as the place where the environmentalistic psychologist has to look. You have to find out what it is that people who have certain genes that produce certain personalities—what kind of environments they seek out which get them into trouble. And then you have to break that co-variation.

"As an environmentalist, whenever I find effects of trauma on adulthood, that's very important to me, because it means you can intervene," he concludes. "It's grist for the mill that I work on. But I'm also a skeptic—and you really have to show me that these things have effects."

Certain passages in *What You Can Change and What You Can't* may leave some readers with the impression that Seligman's intention was more to rattle cages and shock people into looking at things in a new way than to present a measured, sober analysis. At one point, for example, he states: "If you want to blame your parents for your adult problems, you are entitled to blame the genes they gave you, but you are not, by any facts I know, entitled to blame the way they treated you."

Even some of his colleagues are taken aback by his bluntness—though many of them agree with the basic premise.

"Marty says everything in black and white, but that is his nature," says Henry Gleitman. "I think he's exaggerating, but I also think it is a wise exaggeration, because the American ethos is absurdly in the other direction, and every mother and father goes around shaking in their boots lest they do something that the child will tell their psychoanalyst about. And Marty will be the first to say that that psychoanalyst doesn't do a damn thing—which, again, is what the evidence is. This old idea—which is very American and which Freud fit into beautifully, especially as misconstrued by Americans—that all is experience, and also all is early experience . . . . Most of that has come under so much disrepute scientifically.

"This is not Marty's idea," he adds. "Marty is just reflecting what's going on."

"I have spent the last 25 years investigating optimism, and it is certainly not my purpose to destroy your optimism about change," writes Seligman. "But it is also not my purpose to assure everybody that they can change in every way. That would be yet another false promise."

Seligman's current project is a book based on the work of some of his graduate students—Dr. Lisa Jaycox, Karen Reivich, and Jane Gillham—to prevent depressive symptoms in schoolchildren. Titled *The Optimistic Child*, it was inspired partly by a conversation with Jonas Salk, who said that if *he* were starting over again, he would still devote his life to the immunization of children—but he would do so psychologically.

Asked about all of his recent work, Seligman is, as usual, mercilessly realistic.

"I think I'm doing my best work now, whereas I think if you asked people, they would say I did my best work in my twenties, maybe my thirties. It's all been downhill. I'm just captured by my own work now. It seems to me to be the best stuff I've ever done. But history's not going to view it that way."

Once again, the optimist and the pessimist have squared off, and the pessimist has had the last word. But the optimist doesn't seem particularly upset. Swashbucklers are like that.

STRANGE LABYRINTH

JOSEPHINE ROBERTS

(First published in November/December 2004.)

T he ink by now is rust-colored. The words, penned in a fine, cursive italic, appear mostly in the margins, which are browning at the edges. The hand belonged to the book's author, Lady Mary Wroth, who made her notations soon after *The Countess of Montgomery's Urania* was published in 1621.

Most of the changes are minor: a *he* to a *she*, an *antiquity* to an *ambiguity*. But some are substantial—and intriguingly autobiographical.

Even without the handwritten annotations, the *Urania* fascinates on several levels. True, it's a long, hard slog: more than 1,000 pages of convoluted plot and rococo prose; more than 300 incestuously entwined characters. But it is the earliest prose romance—novel, if you will—written by a woman in the English language, and a serious work of literature from a time when women were expected to stay away from such things.

The *Urania* was conceived in scandal. Wroth—"unworthily maried on a Jealous husband" (as her friend, the playwright Ben Jonson, put it)—bore two children to her lover, the rakish third Earl of Pembroke, who happened to be her first cousin. When she found herself cast out of Queen Anne's small circle of friends, she threw herself—and her passions—into her epic prose romance. But the *Urania* was more than just a *roman à clef* about the entanglements of love. It also dealt with simmering social and political issues—and volatile personalities. Its thinly disguised sketches of certain powerful courtiers so enraged them that Wroth was forced to write to an influential friend of King James I to say that she was recalling all copies of the book.

There is no evidence that she ever did; yet the fact remains that just 29 copies of the *Urania* are known to have survived. Only one has Wroth's handwritten annotations; it is now in the Rare Books and Manuscripts Department of Van Pelt Library. It was given to Penn last year by Dr. James F. Gaines, professor of French at Mary Washington College, in memory of his late, beloved wife, Dr. Josephine Roberts. And therein hangs a tale.

T hey were reading Marivaux's *La Surprise de l'Amour* when Jim met Jo in the summer of 1972. The two young graduate students were taking Ron Rosbottom's 18th-century French literature seminar, which assembled in Williams Hall. Roberts was an attractive redhead from Virginia, brimming with energy and intelligence. Gaines, the bright son of working-class parents from Massachusetts, had come to Penn from Michigan State to do his graduate work in French literature, and was increasingly drawn to the 17th-century world of Moliére.

She first noticed him when he was cleaning out his wallet—in class—as preparation for an upcoming trip to Dijon, where he would be lecturing. He doesn't remember much about their initial conversation, but he doesn't have any trouble remembering his first impressions.

"There was definitely a wonderful chemistry there," says Gaines. "She was from Virginia, which was a bit exotic for me, being from Massachusetts. I was very intrigued by her."

At the time, Roberts was also working in the Rare Books & Manuscripts Library at Van Pelt, where she welcomed visiting scholars and looked after the rarities. Within a couple of weeks Gaines was stopping by the library after classes, and the two would head out to La Terrasse or an Indian restaurant for a bite.

They had plenty to talk about. Roberts was working on her dissertation on Philip Sidney, author of the *Arcadia*; it was later published under the title *Architectonic Knowledge in the New Arcadia (1590): Sidney's Use of the Heroic Journey*. Sidney, incidentally, was Lady Mary Wroth's uncle—and one of the characters in the *Arcadia* was a shepherdess named Urania. One thing soon led to another.

"Jo was already acquainted with the *Urania*, and thinking about it," recalls Gaines. "Well before she left Penn, she was mentioning this wonderful field of study that relatively few people had gone into, and she was already collecting bibliographical references and talking about visiting England and all these castles to track down some of the literature and references that were fuzzy or lost."

By the time they were married in 1975, Roberts had received her Ph.D. from Penn and Gaines had finished the course requirements for his. Despite the dismal mid-seventies job market, Roberts had a number of offers from universities around the country, and finally accepted a tenure-track position at Louisiana State University. Gaines took a job at a local high school teaching geography and sociology while he worked on his dissertation on "Social Structures in Moliére's Major Plays," then landed a position at Southeastern Louisiana University, some 50 miles away.

Life was different in Baton Rouge—where even Roberts was seen as coming from "up North"—but unquestionably good. Even after they moved to the eastern edge of town, Gaines still had a 40-mile drive to SELU, but Roberts' commute was a relatively easy one across town, mostly along Interstate 10. And in case their lives weren't full enough, they added a baby boy to the mix in 1982. They named him John Manley Roberts Gaines, honoring both of their fathers.

Roberts, who would be named the William A. Read Professor of English Literature, was becoming a very popular professor at LSU, both at the undergraduate and the graduate level.

"She really was beloved," says Gaines. "She had a very strong following, both among her undergraduate and her graduate students. She got several awards at LSU for her teaching and research. Unofficial ones, too—one of her undergraduate English classes got together and gave her a plaque all on their own."

"Jo was a great mentor to me," recalls Dr. Mary Villeponteaux, who chose Roberts to be her dissertation director at LSU and now teaches early modern English literature at the University of Southern Mississippi. "She gently kept me on track; she helped me refine and develop my ideas; and she really never stopped helping me, even after I graduated. I think she was that way with all her students. She didn't just help you with your academic work; she helped you with your life.

"I knew her quite well for several years," adds Villeponteaux, "and in all that time I never once heard her say anything negative about anyone. If you know English departments, you know how rare that is!"

For all her quiet modesty, Roberts was also a rising star as a scholar. In 1983 LSU Press published her landmark collection of Wroth's poetry—*The Poems of Lady Mary Wroth*—complete with a lengthy critical introduction that included a short biography of Wroth. As she put Wroth on the literary map, Roberts was doing the same for herself.

"She seemed to me then, as she does now, the perfect scholar, one who is not driven by a desire for fame, but by a true love of the subject," wrote Dr. Sigrid King, a former graduate student and research assistant of Roberts', in *Pilgrimage for Love: Essays in Early Modern Literature in Honor of Josephine A. Roberts*. The fact that King (now an associate professor of English at Carlow College) undertook such a book speaks volumes about its subject.

One of the best sources of Wroth's work is the Newberry Library in Chicago, which had several copies of the published First Part of the *Urania*, not to mention the only manuscript of the unpublished Second Part. Roberts spent a good deal of time there, often joined by her husband and, later, her son. Jim Gaines would sometimes help her decipher Wroth's handwriting and spelling, and otherwise aid in her scholarly detective work. Once, when Roberts was baffled by a reference in the *Urania* to "the island now called Robollo"—which didn't appear on any maps, new or old—he tapped an unlikely source of knowledge.

"I liked the James Bond movies," he recalls, "and I was watching *For Your Eyes Only*, part of which takes place in the Aegean. At one point Bond has a snack with a character who turns out to be the villain, and they're eating caviar and crab or something, and the villain says, 'May I suggest a white Robolo . . .'"

Gaines soon discovered that Robolo (also known as Robola) was a wine once made by Venetian monks on the island of Cephalonia, and was well known in Wroth's day. Scholarship works in mysterious ways.

Roberts was also making a name for herself in feminist-scholarship circles. "She became increasingly interested in feminist studies, especially in the late '80s and early '90s," recalls Gaines, noting that her interests were widespread, ranging from Hildegard of Bingen in the Middle Ages to Virginia Woolf and other 20th-century British writers. "Had her career gone on longer, she might very well have done something in that area," says Gaines. "She was reading very widely and was beginning to cast out her critical tendrils and develop bibliographical lines."

But for now, she had her hands full with Lady Wroth. And the heart of Wroth's work was the *Urania*.

Soe though in Love I fervently doe burne,
In this strange labourinth how shall I turne?

—from the "Pamphilia to Amphilanthus" sonnet sequence, published as a separate section in the First Part of the *Urania*.

The Urania is not for the intellectually faint-hearted (which may explain why this writer still has not finished it, and probably never will). Nor does it lend itself to quick summaries. At the heart of it, though, is what Roberts called the "intense, ambivalent passion" of Pamphilia—queen of a country by the same name—for Amphilanthus, whose credits include

King of Naples, Holy Roman Emperor, and the first to teach Pamphilia the art of poetry. There is a lot of Lady Wroth in her portrait of Pamphilia, which means "All-Loving," and a lot of William Herbert, third Earl of Pembroke, in Amphilanthus, whose name translates to "the lover of two."

Actually, Wroth created a number of more-or-less autobiographical characters in the *Urania*, and those "multiple self-portraits" indicate a "continuing struggle for self-representation, in which the author seeks to assert and justify her behavior in the face of a disapproving public," wrote Roberts. They also suggest a "progressive attempt to fashion an image of a woman and author who refuses to accept defeat"—and who is willing to subvert conventions, literary and otherwise. No wonder Roberts admired her.

"Jo came to see her as a kind of exemplary woman in many ways," says Gaines. "She was very self-sufficient, as much as a woman could be at that time. Although she came from an illustrious family, her own family disintegrated during her life, and she really had to fend for herself. I think Jo identified with the strength of Wroth in her struggles."

Wroth's family was as literary as it was aristocratic. In addition to her famous Uncle Philip (a soldier and statesman as well as writer), her aunt and godmother, Mary Sidney, was a poet, translator, and "the greatest patronesse of witt and learning of any lady in her time," in the words of Aubrey's *Brief Lives*. Her father, Sir Robert Sidney, was a minor poet; her cousins included Sir Walter Raleigh; and her friends and literary admirers included the likes of Ben Jonson and the Scottish writer William Drummond.

Then there was her handsome first cousin, the third Earl of Pembroke, Sir William Herbert. Pembroke, as he is usually referred to, was a literary man himself, being Jonson's chief patron and one of those to whom Shakespeare dedicated his first folio. (In a way that was fitting, since as a statesman, Pembroke had a reputation as a Hamlet.) While he was "immoderately given up to women," he was fascinated not so much by physical beauty as by "those advantages of the mind, as manifested by an extraordinary wit, and spirit, and knowledge, and administered great pleasure in the conversation." Or so said his biographer, the Earl of Clarendon. But Pembroke had already had an affair with the courtier Mary Fitton (thought by some to be Shakespeare's Dark Lady), who found herself pregnant with his child in 1601. He admitted to being the father but refused to marry Fitton, which prompted Queen Elizabeth to toss him into Fleet Prison for a month, then banish him from court. Only after the accession of King James I in 1603 was he allowed to return.

No one knows exactly when he and Mary, who had known each other since childhood, became lovers. Roberts raises the possibility that they may have entered into a private, *de praesenti* marriage with each other, but since such marriages were based on oral agreements only, they are even harder to prove now than they were when the lovers were alive. In the Second Part of the *Urania*, Pamphilia and Amphilanthus exchange vows in a private ceremony with five witnesses, but although the narrator states flatly that such a vow "can nott bee broken by any lawe whatsoever," it didn't stop both characters from marrying others—to their mutual sorrow. In an essay titled "'The Knott Never to Bee Untide,'" Roberts noted that Wroth raised pertinent questions for women about "exclusively monogamous relationships and how widely such unions need to be acknowledged."

Whatever Wroth's agreement was with Pembroke, she tied her legal knot with Sir Robert Wroth in 1604. It was a bad match. One of the groom's few literary accomplishments was that somebody dedicated a treatise on mad dogs to him, and one of Mary's servants once described another man as "a true imitation of Sir Robert Wroth"—in that he was the "foulest Churle in the world" and "seldom cometh sober to bedd."

Around the time that Mary Sidney became Mary Wroth, Pembroke gave in and married a wealthy heiress named Mary Talbot. But he "paid much too dear for his wife's fortune," his biographer noted, "by taking her person into the bargain."

Behind the scenes lurked one Hugh Sanford, a secretary and tutor who apparently acted as an intermediary in arranging the marriages of Mary Wroth and Pembroke—and in hindering their relationship with each other. Wroth would later paint a caustic portrait of Sanford in the *Urania* through a fictional character who, on his deathbed, admits to Pamphilia that he had tricked Amphilanthus into believing that she had married another man, thus laying the groundwork for Amphilanthus to marry someone else. He begs her to pardon him "for the most treacherous and most deserving-torterous punishment, if hell fire, that ever man deserv'd."

Robert Wroth did have one thing to offer: his friendship with King James, which gave the well-born Mary further entrée to the Jacobean court. In Queen Anne's first masque—*The Masque of Blackness*, designed by Ben Jonson and Inigo Jones—Wroth was given a plum role, joining the queen and 11 of her friends "in disguising themselves as black, Ethiopian nymphs," as Roberts noted. That and other elaborate masques would find their fictionalized way into the *Urania*.

But after Robert Wroth died in 1614, and their one son died two years later, much of the estate passed to her late husband's uncle, and Lady Mary found herself deeply in debt. She would soon have other issues to contend with. One letter-writer said he had heard "whispering of a lady that hath ben a widow above seven years, though she had lately two children at a birth. I must not name her, though she be saide to be learned and in print."

Those love-children by Pembroke cost Wroth dearly in the Court of Royal Opinion. One of her self-modeled characters in the *Urania* is described as having fallen from the queen's favor after "fourteen years unchang'd affection," and having been forced to retire from court, "her honor not touched, but cast downe, and laid open to all mens toungs and eares, to be used as they pleas'd."

Wroth took solace—and some revenge—in writing *The Countess of Montgomery's Urania*, which she dedicated to her close friend and neighbor, Susan Vere Herbert, Countess of Montgomery, an independent-minded woman who could appreciate the world Wroth created. The role of women in society was just one of the charged issues explored in the *Urania*, which was written "at the height of the Jacobean debates concerning the nature and status of women," as Roberts pointed out. Wroth was keenly aware of "how little voice women had in determining their own destinies or even choosing their life partners," and the *Urania*'s "vast panorama of women characters" explored some unorthodox options. "In transgressing the traditional boundaries that restricted women," Roberts noted, "Wroth ventured into a territory that offered rich possibilities for women to reshape Jacobean culture by addressing and representing it."

That territory—and some of the men who inhabited it—proved to be hostile. Shortly after the *Urania* was published in 1621, Lord Edward Denny, who apparently saw more of himself in the book than he cared to, "charged that he and his family had been maliciously slandered in the work and that his personal affairs had been thinly disguised in the episode of Seralius and his father-in-law," Roberts noted. Denny also wrote a furious poem in revenge, titled "To Pamphilia from the father-in-law of Seralius," which began:

> *Hermophradite in show, in deed a monster*
> *As by thy words and works all men may conster*
> *Thy wrathfull spite conceived an Idell book . . .*

Halfway through, Denny took nasty to a new level:

> *Yet common oysters such as thine gape wide*
> *And take in pearles or worse at every tide.*

Denny concluded by advising Wroth to

> *. . . leave idle bookes alone*
> *For wise and worthyer women have writte none.*

Wroth responded line for line with "Railing Rimes Returned upon the Author":

> *Hirmophradite in sense in Art a monster*
> *As by your railing rimes the world may conster*
> *Your spitefull words against a harmless booke*
> *Shows that an ass much like the sire doth look . . .*
> *Take this then now lett railing rimes alone*
> *For wise and worthier men have written none.*

Wroth may have had the last word, but she was now in very hot water. She wrote to the powerful Duke of Buckingham, assuring him that she never intended the *Urania* to offend anyone and that she had already stopped sales of it. In fact, she added disingenuously, the books "were solde against my minde I never purposing to have had them published." (This ignores the fact that she had already sent him his own personal copy.) She also requested the king's warrant to recall copies of it—though no record of such a recall exists—and claimed to have had the remaining books withdrawn from sale and "left to bee shut up."

Whatever the extent of Wroth's efforts, she set aside "at least one copy in which she sought to correct the major errors in the text and to revise selected passages," Roberts pointed out. "The meticulous care which she devoted to the task is one reflection of her determined dedication to authorship, even in the face of her society's hostile reception."

Even though the First Part was consigned to a sort of permanent exile, Wroth still churned out some 500 manuscript pages of the Second Part. But eventually she lost interest in it—perhaps in 1626, when Pembroke assigned his estate to his seven-year-old nephew, thus dashing Wroth's hopes that he would provide for the two children he had fathered, one of whom she had named William Herbert. At that point, the romance was probably over.

Four years later, Pembroke died suddenly, and though Wroth lived on for more than two decades, she apparently wrote little during that time. When she passed away in the early 1650s, her literary name died with her. Almost.

In a certain neighborhood of Baton Rouge, word began to spread of a mysterious investigation. It was called Project Urania, and according to the rumor's perpetrator—a very young man named John Gaines—it involved nothing less than a "top-secret NASA mission." John's mother, Jo Roberts, documented that story with considerable amusement in her acknowledgements section of the First Part of the *Urania*, which was published by Medieval & Renaissance Texts & Studies in 1995.

Project Urania was an immense undertaking, and an important one for Renaissance scholars. Until Roberts came along, the only way to read the *Urania* was to track down one of the 29 surviving copies from the 1621 print run. Even then, you could only read the First Part, since the Second Part existed only in Wroth's handwritten manuscript at the Newberry.

"As feminist scholars and Renaissance scholars, Josephine Roberts and I felt it was a hugely important project to get the *Urania* published," says Dr. Mary Beth Rose, the former director of the Newberry's Center for Renaissance Studies.

Roberts' original idea was to edit only the Second Part, using the handwritten manuscript, since "requests to see the manuscript were becoming frequent, and the manuscript itself is fragile," notes Dr. Suzanne Gossett, a member of the editorial board overseeing the project. Roberts applied for a grant from the National Endowment for the Humanities—which turned it down on the grounds that it was "illogical" to edit the Second Part but not the First, Gossett recalls. Roberts then reapplied for a grant to edit both parts, and in 1989, the NEH came through with a $130,000 grant, the largest in the history of LSU's English department.

"This was indeed a project of enormous ambition—genuinely Renaissance, outsize dimensions—dictated by a unique combination of circumstances," says Dr. Janel Mueller, another member of the editorial board. "No wonder Jo Roberts found her Wroth project becoming her life's vocation—it would have been that even if she had been permitted a longer life."

One of Roberts' self-appointed tasks involved tracking down all 29 copies of the First Part of the *Urania*, a process she described as "an adventure, full of delight and frustration." In 1989, she learned about a copy owned by Dr. Charlotte Kohler, former editor of *The Virginia Quarterly*, who had written her doctoral dissertation on "The Elizabethan Woman of Letters" in 1934. Kohler had bought the copy in 1948 from an Elizabethan bookseller in Waukegan, Illinois, and agreed to let Roberts see it.

Since Roberts had already examined 26 copies of the *Urania* by then, she had no reason to think that this one would contain anything unusual. "Imagine my surprise," she wrote, "as I turned over the leaves and saw Wroth's own distinctive italic handwriting in the margins!"

"She passed it to me," recalls Jim Gaines, "and said, 'Is this what I think it is?'"

Kohler was kind enough to let Roberts examine the copy for her project, and gave her permission to publish the manuscript corrections—of which there were hundreds, all incorporated into the new edition. While most were either misspellings or simple mistakes by the printer, some were substantial rewritings.

Kohler had one more contribution to make. On August 11, 1994, she presented it with the following inscription: "For Josephine Roberts/with love and gratitude/Charlotte Kohler."

It was an "absolutely unexpected gesture," says Janel Mueller. "Jo's understated pleasure in telling the story gave me pleasure, because Kohler had clearly recognized that Jo was the volume's ideal possessor, and then had the generosity to act on her recognition."

The First Part of the Countess of Montgomery's Urania was published in 1995, and represented a "model for scholarly excellence," in the words of Sigrid King. It bore the simple dedication: "For Charlotte."

Kohler, now well into her 90s, is still living in Charlottesville, though she had not realized that the book had been given to Penn. "I'm not interested in it anymore," she said when contacted by telephone in September. "Thank you for calling."

Roberts now set her sights on the Second Part of the *Urania*. It was, in many ways, a far more difficult task than the First Part, given the difficulties of deciphering a 375-year-old handwritten manuscript. But Roberts wasn't too worried about that.

"She would sometimes say, 'If anything happens to me, make sure the edition of the *Urania* gets completed,'" says Gaines. "I'd say, 'Don't worry, I'll make sure that it does.'"

A ugust 26, 1996. Most people won't remember what they were doing that day. Jim and John Gaines will never have the luxury of forgetting.

At LSU, the semester had just gotten under way. Roberts had gone to a meeting at the Office of Academic Affairs, and had taken John, then 13, with her. After the meeting, they began to drive back to their home at 464 Wilton Drive, heading east on Interstate 10. As they approached Jefferson Highway, a pickup truck with a flatbed trailer attached to the rear came barreling over the bridge at a high rate of speed. The hitch to the trailer was jolted loose, suddenly, violently.

There was no chance for evasive action. The trailer was on top of them almost instantly. But Roberts did have one split second to prevent a head-on collision by jerking the wheel to one side. Had she not, both she and John would have been killed instantly. Had she turned it to the left, the trailer would have smashed into the side occupied by her son.

Instead she turned—hard—to the right.

Jim Gaines was at Southeastern Louisiana, teaching. After class, he went back to his office. A grim-faced secretary thrust a piece of paper into his hand: *Go to Our Lady of the Lake hospital at once.* At the bottom was an even more ominous note: *See the chaplain.*

"I was in a very disturbed state of mind," he says, convincingly. "I was trying not to drive so fast that I would get into an accident myself." Then, as he began to cross the bridge over Jefferson Highway, he saw a car on the other side of the road, horribly mangled. It was Jo's.

"I tried not to think about what the possibilities were," he says. "Then I got there and went to the emergency room. The ER doctors were hovering there and pulled me aside."

Roberts was dead on arrival. She had died from massive injuries there in the car, while her son, dazed and bleeding from his own serious wounds, watched helplessly. John was in the intensive-care ward, but he was expected to survive.

"She took the hit," says Gaines quietly. "I think she was deliberately trying to protect John. Her whole side of the car was crushed in."

Jim spent some time alone with the body of his wife, saying goodbye. They had been together for 24 years, since that first class in Williams Hall when they read *La Surprise de l'Amour.* She would have turned 48 that November.

Finally he pulled himself together and went to see his son, who had a ruptured spleen (fortunately still encapsulated) and multiple lacerations, but was otherwise in stable, if groggy, condition.

"He was able to talk about it," says Gaines. "He handled it pretty well; he didn't like to go over it, but he didn't clam up and internalize it. He stayed there until his spleen was OK, and then he was able to go back after a few days."

Roberts' LSU colleagues and church congregation poured out sympathy, food, and general assistance. The English department immediately put up a memorial website that listed many of the funds, seminar rooms, dissertation awards, and festschrifts named in her honor. Around the country and beyond, the community of Renaissance scholars mourned.

"I was so horrified I couldn't even talk about it," says Suzanne Gossett. "This was a youngish woman in her 40s, driving with a 14-year-old child on what was probably a simple local errand."

"Josephine's death was so terrible; nothing can replace her," says Mary Beth Rose. "She had a husband and son who adored her and whom she adored. She was also a kind and wonderful person. I miss her, and I am still shocked and saddened."

"The world of Renaissance studies has lost a pioneering scholar and a gentle, loving person," the memorial page concluded. "She leaves the world an emptier place, yet having been blessed by her gracious presence."

L ife—somehow—went on for Jim and John Gaines. So did Project Urania, as Gossett and Mueller suddenly found themselves in the difficult position of having to finish the Second Part themselves. It would prove to be, in Mueller's words, "one of the most challenging and solemnly satisfying tasks we have encountered in our professional lives."

The details are probably best left to the article Gossett wrote titled "The Ethics of Post-Mortem Editing"; suffice it to say that it was a huge job, made more complicated by the fact that Gossett and Mueller occasionally found minor mistakes in Roberts' interpretations of the text but weren't sure if a final version of her interpretations existed—somewhere. Wroth's handwriting, Gossett has noted, is "very difficult," and certain parts of the manuscript had suffered "extensive bleed-through, making it harder to decipher." Furthermore, she adds, "Lady Mary's concept of punctuation is not ours."

Equally daunting was the fact that Roberts had not yet written the textual introduction or the five-part critical introduction she had planned.

Back in Baton Rouge, Jim Gaines was dealing with the devastating loss of his wife and his son's mother. But he had promised her that the *Urania* would be completed, and though it took him nearly a year, eventually he organized and sent boxes of notes, paper files, and a disk copying a series of *Urania* files from the hard drive of the computer they had used together. Considering what had happened to him, says Gossett, "this was a heroic effort."

There was one other thing that Roberts had not been able to do before her death: provide a dedication for the Second Part, which was published in 1999. Gossett and Mueller knew what they had to do. The book bears a simple dedication: "For James F. and John Gaines."

T hree hundred and fifty years after her death, Lady Mary Wroth is part of the canon. It hasn't always been that way.

"The whole shift in the ability to study women in the early modern period as if they were creators, rather than passive recipients as readers of male literature, is a change since I was in graduate school," says Dr. Daniel

Traister, curator in the Rare Books and Manuscripts Department at Van Pelt and an adjunct professor of English. "Now all of this has changed, because of the work of people like Jo Roberts."

"Wroth is now perhaps the most—certainly one of the most—studied of all early modern English women writers," says Suzanne Gossett. "But without the editions of her poems and of the *Urania* that Jo Roberts published or started, this would be impossible."

Furthermore, points out Mary Beth Rose: "The availability and subsequent interpretations of the *Urania* will alter our view of women writers in the Renaissance. Just think of Virginia Woolf's assertions in *A Room of One's Own* that women in the 16th and 17th centuries didn't write. It will enrich gender studies in all of the centuries."

Dr. Maureen Quilligan, former professor of English at Penn and now chair of the English department at Duke University, recently finished a book titled *Incest and Agency in Elizabeth's England*, which will be published next year by the University of Pennsylvania Press. It takes the *Urania* as its central text, and Quilligan freely acknowledges that she could not have written it without Roberts' work. She also notes that the insights she gained from it were enormously helpful to her understanding of other English Renaissance writers—including Shakespeare. "I think [women writers like Wroth] are absolutely crucial for a far more historically accurate understanding of what everybody was doing at the time," she says. "Reading the women makes us understand how badly we've read the men."

Jim and John Gaines soon left Louisiana and its memories. Jim accepted a position at Mary Washington College in Virginia, where he is chair of the Department of Modern Foreign Languages. John is now a student there—majoring in English literature.

"Time passes, and you have to adapt and carry on," says Jim. He pauses for a moment. "One of the things Jo made me promise is that if anything happened to her, I would remarry—which I have not done."

Having done his part to get the Second Part of the *Urania* finished, he had one more matter to deal with—what to do with the annotated copy of the *Urania*. He knew that Jo wanted it to go to a good research library, where it would be available to scholars in the field. She had given one original copy of the book to LSU, and another deserving candidate, the Newberry Library, already had an abundance of Wroth texts, including published and manuscript versions of the *Urania*. Finally, after thinking about it a lot, and consulting with a number of her colleagues, he concluded that Penn was the right place for it to go. It was there that she first became interested in Wroth. It was there that she and Gaines had fallen in love. The rare-books department had been "extremely encouraging and helpful," he says, especially Dan Traister, who had been the point person from the beginning, and who had made him feel "very welcome" when he came to deliver the volume last year.

In Traister's eyes, the choice made good sense even beyond the intense emotional connection. Penn already has a "truly wonderful collection of English Renaissance literature," he says, and the *Urania* "is therefore something that, at Penn, has a context: it's not an isolated object." That literature is also "avidly studied at Penn, by undergraduates, graduates, and by some of the finest scholars of the English literary renaissance at work in the field today."

Furthermore, he says, a number of Penn scholars are deeply interested in the "material ways—the physical manuscripts, the physical printed books—in which this body of literature has survived." That includes the various ways in which the books have been marked and written in by their owners. "And for us to have the physical copy of one of those books, which turns out to be an extraordinarily useful book for students of early modern literature and early modern women's literature, in the copy annotated by its own author—*rare* is putting it mildly. Its importance for the people who care can't be overestimated."

"For Penn to have it is fabulous—spectacular," says Maureen Quilligan. "I mean, having an author correcting their own printed text—this is a unique experience. I'm sure there are others, but I don't know of any. To get an author's second thoughts and revisions, to see how the mind continues to work, is staggering. Even though Jo Roberts has given it to you in the notes, having it in the physical text can tell you so many things that a modern edition can't, however well-edited. And that's the sort of thing that [history professor Roger] Chartier does at Penn, and [English professors] Peter Stallybrass and Margreta de Grazia. It's perfect to have it there."

I ask Jim Gaines if Jo would be pleased by the choice.

"I hope so," he says. "I think she would. I feel good about it. I'm sure that's exactly what she would have done with it."